T0413261

THE VERY LATE GOETHE
SELF-CONSCIOUSNESS AND THE ART OF AGEING

LEGENDA

LEGENDA, founded in 1995 by the European Humanities Research Centre of the University of Oxford, is now a joint imprint of the Modern Humanities Research Association and Maney Publishing. Titles range from medieval texts to contemporary cinema and form a widely comparative view of the modern humanities, including works on Arabic, Catalan, English, French, German, Greek, Italian, Portuguese, Russian, Spanish, and Yiddish literature. An Editorial Board of distinguished academic specialists works in collaboration with leading scholarly bodies such as the Society for French Studies, the British Comparative Literature Association and the Association of Hispanists of Great Britain & Ireland.

MHRA

The Modern Humanities Research Association (MHRA) encourages and promotes advanced study and research in the field of the modern humanities, especially modern European languages and literature, including English, and also cinema. It also aims to break down the barriers between scholars working in different disciplines and to maintain the unity of humanistic scholarship in the face of increasing specialization. The Association fulfils this purpose primarily through the publication of journals, bibliographies, monographs and other aids to research.

Maney Publishing is one of the few remaining independent British academic publishers. Founded in 1900 the company has offices both in the UK, in Leeds and London, and in North America, in Philadelphia. Since 1945 Maney Publishing has worked closely with learned societies, their editors, authors, and members, in publishing academic books and journals to the highest traditional standards of materials and production.

GERMANIC LITERATURES

Germanic Literatures includes monographs and essay collections on literature originally written not only in German, but also in Dutch and the Scandinavian languages. Within the German-speaking area, it seeks also to publish studies of other national literatures such as those of Austria and Switzerland. The chronological scope of the series extends from the early Middle Ages down to the present day.

Managing Editor
Dr Graham Nelson, 41 Wellington Square, Oxford OX1 2JF, UK
www.legendabooks.com

The Very Late Goethe

Self-Consciousness and the Art of Ageing

CHARLOTTE LEE

LEGENDA

Germanic Literatures 5
Modern Humanities Research Association and Maney Publishing
2014

Published by the
Modern Humanities Research Association and Maney Publishing
1 Carlton House Terrace
London SW1Y 5AF
United Kingdom

LEGENDA is an imprint of the
Modern Humanities Research Association and Maney Publishing

Maney Publishing is the trading name of W. S. Maney & Son Ltd,
whose registered office is at Suite 1C, Joseph's Well, Hanover Walk, Leeds LS3 1AB

ISBN 978-1-909662-12-4

First published 2014

Printed in Great Britain

Cover: 875 Design

Copy-Editor: Nigel Hope

CONTENTS

FOR MY PARENTS

ACKNOWLEDGEMENTS

I owe my greatest debt to Nicholas Boyle, who supervised the doctoral thesis on which this book is based. Without his remarkable learning, his generosity with his time and insight, and above all his kindness, this study quite simply could not have been. It has been my great privilege to work with him.

It is with pleasure and gratitude that I acknowledge the Arts and Humanities Research Council, which funded the PhD in its entirety; in Cambridge, Gonville and Caius College and the Tiarks Fund of the German Department, for their generosity in providing grants; and, in Berlin, the Friedrich Schlegel Graduiertenschule at the Freie Universität, which hosted me for a semester. I am particularly grateful to the community at Murray Edwards College for electing me to a research fellowship, and for being forthcoming with support of every kind since my arrival.

I am indebted to the team at Legenda, especially to Nigel Hope, whose scrupulous copy-editing saved me from many embarrassing errors, and to Graham Nelson for all his good-humoured efficiency.

Many other individuals have contributed to the development of the project. Joyce Darby's inspiring teaching first kindled my interest in German some thirteen years ago. Anita Bunyan has been unstinting in her encouragement since the beginning of my time as an undergraduate, and Peter Hutchinson helped in more ways than I can count during the PhD, not least with the generous gift of so many of his books. As examiners, he and Angus Nicholls were supportive and challenging in equal measure, and I benefited greatly from their insightful comments. I am also very grateful to Roger Paulin and Martin Swales for their input during a particularly rigorous period of assessment. John Guthrie and Joachim Whaley have both been invaluable sources of advice, and, in earlier years, Stephen Fennell encouraged the development of some of the ideas underlying this project.

Sincere thanks also to many friends in Cambridge and Berlin, who have been both great interlocutors and great fun, and especially to Semele Assinder, Lucy Bell, James Jones, Regina Sachers, Ed Saunders, Catherine Smale, Anja Stadeler, and Hanna Takeuchi for boosting me whenever confidence has been on the wane, and to Rosemary Boyle for being so welcoming.

Finally, my dear parents, Margaret and Stephen: with their love and wisdom, their belief in education and humanity, they have brought me to this point. I cannot adequately express what they mean to me, but this book is dedicated to them.

C. L., Cambridge, February 2014

ABBREVIATIONS

Critical editions of Goethe's works

FA   Johann Wolfgang Goethe, *Sämtliche Werke: Briefe, Tagebücher und Gespräche,*
      ed. by Dieter Borchmeyer, Karl Eibel, Albrecht Schöne, and others
      (Frankfurt am Main: Deutscher Klassiker Verlag, 1985–99)
HA   *Goethes Werke. Hamburger Ausgabe in 14 Bänden,* XIII, ed. by Erich Trunz
      (Munich: Beck, 1981)
MA   Johann Wolfgang Goethe, *Sämtliche Werke nach Epochen seines Schaffens:
      Münchener Ausgabe,* ed. by Karl Richter and others (Munich: Hanser,
      1985–98)
WA   *Goethes Werke. Hrsg. im Auftrage der Großherzogin Sophie von Sachsen*
      (Weimar: H. Böhlau, 1887–1919)

Journals

DVjs   *Deutsche Vierteljahrsschrift für Literaturwissenschaft und Geistesgeschichte*
GJb   *Goethe-Jahrbuch*
GLL   *German Life and Letters*
GY   *Goethe Yearbook*
JDS   *Jahrbuch der Deutschen Schillergesellschaft*
JFDH   *Jahrbuch des Freien Deutschen Hochstifts*
JGG   *Jahrbuch der Goethe-Gesellschaft*
JWGV   *Jahrbuch des Wiener Goethe Vereins*
MLN   *Modern Language Notes*
MLQ   *Modern Language Quarterly*
MLR   *Modern Language Review*
OGS   *Oxford German Studies*
PEGS   *Publications of the English Goethe Society*
PMLA   *Publications of the Modern Language Association of America*

Translations in the text are my own unless stated.

INTRODUCTION

I

The note which Goethe made in his diary on the completion, after nearly sixty years of work, of his *Faust*, is peculiarly casual: 'Das Hauptgeschäft zustande gebracht. Letztes Mundum. Alles rein Geschriebene eingeheftet' [Main business achieved. Final version. All pages of fair copy fastened together].[1] The entry continues simply with the letters he wrote that day, the visitors he received. Yet the understatement of these lines does not detract from the significance of that little word 'Hauptgeschäft', which, in various permutations, including 'Hauptzweck' [main goal], is a recurring motif in his diary for 1831, and especially for July. Its frame of reference is both quite local — the completion of *Faust* as the most important of a number of jobs to be done, which include writing letters and receiving visitors — and very broad, for it refers also to the summation of his life's activity.[2] The reticence of the diary entry suggests that there is little more to say: and indeed, *Faust. Zweiter Teil* [*Faust. Part Two*] was Goethe's last major work, apart from the conclusion of *Dichtung und Wahrheit* [*Poetry and Truth*], before his death at the age of eighty-two. The word 'Hauptgeschäft' is, moreover, a clue to the situation of the person who has opted to use it: someone, namely, who feels that the end is near, and that what he has left to say surpasses all that he has said — in short, someone who is old, but who is still driven to create. This study is concerned with the six or so years of activity leading up to the completion of the 'Hauptgeschäft'. My contention is that the major literary works, from the *Trilogie der Leidenschaft* [*Trilogy of Passion*] onwards, form a distinct group — which I shall call the 'very late' works — and are marked by the particular creative energy which knows that the 'Hauptzweck' has yet to be achieved, and so by what I here define as 'self-consciousness'.

The thrust towards a goal, the finality of which cannot be matched at any other stage of life, is offset in these works by retrospection: the tendency, that is, of an elderly person to reflect upon what he has done in his life, on the versions of his self. Self-consciousness is the necessary consequence of a very late author's memory; but it is also a non-psychological feature of the texts themselves. There are two aspects to this. First, all the major literary works of this phase display — in varying combinations — standard[3] reflexive features: self-irony, overt allusions to and transformations of the literary and mythological canon, or the thematization of the process of writing. Yet, although they appear with greater frequency in the very late works, these moments are not innovations, but the continuation of practices which Goethe adopted throughout his writing career.[4] The second aspect of the self-consciousness of these texts, however, *is* new to this period: their replication, namely, of the work of memory, by incorporating and reconsidering material from earlier works of Goethe's own. Of course, the psychological and the literary senses of self-consciousness cannot be fully severed from one another. In respect of 'Über allen Gipfeln' ['Over all the hilltops'], Martin Swales and Erika Swales observe that:

> within the lyrical formation there is also a drama of self-reflexivity [...] Grammatically and cognitively, the subject is self-conscious, and is, by virtue of that condition, more unquiet than the mountain tops, the tree tops, and the birds, more complexly constituted.[5]

And 'Über allen Gipfeln' is a relatively early poem (1780). The centrality of memory to the very late period of Goethe's work causes the psychological and the purely literary to slide over into one another more than ever. It is for this reason that 'self-consciousness' will be the preferred term in this study. It expresses more completely than other, related concepts (such as reflexivity, self-reference, or metafiction) the human dimension of the phenomenon: the fact that these texts emanate from a person, and that their reflexive, self-referential features are not only a function of themselves, but also of the mind, the consciousness behind them.

This position is hardly free from controversy. Throughout the twentieth century, formalist, structuralist, and poststructuralist theorists advocated attention to the internal logic and composition of the text, its rhetoricity, rather than to its supposed field of reference (including the feelings and preoccupations of its author). A particularly provocative contribution was 'The Death of the Author' (1967), in which Roland Barthes contended that: '[t]o give a text an Author is to impose a limit on that text, to furnish it with a final signified, to close the writing'.[6] The essay was an important moment in ridding literary criticism of the shackles of straightforwardly biographical interpretation: a limiting force which for decades dogged Goethe studies,[7] and one of which Goethe himself was only too aware. When, in 1820, Goethe received an interpretation of his 'Harzreise im Winter' ['Winter Journey in the Harz Mountains'] (1777) from one Karl Friedrich Ludwig Kannengießer, who had tried to deduce Goethe's personal situation from the symbolism of the poem, he responded with a biographical gloss on the text, which was published in *Kunst und Altertum* [*Art and Antiquity*] in 1821.[8] The piece purports to confirm the perspicacity of Kannengießer's reading, and to offer 'nähere Aufklärung' [further elucidation] of the poem; but it is little more than a paraphrase, with some additional details about his itinerary and the meteorological conditions, which tells us nothing new about the text itself. It is a strange essay, but it hardly seems likely that, as Klaus Weimar claims, Goethe was not fully aware of the interpretative complexity of his own texts.[9] Rather, for all his professed support for Kannengießer, his response is, I think, deliberately disingenuous: another example, like the diary entries concerning the completion of *Faust*, of his deliberate and maddening reticence at moments when the reader craves more. His essay suggests, by means of a tacit parody of naively literal reading, that poetry not only is, but must be about more than the person and the situation behind it.[10] He is concerned to protect the ineffability of the poem's meaning, but also that of the private life of the self: his commentary actually suppresses one of the most important motivating forces behind 'Harzreise im Winter', namely the crisis of his 'vocation' at the Weimar court.[11] Here, then, empirical or biographical reality and the reality of the poem are forced apart by the author himself.

Barthes's essay depends, however, on a rather narrow, indeed old-fashioned conception of authorship, as if the historical personage, who is 'thought to *nourish* the book, [...] is in the same relation of antecedence to his work as a father to his child',[12] and could be confidently separated from what he calls 'the modern scriptor', who is 'born simultaneously with the text [...] [and] is not the subject with the book as predicate'.[13] It is perhaps more plausible to imagine a continuum between Barthes's 'author' and 'modern scriptor'. As Angus Nicholls observes, ' "Goethe" is in a sense a product of the poems, letters and conversations rather than an ontologically secure historical origin from which they emerged and according to which they can be interpreted',[14] but this does not render redundant the '[careful examination of] his life, historical contexts, correspondence, and opinions in relation to the works'.[15] Barthes's actual preoccupation, and the real issue affecting Goethe studies, Nicholls contends, is the question of authority: 'Goethe's authority as an interpreter of these works should not simply be accepted and must continually be questioned'.[16] My own argument proceeds from a similar, though not identical, assumption. Goethe's own pronouncements on his work and on theories of literature should be treated with caution, and the temptation to equate them unreservedly with his own poetic practice should be resisted, not least because of the impish presence, in many of his public statements, of what Katrin Kohl has called his 'strategies of self-projection'.[17] These strategies can veer between the inventive and, as we saw with his response to Kannengießer, the deliberately misleading. Goethe had (*pace* Klaus Weimar) a very sophisticated understanding of his own poetry, and in that respect can be credited with some authority, just not necessarily in those places where he purports to offer the last word.

Yet to accept that a text was written by a particular person, and that it *does* matter who that person was, is not necessarily to claim a single, immutable message for it. After all, human nature — and, consequently, that of both author and reader — is itself constantly shifting, is every bit as much 'a multi-dimensional space in which a variety of writings, none of them original, blend and clash'[18] as a written text. It is now self-evident that texts have an existence independent of the circumstances of their composition, but that does not make them empty vessels ready to be filled by the reader; and sometimes — as, I shall argue, in the case of Goethe's very late works — those circumstances may shape them in lasting ways, in ways, moreover, which themselves allow for the quality of 'multiplicity' which Barthes is so anxious to claim back for writing.

II

There have been various book-length studies of literary self-consciousness in Goethe's writing, but their emphasis is quite different from my own. It is evident even from the titles of two of the most recent contributions — Joan Wright's *The Novel Poetics of Goethe's 'Wilhelm Meisters Wanderjahre': Eine zarte Empirie* (2003) and Sebastian Kaufmann's *'Schöpft des Dichters reine Hand ...': Studien zu Goethes poetologischer Lyrik* (2011) — that the chief focus of critics' attention has been the reflexive play with genre within these texts, 'the ways in which the work succeeds in being both a novel and a poetics of the novel'[19] (or poem, or play).[20] The purpose, and achievement, of these studies is indeed more than simply to extract an aesthetic theory from the literary works.[21] Nonetheless, the main interest of self-conscious tendencies lies for these critics in the evidence which they provide of a theorizing edge to texts which, far from being 'naive',[22] incorporate into themselves an awareness of 'the infinite and boundless nature of the interpretative task'.[23] The distinguished contribution in this 'poetological' vein remains David Wellbery's 1996 study, *The Specular Moment: Goethe's Early Lyric and the Beginnings of Romanticism*. Although self-consciousness is not explicitly designated as the focus of the book, it is concerned with the self-making of poetry, and, through it, of humanity:

> The poetic vocation envisioned and enacted in the 'Prometheus' ode is the declaration of autonomy. Poised at the peripeteia of history, where it herme-neutically discloses the truth of the mythic past as the promise of a self-forming humanity, the poetic utterance becomes the paradoxical figure through which humanity freely constitutes itself.[24]

It is impossible to do justice to the book's full argument here, and indeed there are moments in it which are not without question. The passage above, for example, makes perhaps excessively grand claims for 'Prometheus', magnificent and challenging though the poem is. However, Wellbery's interest in the recodification of established discursive practices, such as the idyll or the poetry of religious quest, in Goethe's early lyric poetry is of particular resonance for this study. For he understands that process as intimately linked with the creation of a new space for the elaboration of subjectivity; and the remodelling of past forms to free up new paths of exploration for the self is also a central process in Goethe's last works, although it manifests itself very differently there.

There is a (productive) tension in the appeal which Wellbery makes, both implicitly and explicitly, to the *objectivity*, or autonomy, of the text in order to highlight its figurations of subjectivity. His suggestion at various points that the subjectivity elaborated in the early poems is, for example, 'a metaphorical presence'[25] worked out within a 'network of reference'[26] makes it plain that, in his use of the term, the self does not mean individual, personal identity; rather, it is potential, which is shaped within a community of readers and writers. This is particularly important where the identity of the poet is concerned. We have already seen that a methodology grounded simply in biographical data will not do, and in that respect I do not dispute Wellbery's assertion that:

> a biographical construal of the lines [of 'Harzreise im Winter'] that links them to Goethe's ascent of the 'Brocken' is entirely out of place. Such a derivation of the figure misses the essential issue, that the autonomy of poetic cognition is here being thematized.[27]

This is, however, somewhat overstated: is Goethe's ascent of the Brocken *entirely* irrelevant? And if so, who decrees the relevance of other types of context, such as that of contemporary discourse, to which Wellbery — I think rightly — attaches such importance in his study? His argument, as I understand it, rests on a conception of art and life as fundamentally separate. But what happens when the course of the poet's career is written in to his work — as, for example, in 'An Werther' ['To Werther'], the first poem in the *Trilogie der Leidenschaft*? When his poetry, whilst it can still be the figuration of 'a' subjectivity, is now also, by means both indirect and overt, *a* figuration of *this* subjectivity, that of the author of *Werther*?[28] This book is addressed to that question. The interpretations which it offers do not seek to reduce the texts in its corpus to the direct expression of a particular 'Erlebnis' [experience], but do take into account the perspective from which they emerged, which profoundly affects how they are written: the perspective, namely, of an old man, with an immense writing career behind him. This is where the term 'self-consciousness' is so helpful. It allows the text the independence of a 'discursive event'[29] — that is, an autonomous system with its own performative field of reference and self-reference. Yet, at the same time, it upholds an essential connection to the life, to the human being behind it, who is, in this particular case, manifestly not dead to it. Goethe's major literary works of this period are not straightforward descriptions of his situation, but they can be read as a reflective response to it. In this study, then, the strictly poetological aspect of self-consciousness will be considered together with its other forms, above all memory.[30]

It is the predominance of memory in Goethe's last works which links them to one another and makes them a distinct subset of his oeuvre. As Karl Pestalozzi writes:

> Das kennt man nun gerade als eine Besonderheit des Alters, dass man nicht auf das jedermann vor Augen Liegende reagiert, sondern eigene Assoziationen, Erinnerungen, selbst gemachte und von Fremden übernommene Erfahrungen das Wahrgenommene förmlich überschwemmen.[31]

> [It is, we know, a peculiarity of old age that one does not simply react to things which lie plain for all to see, but that one's perceptions are positively flooded with personal associations and memories, with experiences both of one's own and appropriated from others.]

At no other point in Goethe's career is his writing so saturated with allusions to the past, to *his* past, or indeed with reflections on the nature of memory. It is for this reason that I apply the term 'very late' to these works. This move, too, may provoke debate. Goethe's life has already been subdivided into a number of periods, and readers are bound to ask whether another one is necessary, or even desirable. The issue of periodization, of course, is itself far from straightforward, and has received intense scrutiny at least since the late 1960s.[32] Timothy J. Reiss suggests that establishing discrete time frames can seriously interfere with our understanding of historical change and continuity:

> If we slice the 'line' into happily self-contained points (although to speak of lines belittles the endlessly broad complexities of experienced times and places), do we not hopelessly flaw analysis and understanding? Even the possibilities of understanding?[33]

Moreover, not all literary periods are helpful: they may receive an ideological impetus early in their formation which can distort our reading of those texts in which that phase is allegedly enshrined. The prime example of this from Goethe's own career is Weimar Classicism: a denomination which, as Reinhold Grimm, Jost Hermand, and the other contributors to *Die Klassik-Legende* show, had as much to do with nation-building after German unification in 1871 as it did with the enthusiasm of Goethe and Schiller for the ancient world, but which has nonetheless proved remarkably tenacious.[34] Yet, as Lawrence Besserman observes, the out-and-out rejection of periodization can lead, indeed has led, to the development of 'a counter-myth: that we are the giants [...], liberated from tyrannical and specious claims of continuity and segmentation forged and passed along by a chain of white male dwarves'.[35] This comment (or 'warning', as he calls it) comes at the end of a thorough survey of the debates surrounding the issue of periodization, and Besserman's concern here is to show that revisionism, too, can be ideologically motivated. His words suggest that *all* methods of historiography must be reflexively undertaken, for none is innocent. It is on that understanding that I mount my own argument: in the full knowledge that all time frames are fallible and to an extent (but only to an extent) artificial, but in the belief that, if managed with care, the designation of a period for study can train the eye on distinctive, perhaps even unique, occurrences.

For there is a compelling case to be made for positing a very late period in Goethe's writing. First of all, there is a need to distinguish between the period roughly from the *Trilogie der Leidenschaft* onwards, and the rest of Goethe's so-called *Spätwerk* [late works], which is commonly held to extend as far back as *Die Wahlverwandtschaften* [*Elective Affinities*] (1809)[36] and the first stages of work on *Dichtung und Wahrheit* (1810/11). Peter Eichhorn is unquestioning in his acceptance of the supposed consensus that Schiller's death and the collapse of the Holy Roman Empire mark the point in Goethe's career which ushers in his 'Spätzeitlichkeit' [lateness].[37] Yet, although the 'crisis' of 1805/6 is indubitably a pivotal moment for Goethe, and the point of transition to a more mature phase, the single designation 'spät' or 'spätzeitlich' is not commensurate with the long twenty-six years between 1806 and Goethe's death, or with the extraordinary variety of the material which he produced in that time. Moreover, there is a difference between Goethe's last works and those of, for example, Mozart or Jane Austen: the term 'late work' is sometimes applied in cases such as theirs to denote a shift in style which, with the benefit of hindsight, we know to be chronologically 'late' or last because their career was brought to an end by premature death. In Goethe's case, however, lateness — or, as I prefer to call it, very-lateness — is about being old: it is about having memories, and about being towards the end of a long life. Again, this sense of death's waiting is not the same (though it is not necessarily any less difficult) for an elderly person as for, say, the 31-year-old Schubert, gravely ill with syphilis and writing the songs which would posthumously be collected together as *Schwanengesang*: for in the first case, lateness is a function of the depth of memory and experience, whereas in the second, it is the unhappy anticipation of an untimely ending. Goethe's very late phase, then, is a singular one, which he has not yet reached in *Die Wahlverwandtschaften*, or even in the *West-östlicher Divan* [*West-eastern Divan*], when he is still 'within hailing distance of middle age'.[38] A literary-critical construct it may be, but it is by no means arbitrarily imposed: rather, it takes its cue from trends within the texts with which it is concerned, and is grounded in the empirical fact that Goethe was nearing the end of a long life when he composed them. The point in time which, I shall recommend, we might see as its beginning is just that — a recommendation; but, unlike most literary periods, its end is non-negotiable. It is, to borrow a notion from Timothy Reiss, only one possible 'story', but it is a story that needs to be told.[39]

This book is the first full exploration of the implications of very-lateness in relation to Goethe.[40] In his own last book, *On Late Style* (published posthumously in 2006), a study of the work which, among others, Beethoven, Thomas Mann, and Jean Genet produced at the end of their lives, Edward Said identifies two kinds of 'last work': first, 'a special maturity, a new spirit of reconciliation and serenity often expressed in terms of a miraculous transfiguration of common reality';[41] but second, and, for his purposes, more interestingly, 'artistic lateness not as harmony and resolution but as intransigence, difficulty, and unresolved contradiction'.[42] This second, 'catastrophic'[43] type of lateness is not exactly the note which Goethe strikes, but it is useful to keep it in mind. Once the characterization, dominant in the nineteenth century, of Goethe's later work as a time of senility, of 'bedauerliches Erstarren und Absinken [...] Schwäche und Verknöcherung' [a regrettable paralysis and subsidence, [...] weakness and ossification][44] had been overcome, a countervailing tendency developed among many critics, who wanted to see serenity above all in that same period of his output. Christine Wagner-Dittmar, for example, writes of '[d]ie Freiheit und Gelassenheit des Alters' [the freedom and serenity of old age], '[d]ie innere Entspannung' [inner relaxation].[45] A related trope is the notion of an Olympian distance (the distance, that is, of wisdom rather than of exile), of 'objectivity' as the defining quality of these works.[46] The problem with appraisals such as these is that they overlook the flashes of pain, of doubt — indeed, to use Said's word, of *difficulty* — which, though they by no means set the entire tone for the last works, are undeniably there. Here, once again, the term 'self-consciousness' has valuable work to do: for it implies a dichotomy of self-knowledge and self-limitation, which, in Goethe's case, is at the heart of very-lateness. Critique and questioning (including self-questioning) are implicit in the metafictional or metapoetic model;[47] and if reflection on the past, on one's development, can sharpen self-knowledge, it must also (if done honestly) oblige one to confront the limitations of memory and of understanding. Thus two main forces run through the works of the very late Goethe: a new and remarkable flowering of creativity on the one hand, and a constant preoccupation with the deficiencies of knowledge and self-knowledge on the other. That is their difficulty, but also their strength.

In Goethe's case, self-consciousness is a mode of writing rather than a theory which is elaborated: it is writing which reflects on its own making, and, in the very late phase, does so in cooperation with memory. Yet his thought bears considerable relation to the speculative work of some of his contemporaries on the nature of being and consciousness. There has been a recent upsurge in research on Goethe's relationship to Kant, and to post-Kantian Idealism,[48] and there is plenty more work to be done. Although that is beyond the remit of this study, a brief sketch of the most important aspects of that relationship will bring sharper definition to the particular variant of the self-consciousness which can be discerned in Goethe's work. Common to both Kant and Goethe is extensive reflection on the nature of human cognition. The tenets of Kant's *Kritik der praktischen Vernunft* [*Critique of Practical Reason*] harmonized relatively easily with Goethe's own thought — or so he claimed in his 1820 essay 'Einwirkung der neueren Philosophie' ['Influence of Recent Philosophy'],[49] possibly in tacit acknowledgement of the overriding preoccupation, on the part of Schiller and others, with Kant as a moral philosopher, rather than as a philosopher of science and cognition, which was the real substance of his interest for Goethe. Goethe's experience of the first *Kritik*, on the other hand, was a little more fraught. In 'Einwirkung der neueren Philosophie', Goethe describes the impenetrability of some of Kant's ideas; and, although he did not agree with it, Herder's contempt for the text compounded its difficulty for him.[50] Nonetheless, Goethe's encounter with the *Kritik der reinen Vernunft* [*Critique of Pure Reason*], and especially with the *Kritik der Urteilskraft* [*Critique of Judgement*], was a productive one, as Geza von Molnár has shown.[51] Yet Molnár's strategy in his book *Goethes Kantstudien* is to keep to the markings which Goethe made in his copies of the various texts; and this leads to an overstatement of the importance of the first *Kritik* at the expense of the third. For, even if it bears less of his marginalia, it was the text of Kant's which held the greatest pleasure for him; indeed, his reading of the first *Kritik* was mediated through the third.[52]

An aspect of the relationship between Goethe and Kant which has been somewhat overlooked, but which is crucial to this study, is their shared commitment to the 'Ding an sich' [thing in itself]. I cannot accept Frederick Amrine's claim, in his essay on intellectual intuition, that '[a]t no point and in no way did Goethe ever agree with Kant's attempt to limit human knowledge'.[53] Although Goethe was passionate about developing methods of cognition — including, as Amrine shows, the very un-Kantian intellectual intuition — which might bring us closer to ideal knowledge, there is a persistent awareness in his writing of the limitations of human understanding. As we shall see, this acquires particular prominence in his very late works, but it took root much earlier. The preface to the *Farbenlehre* [*Colour Theory*] (1810), for example, opens with the caveat: 'eigentlich unternehmen wir umsonst, das Wesen eines Dinges auszudrücken. Wirkungen werden wir gewahr, und eine vollständige Geschichte dieser Wirkungen umfaßte wohl allenfalls das Wesen eines Dinges'[54] [the endeavour to express the basic nature of a thing is in fact a vain one. We become aware of effects, and a complete survey of these effects would at best provide a thorough conspectus of the nature of a thing]. The element of hesitation is particularly clear in the German: for, although it is generally used to suggest comprehensiveness, the word 'umfassen' also has the sense here of surrounding the 'Wesen eines Dinges' rather than penetrating right through to it. Although more mildly formulated, both this excerpt and the continuation of the preface are strongly reminiscent of Kant's assertion in the *Transzendentale Ästhetik* that space and time are 'bloß subjektive Bedingungen aller unsrer Anschauung [...], im Verhältnis auf welche daher alle Gegenstände bloße Erscheinungen' [simply subjective conditions of our perception, in relation to which all objects are thus mere appearances].[55] The predominance of the words 'Erscheinungen' and 'Wirkungen' in Goethe's preface makes plain that his investigations are underpinned by an awareness of colour as a subjectively conditioned phenomenon. Like Kant, Goethe resists the radical scepticism of Hume and Berkeley by upholding the possibility that, sometimes, the 'Wesen eines Dinges', the 'Ding an sich selbst', may indeed be apprehended; but, for him, this is a matter of revelation, a gift from nature, not the direct result of human intuition.[56] Therefore, although Goethe would diverge from Kant at points (as, for example, in his 1820 essay 'Anschauende Urteilskraft' ['Intellectual Intuition']), his priority was not, as it was for the Idealists, to eliminate the notion of the 'Ding an sich'. For all that, ultimately, Fichte 'stressed the regulative status of [the] idea [of the absolute subject], and firmly rejected the thesis of "dogmatic idealism" that the absolute subject creates the entire world',[57] this aspect of the *Wissenschaftslehre* [*Doctrine of Science*] (1794) was still a step further than Goethe ever went. Nonetheless, his thought resonates with post-Kantian Idealism in important ways, and especially with the work of Hegel.

'Self-consciousness', as I use it in relation to Goethe, is not coterminous with Hegelian 'Selbstbewußtsein': the former denotes a highly sophisticated literary practice, whereas the latter refers to a relatively primitive stage in the development of *Geist*, as described in the fourth chapter of the *Phänomenologie des Geistes* [*Phenomenology of Spirit*]. But there are plenty of other points of resonance between the two thinkers. Goethe and Hegel corresponded intermittently for some two decades, and there was significant mutual respect, even admiration, between them. Hegel was outspoken in his defence of Goethe's *Farbenlehre*, which had been harshly received, and he was deeply influenced by Goethe's theory of morphology. Goethe, for his part, valued Hegel's unique mind, and commented on more than one occasion on Hegel's sensitivity to his own ideas.[58] Of course, they remained profoundly different thinkers. It goes without saying that Goethe did not share Hegel's conception of *Geist*, and that he did not seek, as Hegel did, to develop an all-encompassing philosophical system. Moreover, in his drafted letter to Seebeck of 28 November 1812,[59] Goethe expresses disquiet at the concept of negation which Hegel deploys in his account of natural development in the *Vorwort* to the *Phänomenologie* (not, as Goethe calls it in the letter, the *Logik*, which at the time was unpublished): 'Die Knospe verschwindet in dem Hervorbrechen der Blüte, und man könnte sagen, daß jene von dieser widerlegt wird' [The bud disappears as the blossom bursts forth, and it could be said that the former is invalidated by the latter].[60] Although Goethe retracted his initial, scathing comments almost immediately,[61] and declared himself to be more satisfied once Seebeck had explained the context of the remark to him,[62] negation was one aspect of Hegel's system which remained foreign to him.[63]

Yet other moments in the *Phänomenologie* bear a much stronger relation to Goethe's way of thinking. For Hegel, just as the Other is *aufgehoben*, both upheld and transcended, in the ongoing life of *Geist*, so the past endures even as it is left behind:

> die *Er-Innerung* hat [die Erfahrung der früheren Geister] aufbewahrt und ist das Innere und die in der Tat höhere Form der Substanz. Wenn also dieser Geist seine Bildung [...] wieder von vorn anfängt, so ist es zugleich auf einer höheren Stufe, daß er anfängt.[64]

> [memory has preserved, internalized the experience of earlier spirits, and it is the inner, and indeed higher, form of the essence. Therefore, when this spirit begins its formation anew, it starts as it were from a higher level]

That term 'Stufen' is key, recurring in the work of both Hegel and Goethe, albeit in different contexts. Hegel frequently uses it to describe the career of *Geist*,[65] and it is a central concept in Goethe's morphology.[66] Similarly, Goethe conceives of the twin processes of *Polarität* [polarity] and *Steigerung* [heightening] as the motor of nature; and Hegel's notion of the development of *Geist* also suggests a helical movement, one of repeated return to the same place, but on a higher level. Although, therefore, they may not be in agreement about *what* is developing, the form which they conceive for that development is strikingly similar. Moreover, Hegel's notion of *Er-Innerung* fits very comfortably with Goethe's poetic practice later on in his career. The *West-östlicher Divan*, for example, is an oscillation between the present and the past, a movement which preserves the legacy of what has been, without stifling new ideas; and this becomes common practice in the very late phase.[67] The poetry of the *Divan* — and, as we shall see, of *Faust* — is mediated through engagement with traditions both familiar and foreign: that is, through reflections on the history of poetry, or through what Hegel might call 'das *wissende, sich vermittelnde* Werden' [the *knowing, self-mediating* becoming][68] (that is, history, one of the two types of 'Entäußerung' which he posits for *Geist*). Thus Goethe's reflexive poetic practice, which incorporates earlier manifestations of itself into its innovations, bears a striking resemblance to moments in Hegel's argument; and this is suggestive less of any direct influence on Hegel's part than of enduring Idealist patterns in Goethe's thought.

III

This book examines self-consciousness and very-lateness, those two intimately related phenomena, in each of Goethe's last major literary works. Indeed, it is the first cross-genre study of literary self-consciousness in any period of his oeuvre. Chapter 1 will tease out the distinctive features of Goethe's very late style through an analysis of his lyric poetry. The phase begins, it will be argued, with the rearrangement in 1826 of three poems written a couple of years earlier — 'Aussöhnung' ['Reconcilement'], 'Elegie' ['Elegy'], and 'An Werther' ['To Werther'], in that order — to form *Trilogie der Leidenschaft*, which begins with 'An Werther'. The new cycle reverses the downward spiral into depression suggested by the original order of composition, and proceeds instead from intense reflection on the past, both distant and recent, to the cautious restoration of life and hope in the present. One of the hallmarks of Goethe's very late style is established with 'An Werther': the invocation, namely, of a very particular poetic past, that of his own career. This practice begins to soar in the *Chinesisch-deutsche Jahres- und Tageszeiten* [*The Chinese-German Book of Hours and Seasons*] (written in 1827), and in the Dornburg poems of 1828: these are full of little echoes of earlier works by Goethe — indeed, they are full of memory. Yet, far from being simple recapitulations, these poems are very different from what has gone before. A further characteristic of the very late phase, then, is what I shall call poetic 'Steigerung': the self-conscious transformation of motifs from the past to yield strikingly new work in the present. This overwhelming sense of renewed creativity is matched in the *Jahres- und Tageszeiten* and the Dornburg poems by frequent moments of recognition and self-knowledge, although these are always balanced by flashes of pain, or by reminders of the limitations, both of old age and of human cognition in general, that persist.

Chapter 2 will see an intensification of that element of dissonance which sounds quietly in the — mostly harmonious — poetry: for as our focus shifts to Goethe's autobiographical writing, limitation becomes the dominant note. It befits the ambivalence of the very late phase that the genre most overtly concerned with memory should also contain the most explicit doubts about its effectiveness. Both the *Zweiter Römischer Aufenthalt* [*Second Roman Sojourn*] (1829) and *Dichtung und Wahrheit. Vierter Teil* [*Poetry and Truth. Part Four*] (1830–31) place continuous emphasis on the distance between the older, narrating self and the younger avatar, and thereby on the impossibility of fully uncovering the past. At the heart of the *Zweiter Römischer Aufenthalt*, there is absence: it is, after all, the intrinsic concern of both retrospective writing and ekphrasis (the two dominant modes of the work) to compensate for something which is missing, to unmake loss. *Dichtung und Wahrheit IV*, moreover, breaks with the seamless storytelling of Parts I–III: the narrative is frequently interrupted as Goethe refers to the insufficiencies of his memory, or the difficulty of recreating the perspective of his younger self. If the very late poetry is notable for its overwhelming sense of creative self-renewal, the last autobiographical works express significant reservations about the possibility of complete self-knowledge.

Chapters 3 and 4 will treat Goethe's last major works in prose and drama (or dramatic poetry) respectively, namely *Novelle* (1826–27), *Wilhelm Meisters Wanderjahre* [*Wilhelm Meister's Journeyman Years*] (the second edition, completed in 1829), and *Faust II* (completed in 1831). These absorb the tension which can be discerned between the dominant mood of the lyric poetry and that of the retrospective writings — broadly, reconciliation and recognition on the one hand, and doubt and limitation on the other — sharing the hallmarks and preoccupations of both. Evidently, their scope and scale is very different: and those concerns which, in the poetry and the autobiographies, were the province of the individual self, are now addressed more broadly to humanity. Goethe's very late prose fiction, the *Wanderjahre* above all, is well known for its reflexive qualities; but Chapter 3 will deepen our understanding of this, bringing to the fore aspects of its self-consciousness which have not previously been noticed. In addition to the traits common to most metafictional prose — interruptions from the narrator, allusions to the process of writing, the inclusion of extraneous material to throw into relief the constructed nature of even the main narrative — the *Wanderjahre* displays features specific to this phase of Goethe's work. Foremost among these is rewriting: poetic *Steigerung* now takes place on a far grander scale, with scenes and motifs from *Wilhelm Meisters Lehrjahre* [*Wilhelm Meister's Years of Apprenticeship*] recast in a very different mould, and occasionally in ways that incorporate references to the public reception of that novel. The *Wanderjahre* is no straightforward sequel or continuation; rather, its experimental energy comes from the mediation and transformation of its own textual past. It is in this work that our themes of self-consciousness and limitation converge most clearly. For one of its main motifs, and a key compositional principle, is the secret: the *Wanderjahre* refuses to offer easy, final meanings, just as its structure is by turns highly patterned and minutely controlled, and baffling and untransparent. Bound up in the frequent allusions to and reflections on the text's own making is an awareness of its own inadequacies, which is intimately related to the undercurrent of doubt which could be detected in the autobiographical works. Both the *Wanderjahre* and *Novelle* enact a gesture of self-limitation, which we shall meet again in *Faust*: they uphold a commitment to the improvement of human understanding, and to the existence of the ideal, but refuse to represent that ideal, preferring instead to gesture towards it.

Chapter 4, finally, will seek to reconcile two utterly opposed strands of *Faust* criticism: the understanding of the play as, on the one hand, a grand poetic affirmation, and on the other, a despairing parody — 'catastrophic', to use the term favoured by Said in relation to lateness. The self-consciousness of the work, it will be argued, allows it to be both. All the aspects of self-consciousness worked out in the preceding chapters, from poetic *Steigerung* to self-limitation, are present in *Faust II*. The play's poetry displays the qualities of self-renewal and experimentation now familiar from the very late poems and prose, yet it remains cautious about the potentialities of the human mind and human discourse — above all, paradoxically, in its closing scene, which appears so extravagant. This work, too, is full of memory: not only of *Faust I* and Goethe's oeuvre, but of the mythological, religious, and literary heritage of Goethe's Europe. Yet the transformative energy which runs through *Faust II* ensures that, as in the poetry, remembered motifs are not dry scraps of a lost past, but are animated by the spark of innovation. There is, though, a crucial split in the work, one which is simple, obvious, but has not been fully articulated in critical analyses: those highly reflective qualities which make *Faust*, the text, so remarkable are not shared by Faust, the character. His whole career, from the beginning of Part I to the end of Part II, is marked by a refusal to recognize limitations: 'Und was der ganzen Menschheit zugeteilt ist | Will ich in meinem innern Selbst genießen' [And I wish to experience the pleasure of man's whole lot within my inner self]. Furthermore, through his wager with Mephistopheles, a condition of which is that he may not linger on any one experience, he has contracted himself to eschew all forms of reflection, including memory: a disastrous miscalculation, which is at the heart of many of his subsequent errors. It is this disparity between *Faust* and Faust, between the self-conscious text and its (for the most part) unselfconscious central figure, which accounts for the simultaneously heroic and anti-heroic feel of the work.

Notes to the Introduction

1. Johann Wolfgang Goethe, *Sämtliche Werke: Briefe, Tagebücher und Gespräche*, ed. by Dieter Borchmeyer, Karl Eibel, Albrecht Schöne, and others (Frankfurt am Main: Deutscher Klassiker Verlag, 1985–99), XI (38), 431. All references will be taken from this edition (hereafter FA) unless otherwise stated.
2. Although, in earlier entries, the word 'Hauptgeschäft' has quite a different frame of reference, *Faust* and the climax which it represents have come by 1831 to be the main overtones of the word.
3. See, for example, Patricia Waugh in *Metafiction*, 2nd edn (London: Routledge, 2003), p. 2:

> *Metafiction* is a term given to fictional writing which self-consciously and systematically draws attention to its status as an artefact in order to pose questions about the relationship between fiction and reality. In providing a critique of their own methods of construction, such writings not only examine the fundamental structures of narrative fiction, they also explore the possible fictionality of the world outside the literary fictional text.

4. Critical analyses of this aspect of the earlier works include those by Monika Lemmel, *Poetologie in Goethes West-östliche Divan* (Heidelberg: Winter, 1987); Nicholas Boyle on the *Römische Elegien* in *Goethe: The Poet and the Age*, 2 vols (Oxford: Oxford University Press, 1991–2000), I, 632–41; David E. Wellbery, *The Specular Moment: Goethe's Early Lyric and the Beginnings of Romanticism* (Stanford: Stanford University Press, 1996); Kevin Hilliard, 'Römische Elegien XX: Metapoetic Reflection in Goethe's Classical Poetry', in *Goethe at 250: London Symposium. Goethe mit 250: Londoner Symposium*, ed. by T. J. Reed, Martin Swales, and Jeremy Adler (Munich: Iudicium, 2000), pp. 223–32; Joan Wright on *Die Leiden des jungen Werthers*, *Wilhelm Meisters Lehrjahre* and *Die Wahlverwandtschaften*, in *The Novel Poetics of Goethe's 'Wilhelm Meisters Wanderjahre': Eine zarte Empirie* (Lewiston, NY: Edwin Mellen Press, 2003), pp. 89–112; Charlie Louth, 'Goethe's Sonnets', *PEGS*, 72 (2002), 15–24, and Louth, 'Reflections: Goethe's "Auf dem See" and Hölderlin's "Hälfte des Lebens"', *OGS*, 33 (2004), 167–75.

5. Martin Swales and Erika Swales, *Reading Goethe: A Critical Introduction to the Literary Work* (Rochester, NY: Camden House, 2002), p. 27.

6. Roland Barthes, 'The Death of the Author', in *Image, Music, Text*, trans. by Stephen Heath (London: Fontana 1977), pp. 142–48 (p. 147).

7. See, for example, Wellbery, *The Specular Moment*, pp. 7–9, or Angus Nicholls, 'Goethe and Twentieth-Century Theory: An Introduction', *GY*, 16 (2009), 163–72 (esp. pp. 168–69).

8. *FA* XXI, 131–39.

9. See Klaus Weimar in Weimar and Wellbery, *Goethe, 'Harzreise im Winter': Eine Deutungskontroverse* (Paderborn: Schöningh, 1984), p. 37.

10. The editors of this volume (*FA* XXI) also allude in their commentary to Goethe's general reluctance 'das bessere Verständnis eines ästhetisch in sich geschlossenen Werkes von der Kenntnis der entstehungsgeschichtlichen Hintergründe abhängig zu machen' (p. 818).

11. See Boyle, *Goethe: The Poet and the Age*, I, 316.

12. Barthes, 'The Death of the Author', p. 145.

13. Ibid.

14. Nicholls, 'Goethe and Twentieth-Century Theory', p. 169.

15. Ibid.

16. Ibid.

17. Katrin Kohl, 'No Escape? Goethe's Strategies of Self-Projection and their Role in German Literary Historiography', *GY*, 16 (2009), 173–91.

18. 'The Death of the Author', p. 146.

19. Wright, *Novel Poetics*, p. 3.

20. Benjamin Bennett's study *Goethe's Theory of Poetry: 'Faust' and the Regeneration of Language* (Ithaca: Cornell University Press, 1986) is in a category of its own, and I shall engage with it at greater length in the chapter on *Faust*.

21. Sebastian Kaufmann writes that the purpose of his study is not 'aus den behandelten poetologischen Gedichten bloß eine Kunsttheorie zu extrahieren, die schon durch Goethes expositorische Schriften zur Ästhetik vorgegeben wäre' (*'Schöpft des Dichers reine Hand ...': Studien zu Goethes poetologischer Lyrik* (Heidelberg: Winter, 2011), p. 24).

22. In his highly influential essay, *Über naive und sentimentalische Dichtung* (1795), Schiller proposed a dichotomy of the 'naive' (i.e. unreflective) and the 'sentimental' (reflective) mind, of which Goethe and he respectively could be seen as embodiments. The 'naive' is held up by Schiller as an ideal, characteristic of the ancient Greeks and lost to all but the most exceptional of moderns, who are otherwise condemned, almost, to reflection. The notion proved appealing, and arguably had its part to play in the general image, tenacious until at least the middle of the twentieth century, of Goethe as a spontaneous and unreflective poet.

23. Wright, *Novel Poetics*, p. 269.
24. Wellbery, *The Specular Moment*, p. 346.
25. Ibid., p. 244.
26. Ibid.
27. Ibid., p. 384.
28. Wellbery's own contribution on *Trilogie der Leidenschaft* once again takes an approach which is *textimmanent*. See 'Wahnsinn der Zeit: Zur Dialektik von Idee und Erfahrung in Goethes *Elegie*', in *Die Gabe des Gedichts: Goethes Lyrik im Wechsel der Töne*, ed. by Gerhard Neumann and David E. Wellbery (Freiburg im Breisgau: Rombach, 2008), pp. 319–52. I discuss both the importance and the pitfalls of incorporating details from Goethe's biography into an interpretation of these poems, especially 'Elegie', in Chapter 1.
29. Ibid., p. 9.
30. On the link between memory and self-consciousness, see for example Jérôme Dokic:

    there is a sense in which (episodic) memory is a kind of 'vision' through our past life to the remembered experience. Now perhaps such a 'vision' is possible only if the subject is at least *capable* of self consciousness [sic] at any time between the remembered experience and the present. How can we 'see' through our past life if it consists in a mere succession of first-order mental states and episodes, neither unified nor bound together by any reflection?

    (Dokic, 'Is Memory Purely Preservative?', in *Time and Memory: Issues in Philosophy and Psychology*, ed. by Christoph Hoerl and Teresa McCormack (Oxford: Clarendon Press, 2001), pp. 213–32 (p. 231))
31. Karl Pestalozzi, 'Goethes Darstellung des Alters im Gedichtzyklus *Chinesisch-deutsche Jahres- und Tageszeiten*', in *Goethe. Freiburger Literaturpsychologische Gespräche: Jahrbuch für Literatur und Psychologie*, XXIX, ed. by Wolfram Mauser, Joachim Pfeiffer, and Carl Pietzscher (Würzburg: Königshausen und Neumann, 2010), pp. 219–37 (p. 226).
32. Lawrence Besserman provides a useful survey of the stages in this debate in his essay 'The Challenge of Periodization: Old Paradigms and New Perspectives' in a collection of essays edited by him and also entitled *The Challenge of Periodization: Old Paradigms and New Perspectives* (New York: Garland, 1996), pp. 3–27.
33. Timothy J. Reiss, 'Perioddity: Considerations on the Geography of Histories', *MLQ*, 62 (2001), 425–52 (p. 429).
34. *Die Klassik-Legende*, ed. by Reinhold Grimm and Jost Hermand, (Frankfurt am Main: Athenäum, 1971). Although this outstanding work was published some forty years ago, and there have been other reviews of the issue since then (for example, *The Literature of Weimar Classicism*, ed. by Simon Richter (Rochester, NY: Camden House, 2005)), I still do not believe that the debate about the efficacy of the term 'Weimar Classicism' has been satisfactorily resolved.
35. 'The Challenge of Periodization', p. 19.
36. See, for example, Wilhelm Flitner, *Goethe im Spätwerk: Glaube, Weltsicht, Ethos* (Schöningh: Paderborn, 1983; first published Hamburg: Claaßen, 1947), p. 16.
37. See Peter Eichhorn, *Idee und Erfahrung im Spätwerk Goethes* (Freiburg and Munich: Alber, 1971), p. 27.
38. Diana Athill, *Somewhere towards the End* (London: Granta, 2008), p. 13.
39. 'My point [...] is the need to formulate and implement the thought that places and practices involve varieties of temporalities and topologies that consequently enable and produce diversities of story. These are diversities in the very conditions of story: not what can be told but how and why.' 'Perioddity', p. 447.
40. Gerhard Wild's study *Goethes Versöhnungsbilder: Eine geschichtsphilosophische Untersuchung zu Goethes späten Werken* (Stuttgart: Metzler, 1991), is similar in scope, treating *Trilogie der Leidenschaft* and the Dornburg poems, *Novelle*, *Wilhelm Meisters Wanderjahre* and *Faust*, but very different in emphasis. The theme of the investigation is Goethe's aesthetic response to the challenges of modernity in the early nineteenth century, his attempt 'die *Entzweiung* von Arbeit und Liebe bzw. die durch die Ökonomie bedingte *Entfremdung* von Mensch und Natur aufzuheben' (p. 138). Wild's interest, therefore, is in the reaction of the late Goethe to the modern world, rather than in (very-) lateness *per se*, and self-consciousness is not a theme which he treats.

41. Edward Said, *On Late Style: Music and Literature against the Grain* (New York: Pantheon Books, 2006), p. 6.

42. Ibid., p. 7. R. T. Llewellyn specifically compares Beethoven's late quartets to *Wilhelm Meisters Wanderjahre* in 'Parallel Attitudes to Form in Late Beethoven and Late Goethe: Throwing Aside the Appearance of Art', *MLR*, 63 (1968), 407–16.

43. Ibid., p. 8. Said derives the term from Adorno's essay 'Spätstil Beethovens' in *Moments musicaux*.

44. Erich Trunz, 'Altersstil', in *Goethe Handbuch. Goethe, seine Welt und Zeit in Werk und Wirkung*, 1, ed. by Alfred Zastrau (Stuttgart: Metzler, 1961), p. 178. This quotation is Trunz's summary of nineteenth-century opinions, not his own view.

45. Christine Wagner-Dittmar, 'Goethe und die chinesische Literatur', in *Studien zu Goethes Alterswerken*, ed. by Erich Trunz (Frankfurt: Athenäum, 1971), pp. 122–228 (p. 202).

46. See, for example, Trunz, 'Altersstil', p. 180; or, more recently, Jane K. Brown, 'Theatricality and Experiment: Identity in *Faust*', in *Goethe's Faust: Theatre of Modernity*, ed. by Hans Schulte, John Noyes, and Pia Kleber (Cambridge: Cambridge University Press, 2011), pp. 235–52 (esp. pp. 247–48). Paul Stöcklein, similarly, writes of a 'Gesamtstil zeremonieller Langsamkeit und weiser Entrücktheit'. *Wege zum späten Goethe. Dichtung — Gedanke — Zeichnung: Interpretationen um ein Thema*, 2nd edn (Hamburg: Schröder, 1960), p. 331.

47. Again, see Waugh, *Metafiction*, p. 2.

48. In 2011, for example, the American *Goethe Yearbook* produced a special issue devoted to the topic.

49. See 'Einwirkung der neueren Philosophie', in *Goethes Werke: Hamburger Ausgabe in 14 Bänden*, XIII, ed. by Erich Trunz (Munich: Beck, 1981; hereafter HA), p. 28.

50. *HA* XIII, 27.

51. See Geza von Molnár, *Goethes Kantstudien: Eine Zusammenstellung nach Eintragungen in seinen Handexemplaren der 'Kritik der reinen Vernunft' und der 'Kritik der Urteilskraft'* (Weimar: Böhlaus Nachfolger, 1994).

52. See Boyle, *Goethe: The Poet and the Age*, II, 80–81.

53. Frederick Amrine, 'Goethean Intuitions', *GY*, 18 (2011), 35–50 (p. 38). Contrast Angus Nicholls: '[Goethe's] *Urphänomen* marks both the internal (subjective) and external (objective) limits of cognition, and in this sense it is also a principle or law of existence that tells one something about the very essence of Being' (*Goethe's Concept of the Daemonic: After the Ancients* (Columbia, SC: Camden House, 2006), p. 188).

54. *FA* XXIII.1, 12.

55. *Immanuel Kants Werke*, III (*Kritik der reinen Vernunft*), ed. by Ernst Cassirer and others (Hildesheim: Gerstenberg, 1973), p. 75. Geza von Molnár explains the lack of underlining at this point in Goethe's copy with the reminder that 'ihm [Goethe], wie fast allen Gebildeten der Zeit, das allgemeine Anliegen der "Kritik", so wie es in der Haupteinleitung vorgebracht wird, wohl schon längst vertraut war, was auch für das zentrale Thema der transzendentalen Ästhetik gelten mag' (*Goethes Kantstudien*, p. 25).

56. Goethe already uses the term 'sich offenbaren' in the preface to the *Farbenlehre* (*FA* XXIII.1, 12); and, like the theme of limitation itself, it becomes a recurring motif in his very late works.

57. Frederick Beiser, *German Idealism: The Struggle against Subjectivism, 1781–1801* (Cambridge, MA: Harvard University Press, 2002), p. 5.

58. See, for example, his letter to Reinhard of 5 March 1821 (*FA* IX (36), 155–56), or the dedication which accompanied the gift of an opaque wine glass which Goethe made to Hegel (*FA* IX (36), 164).

59. *FA* VII (34), 128–31.

60. Quoted in Goethe's letter; see also Hegel, *Werke*, III, ed. by Eva Moldenhauer and Karl Markus Michel (Frankfurt am Main: Suhrkamp, 1970), p. 12.

61. *FA* VII (34), 131.

62. *FA* VII (34), 151.

63. See Jeffrey Champlin, 'Hegel's *Faust*', *GY*, 18 (2011), 115–25.

64. Hegel, *Werke*, III, 591.

65. See, for example, the *Philosophie der Geschichte*, in *Werke*, XII, 105.

66. See *Versuch, die Metamorphose der Pflanzen zu erklären* (1790), *FA* XXIV, 110.
67. The *Divan* in many ways anticipates this last phase, but its self-consciousness, though very pronounced, is still not quite as intense as that of the last works: for it lacks the constant, and often quite overt, drawing of the poet's own (poetic) past (as well as that of humanity in general) into the new work which, as we shall see, runs throughout those works. For a fuller exploration of the relationship between the *Divan* and Hegel, see my article, '*Im flüßgen Element hin und wieder schweifen*: Development and Return in Goethe's Poetry and Hegel's Philosophy', *GY*, 20 (2013), 166–77.
68. Hegel, *Werke*, III, 590.

CHAPTER 1

Poetry

Self-consciousness is peculiarly central to lyric poetry: it is more intrinsic than in the novel or drama, and more subtle than in autobiography. Language is pressed into an unnaturally tight space, and the lyric is wrought out of reflection on the possible senses of each single word. During the eighteenth century, moreover, the life of the subject became a familiar province for lyric poetry.[1] The work which Goethe produced at the end of his life is no less poetry of the subject than his early lyric, though the premises for its exploration of subjectivity are profoundly different. The perspective from which the very late poems are written, the perspective that comes at the end of a long life, is a singular one. No one can know in advance the day or hour of the 'end', of course, but the sense that it is near is in itself a form of recognition, a type of self-knowledge: it is the ability to say 'I am old'. This is due to more than the simple fact of one's age climbing into the seventies, eighties, and beyond, or physical reminders that one is old. It is above all the result of the accumulation of memories, which flood the present; and the self-consciousness of Goethe's very late poetry is intimately linked with the handling of memory. The poems discussed here are all concerned, be it implicitly or explicitly, with the continuation of the self's existence, and with the role that the past has to play in securing the subject in self-understanding.

Two very late poems

There are two slight and little-known poems which are particularly useful in establishing what is meant by the 'very late' perspective. The poem 'Vor die Augen meiner Lieben' ['Before the Eyes of My Beloved'][2] is the clearest indication that Goethe had reached this stage. This was written in March, 1831 to mark his decision to return letters which he had received from Marianne Willemer to her, lest (it is implied) they find their way into the hands of someone else, such as the executor of his estate; and it was finally sent, together with the letters, the following February.

> Vor die Augen meiner Lieben,
> Zu den Fingern die's geschrieben, —
> Einst, mit heißestem Verlangen
> So erwartet, wie empfangen —
> Zu der Brust, der sie entquollen,
> Diese Blätter wandern sollen;
> Immer liebevoll bereit,
> Zeugen allerschönster Zeit.

[Before the eyes of my beloved, to the fingers which wrote them — once awaited as received, with the hottest desire — to the breast from which they sprang, these letters are now to wander; always in loving readiness, witnesses of a time most beautiful.]

This is a poem about burying a private experience away from the public, in the anticipation of the near end of one of the (private) lives which nurtured that secret. The first six lines are concerned with the return of the letters to their source, and thus with the closure of that stream of experience of which the correspondence was a manifestation. Or perhaps it is truer to say that the stream has been diverted: directed back to its source, from where it may yet take another direction. For the anticipated death of one of the correspondents does not mean the death of both, or of the relationship. The word 'wandern', which is assigned to the letters, is active, and the eyes, fingers, and breast which will receive them are, it is implied, very much alive. Moreover, the word 'einst' in line three, which denotes an experience long since departed, is balanced in the penultimate line with 'immer', which seems to promise the persistence of that experience, or of something like it. The optimism of the closing couplet is cautious: the implications of 'immer' are not confirmed by a verb in the present or the future tense; the noun 'Zeugen' is left without a verb to partner it. Nonetheless, the final line makes it clear that, although the original experience has passed, it has become something else, a memory: and the letters are the material instantiation of it. Returning the letters to their author will assist the survival of that most private memory in the mind of the other who shared it; and it is that recognition which enables the poet to part with them.

Memory, then, is clearly a major preoccupation for the very late Goethe, and the 1830 poem 'Erinnerung' ['Remembrance'][3] is a particularly interesting contribution to that theme:

ERINNERUNG

Er
Gedenkst Du noch der Stunden
Wo eins zum andern drang?
Sie
Wenn ich Dich nicht gefunden,
War mir der Tag so lang.
Er
Dann, herrlich! ein Selbander,
Wie es mich noch erfreut.
Sie
Wir irrten uns an einander;
Es war eine schöne Zeit.

[*He*: Do you still think of those hours of our keen desire?
She: If I did not have you close, the day seemed so long.
He: Then, o rapture! to be together — even now it fills me with joy.
She: We were mistaken in one another; it was a lovely time.]

Though it is superficially a piece of fun,[4] this poem is also a comment on the complexity of the relationship between the past and the present. 'Vor die Augen meiner Lieben' sets up a dialectic between 'einst' and 'immer', and, as we have seen, suggests that what has departed may persist in another form. 'Erinnerung' takes the same dialectic and treats it from a slightly different angle. On the one hand, the poem emphasizes the extent to which the past (indicated immediately by the opening words 'Gedenkst du noch') and the present ('Wie es mich noch erfreut') are bound up in one another. Just as the poem alternates between two interlocutors, so it is also concerned with another, implicit type of 'Selbander', namely the continuous flux between what was and what is. Yet the closing couplet, and — *if* we read this as a joke — the 'punch line', punctures the confidence, expressed by the male voice, in the persistence of what was. 'Es war eine schöne Zeit', the female voice contends in line eight, but that time was marked by error, which only becomes clear with hindsight. The deployment of 'es war' to correct the self-deception of the preceding couplet opens up a certain distance between past and present. Remembering, this poem suggests, is both about preserving the relationship between the two, and about detaching the one from the other. The past remains alive in memory — both *Er* and *Sie* are still talking about it — but memory is no buffer against the advance of time, and the development of different perspectives. Again, this suggests a degree of understanding unique to old age: for only in old age can one truly have the depth of experience, but also the courage, necessary to say 'es war'.

Trilogie der Leidenschaft

'Vor die Augen meiner Lieben' and 'Erinnerung' are among Goethe's last poems, and are therefore bound to display features typical of 'very late' style; but the phase begins, in fact, a few years earlier. It is well known that 'An Werther', 'Elegie', and 'Aussöhnung' were not originally conceived as a trilogy. They were written separately, between August 1823 and March 1824, and were only grouped together in 1826 for the *Ausgabe letzter Hand* (the definitive collected edition of Goethe's works, supervised by him). Moreover, that new order, the form in which we now know them, is the inverse of the order of composition: 'Aussöhnung' was actually written first, 'An Werther' last. The reorganization of the poems is clearly a deliberate intervention by Goethe into their semantics, and it is important to ask exactly what he was doing. For Meredith Lee, the *original* sequence of their composition represents a 'process of slowly regained distance and self-understanding'.[5] This is a defensible point: if read backwards, from 'Aussöhnung' through 'Elegie' to 'An Werther', the poems evince an increased willingness or ability on the part of the poet to face the pain of the Marienbad affair, as well as 'a sharpened sense of himself as a poet and as a man with a past and a future in "An Werther" '.[6] Yet the reorganization suggests that a still greater level of self-understanding had been reached in the two years that elapsed between their composition and the preparation of the *Ausgabe letzter Hand*. Now, in that revised version, the poems begin autobiographically: it is nothing less than the precondition of their existence that their poet 'is a man with a past and a future'. They pass through the profound and painful self-searching of 'Elegie' to the cautious reconciliation of 'Aussöhnung'.[7] If, as Meredith Lee argues, the present moment described in 'Aussöhnung' in 1823 was 'immobilized', passive, not properly understood,[8] the opposite is true in the 1826 version. Now the present is full of the past — both the immediate past of the preceding two poems, and the deeper past which stretches behind 'An Werther'; and it is only the active recognition of that past that makes any sort of 'Aussöhnung' in the present possible.

The 1826 version of the poems represents the end of one phase in Goethe's oeuvre, and the beginning of another. It records a biographical watershed: his love for the nineteen-year-old Ulrike von Levetzow, and her refusal of his offer of marriage, brought his annual visits to Marienbad to an end; indeed, he rarely travelled after that time, remaining in Weimar to concentrate on his work. On a more speculative level, it may be supposed that the experience forced him to confront the end of his life as a sexual being. In literary terms, the poems bear features which were to become characteristic of his very late work. Never again would personal circumstances be brought to bear as intensely on his poetry as in 'Elegie'; but the poetic past and future represented in 'An Werther' continue to be essential to the renewed focus on the present to which we are brought, by way of 'Elegie', in 'Aussöhnung', and in the other lyric works which were to follow. In their revised arrangement, the poems run counter to the biographical reality of the last years: the pain which, in the world of the *Trilogie*, is soothed by the end, continued in Goethe's own life after the writing of 'Aussöhnung'. Yet the sense of reordering the poems for the *Trilogie* is not the outright denial of pain, nor its definitive healing. The effect of the new order is, rather, the *Aufhebung*, the acknowledgement and aesthetic transformation of suffering. Pain continues to shoot quietly but sharply through the apparently harmonious poems composed after *Trilogie*; but it coexists in those works with a modest confidence, which might be called wisdom, and a poetic playfulness, so that the general tone is not one of despair, but one of hope. These poems are both touched by life, by Goethe's life, and are transformations of that life. Very late style thus begins with the reordering of 'An Werther', 'Elegie', and 'Aussöhnung' to form *Trilogie der Leidenschaft*.

'An Werther'[9] records an imaginary encounter between the poet and a character of Goethe's own invention. The poet compares their fates, Werther's early suicide as opposed to his own long life, and finds himself apparently unable to enthuse about his own career: 'Zum Bleiben ich, zum Scheiden du, erkoren | Gingst du voran — und hast nicht viel verloren' (ll. 9–10) [My lot was to stay, yours to depart, | And so on you went — and did not miss much]. The shadow of death hovers over the whole poem: in the first stanza, with the reminder of Werther's untimely death; in the middle of the poem, with the assertion that the vividness of life is ultimately deceptive — 'Doch tückisch harrt das Lebewohl zuletzt' (l. 38) [Yet, in the end, the farewell lies cruelly in wait]; and in the final stanza, with the revelation that those who choose a different path from Werther simply become caught in a further labyrinth of passions before the inevitable departure catches up with them. Yet the poem is also about life. Lines 11 to 38 could be interpreted as a reflection on the different stages of human existence: from the blissful innocence and curiosity of childhood in lines 11–14, to the tribulations of adolescence in lines 15–20, when one feels at odds with oneself and the world by turns (l. 16); and from the ecstasy of first love (ll. 21–32) to the twists and turns of the emotional life after that:

> Das Wiedersehn ist froh, das Scheiden schwer,
> Das Wieder-Wiedersehn beglückt noch mehr
> Und Jahre sind im Augenblick ersetzt [...] (ll. 35–37)

[Joyous it is to see her again, painful to be parted from her, it gladdens me still more to see her once again, and in a moment lost years are regained.]

The poem is evidently written from the perspective of someone who is in the position to look back over a life, and the *mise-en-abyme* of repetition itself in 'Wieder-Wiedersehn' indicates that one sense of that phrase is memory, the ultimate form of 'Wiedersehn'. Thus the line 'Und Jahre sind im Augenblick ersetzt' is a reflection not just on the tendency of time to rush between the alternating posts of 'Scheiden' and 'Wiedersehn', but on the power of memory to summon up, if only for a moment, the feelings of long ago.

This theme of retrospection is intertwined with another. The opening lines 'Noch einmal wagst du, vielbeweinter Schatten, | Hervor dich an das Tages-Licht' [Once again, much-lamented shade, you venture up to the daylight] express a level of familiarity with the addressee that can only come from his creator: the words 'wagst du' [literally 'you dare'] might be used by a parent to a child. Yet they also sound surprised, as if so much time had passed since the poet first dreamed up Werther that the character has almost taken on an existence of his own, and rises up in the manner of an involuntary memory. It is clear from the very title, 'An Werther', that this is a poem about being a poet, and specifically about being *this* poet, the one-time author of *Die Leiden des jungen Werthers*. Poetry about poetry is not confined to this period of Goethe's creativity. What *is* new, however — and is characteristic of this last phase of Goethe's writing — is the allusion not just to the poetic process *per se*, or to works by other poets, but to creations of his own; and, in 'An Werther', this is inextricably linked with the depiction of the unfolding of a life which might be his own. It is almost right to claim, as Sebastian Kaufmann does, that the poet's self and the character from the novel are worked out on the same, fictional level,[10] but this is not quite the whole story. There is certainly, in 'An Werther' as in most poems, an element of fictionalization in the creation of a poetic persona; but the words 'vielbeweinter Schatten' (like their cognate in *Faust II*, 'Bewundert viel und viel gescholten' [Much-admired and much-cursed][11]) refer to the public dimension of Werther's existence, the mourning of his fate by a readership which exists beyond the fictional world of either the original novel or the present poem. The poet's self, therefore, is also at a reflexive remove from the character: the fiction of *Werther* gave rise to the fact of its reception, which is now incorporated by the author of the original into the world of this new poem. Although, therefore, it has the autonomy of a fictional construct, 'An Werther' is also continuously, and deliberately, pulled back into history — above all, into the history of the writing career, and the life, of its poet.

For all the experience and the depth of memory that evidently lies behind the poem, the perspective from which it is written does not seem to be a privileged one. The poet draws attention to man's limited understanding and his propensity to self-deception: 'Des Menschen Leben *scheint* ein herrlich Los' (l. 11) [Human life *seems* a magnificent lot], 'Da steht es nah — und man *verkennt* das Glück. | Nun *glauben* wir's zu kennen!' (ll. 20–21) [Happiness is there, nearby — and we fail to recognize it. Now we *think* we recognize it!], 'Doch erst zu früh und dann zu spät gewarnt' (l. 33) [Yet we are warned too early at first, and then too late] (emphasis mine in all cases). This does not seem confined to early adulthood. Even those who reach a level of maturity beyond that of Werther when he died remain playthings of passions largely beyond their control: 'Dann zog uns wieder ungewisse Bahn | Der Leidenschaften labyrinthisch an' (ll. 43–44) [Then the uncertain path of the passions drew us on into its labyrinth]. There are (at least) two senses of 'uns'. First, a genuine first-person plural, meaning Goethe's public, the readers of *Werther*; and second, the editorial or royal 'we', meaning the poet himself, whose own efforts and achievements are increasingly cast into doubt. There is a hint of self-mockery in the words 'Wie klingt es rührend wenn der Dichter singt' (l. 47) [What a moving sound, when the poet sings]. The following line, 'Den Tod zu meiden den das Scheiden bringt!' [To avoid the death which separation brings], implies that poetry can at best provide consolation: the resounding 'bringt' at the end of the line emphasizes that 'Scheiden' is not to be avoided, even if death's sting might possibly be lessened. Moreover, the final line 'Geb' ihm ein Gott zu sagen was er duldet' [May a God help him to tell of his suffering], is a wish or plea rather than an affirmation. It is, of course, also an echo of a line from Goethe's *Torquato Tasso*, which is quoted verbatim at the beginning of 'Elegie'. Although Eckart Goebel exaggerates with his claim that the poem is an admission that human life is devoid of sense,[12] the mood of 'An Werther' is certainly muted, and the poet's confidence in poetry (especially, it could be argued, in his own) seems at a particularly low ebb. The point here is not, as Gerhard Wild argues, that poetry can lead us out of the labyrinth;[13] on the contrary, it refuses to offer any such assurance.[14] Despite the 'Aussöhnung', which does eventually come in the *Trilogie*, and which is upheld for the most part in the poetry written afterwards, this is one of a series of reminders of the limitations of poetry, indeed of all forms human discourse, which extends through Goethe's very late work.

'Elegie'[15] shares many themes with 'An Werther'. It too describes an encounter in the poet's mind, this time with 'Sie', his beloved; and the theme of 'Scheiden', of departure and especially of separation, is again central. 'Elegie' traces the different stages of the poet's love, from the time it first touches him to the period after the departure of the beloved, in which he vacillates between depression over her absence, the comfort of his imagination, and redoubled despair at the reality of things. If 'An Werther' was about both human life in general, and by implication the career of this particular poet, then 'Elegie' is unambiguously about the subjective experience of the speaker. The middle group of stanzas, between lines 43 and 90, makes it clear that the poem is less about the beloved herself than about the poet's experience of loving her. Faced with separation from her, he retreats further from the world into his heart, 'Ins Herz zurück' (l. 45); there he finds her image, which is more vivid than ever, and his love intensifies with it:

> Dort regt sie sich in wechselnden Gestalten;
> Zu Vielen bildet Eine sich hinüber,
> So tausendfach, und immer immer lieber. (ll. 46–48)

> [There she stirs in shifting forms; that single figure is transformed into many more, a thousand times over, and each one lovelier than the last.]

He believes he has found 'der Liebe heitern Frieden' (l. 75) [the bright peace of love], and a warmth which has brought about a thaw in his inner life:

> Vor Ihrem Blick [...]
> Zerschmilzt, so längst sich eisig starr gehalten,
> Der Selbstsinn tief in winterlichen Grüften; (ll. 85–87)

[Before her gaze my sense of self melts, for so long rigid as ice, buried deep in its wintry tomb]

This is an effect not simply of her beauty or grace, but of the poet's own love for her, of that 'tiefsten Sinn, den Sinn Ihr zu gehören' (l. 78) [deepest sense, the sense of belonging to her]. That this is a subjective reality does not make it any less real for the poet; but the preposition 'vor' in lines 85–86 suggests an implicit distance between him and the beloved: 'Vor Ihrem Blick, wie vor der Sonne Walten, | Vor Ihrem Atem, wie vor Frühlingslüften' [Before her gaze, as before the mighty sun, before her breath, as before the breezes of spring]; and in lines 46–48, he invests a great deal in the pictures of his fantasy, which suggests that he is drifting dangerously far from what is objectively possible.

To an even greater extent than in 'An Werther', the poem hints periodically that there is self-deception at work. Whereas most of the poem is written in the present or historic present, strophes two and three, which relate the brief period of time when the beloved was present, are written in the past tense; and this implies that the poet has a certain amount of reflective distance from his experience. The lines 'So warst du denn im Paradies empfangen, | Als wärst du wert des ewig schönen Lebens' (ll. 7–8) [So, then, you were received in paradise, as if you were worth the eternal life of beauty] are more barbed than they at first appear: for the subjunctive 'als wärst du wert' implies that the reality is rather different, and that this 'Paradies' is a flimsy realm — indeed, one that does not exist outside the imagination. We have already seen that the poet's perception is central to the poem, more central than any other reality; and the extraordinary phrase 'Als glich es ihr' (l.39) [As if it resembled her] reveals the extent to which his love and the fantasy that it stimulates have taken over: the wisp of cloud which reminds him of the beloved is not even her likeness, it is 'as if it were' her likeness — a far cry from the fleshly being which first inspired him to love. This implication of self-deception is supported by an extremely subtle, even private, piece of self-reference. That image in lines 37–40 recalls the poem 'Du Schüler Howards' ['You pupil of Howard's']: one of the poems written for or about Ulrike von Levetzow in August 1823 (that is, the month before 'Elegie'), and which were grouped together in the *Ausgabe letzter Hand* under the heading *Inschriften, Denk- und Suche-Blätter* [*Inscriptions, Thoughts, and Queries*]. In 'Du Schüler Howards', the poet wonders whether patterns in the ether might forecast his fortunes in love, just as here they remind him of the beloved. Although that poem does admit the possibility of a rainstorm, it is nonetheless hopeful in tone; but 'Elegie' ends on such a profound sense of futility that the cheeriness of 'Du Schüler Howards' now seems foolhardy. At least the closing line of 'An Werther' admitted the possibility of salvation through poetry. Now, the very gods who once inspired him — 'Der ich noch erst den Göttern Liebling war', (l. 134) [I who was but recently the favourite of the Gods] — have, he believes, conspired to bring about his destruction: 'Sie trennen mich, und richten mich zugrunde' (l. 138) [They tear me apart and bring me to destruction]. Those words 'den Göttern Liebling' are an allusion both to the poet's public profile, in the manner familiar from 'An Werther', and to this highly influential short poem by Goethe, written in 1777:

> Alles geben die Götter, die unendlichen,
> Ihren Lieblingen ganz,
> Alle Freuden, die unendlichen,
> Alle Schmerzen, die unendlichen, ganz.

> [The unending Gods give their favourites all things, complete, all the unending joys, all the unending woes, complete.]

These lines were prompted by the death of Goethe's sister, Cornelia;[16] but they are recalled in darker times still. Whereas before, the poet of 'Elegie' seems to be saying with this allusion, joy and pain were at least showered upon him in equal measure, all that awaits him now in his fall from grace and favour is desolation. Thus the experience of love, when the poet's heart and words surge, is framed in 'Elegie' by a more knowing, more ironic and disillusioned perspective.

The poet who believes himself to be in love (as opposed to his detached other voice, which recounts those experiences in retrospect) is not entirely deluded. He is indeed in love, but that subjective experience has come adrift from the reality of things external to him; and the intrusion, in the form of physical separation ('Nun bin ich fern!', l. 109 [Now I am far away!]), of objective reality seems to reduce to naught that private love, which just now was so vivid. The repetition of her image in his mind ('Er wiederholt Ihr Bild zu tausendmalen', l. 122) now becomes painful and compulsive, whereas in lines 46–48 it had been a delight. A new subjective experience, that of despair, takes the place of love, and the poet feels utterly alienated from the world and, crucially, from himself: 'Mir ist das All, ich bin mir selbst verloren' (l. 133) [I have lost the whole cosmos, I have lost myself]. The deeply disappointed poet rejects pursuits such as science, which no longer console him:

> Verlaßt mich hier, getreue Weggenossen!
> [...]
> Betrachtet, forscht, die Einzelheiten sammlet,
> Naturgeheimnis werde nachgestammelt. (l. 127, ll. 131–32)

> [Leave me here, loyal companions! [...] Contemplate, research, collect details, and may nature's mystery be stutteringly discerned.]

The allusion to science is, of course, a particularly autobiographical touch. This sense of alienation is accompanied by a loss of faith in the present moment: 'Nun bin ich fern! Der jetzigen Minute | Was ziemt denn der?' (ll. 109–10) [Now I am far away! The present moment — what does it require?]. That loss of faith is triggered by more than the absence of the beloved. In the advice, or imagined advice, which she gives him a few stanzas earlier, she counsels him to treasure the present: 'Dem Augenblick ins Auge! Kein Verschieben! | Begegn' ihm schnell, wohlwollend wie lebendig' (ll. 98–99) [Face the present moment! Do not tarry! Confront it quickly, be both kind and lively]. Yet, although he appreciates the value of her words — 'Du hast gut reden dacht' ich, zum Geleite | Gab dir ein Gott die

Gunst des Augenblickes' (ll. 103–04) [It's all very well for you, I thought: a God has given you the grace of the moment] — the poet soon finds himself unable to follow them. This is because the condition which she sets for seizing the present is being 'kindlich', or perceiving his environment with childlike simplicity: 'Nur wo du bist sei alles, immer kindlich' (l. 100) [Only, wherever you are, be everything, always childlike]: and there have been plenty of indications that the poet himself is anything but 'kindlich'. The issue here is not the supposed conflict between a problematic, mature state and an idealized, 'naive' one.[17] Rather, it is the cruel irony of the demand. For the words 'Der Selbstsinn tief in winterlichen Grüften' (l. 88) imply that the poet is old, and feels it; and the extraordinary superlative in 'Den letztesten [Kuß] mir auf die Lippen drückte' (l. 52) [Pressed the most final kiss on my lips] suggests the awareness of an approaching end. Similarly, the words 'Schon rast's und reißt in meiner Brust gewaltsam, | Wo Tod und Leben grausend sich bekämpfen' (ll. 117–18) [Already there is a violent raging, tearing in my breast, where life and death do dreadful battle] could be understood as the words not only of one contemplating suicide (which is the interpretation that suggests itself at first), but also of one at the end of life, when life and death literally tussle for possession of him. The unfortunate mention of childhood only serves to emphasize to the poet the loss of his own youth and its gifts: and the poem ends with his faith in his poetry and in himself at its nadir. The self-consciousness of this poem takes the form of self-questioning more severe than at almost any other point in Goethe's oeuvre.

In the new position accorded it for the *Trilogie*, 'Aussöhnung'[18] both recalls and moves on from the previous two poems. The emotions of 'An Werther' and 'Elegie' are telescoped in the first strophe. Once again, the predominant mode is loss and inadequacy. Our understanding is allegedly limited, 'Trüb' ist der Geist' (l. 5) [The mind is dull], our perceptions too: 'Die hehre Welt wie schwindet sie den Sinnen!' [The sublime world, how it disappears before our senses!] (l. 6). The reconciliation promised by the title is not, therefore, a magic solution, easy and total: the pain of the previous poems persists here. In the second stanza, the gift of music is to release man, however briefly, from the coils of this suffering by turning his gaze away from the earthly. Whereas the first stanza is rooted in the human body and mind ('Herz', 'Sinnen', 'Geist'), and time is divided into earthly units ('die Stunden'), the diction shifts in the second stanza to the transcendent: 'Engelschwingen' [the hovering of angels], 'mit ew'ger Schöne' [with eternal beauty]. Loss and lack are transformed into plenty: 'Verflicht zu Millionen Tön' um Töne' (l. 8) [weaves note upon note, in their millions], 'Zu überfüllen ihn mit ew'ger Schöne' (l. 10) [Flooding him with eternal beauty], and water begins to spring from the soul, which in the first strophe was so barren: 'Das Auge netzt sich' (l. 11) [His eye becomes moist]. The poet himself has not become transcendent; he is still rooted in the earthly, and can only yearn for the divine: 'im höhern *Sehnen*' (l. 11, my emphasis). Nor has his pain disappeared: 'Den Götter-Wert der Töne wie der Tränen' (l. 12) [The divine worth of music as of tears]. But he has been filled with the promise of something greater; and this propels him onward. The third strophe begins with a moment of recognition, even if the verb used to convey it is a very modest one, 'merken' [to notice]. The recognition is that, despite the fact of his ageing ('Wo sind die Stunden überschnell verflüchtigt?', l. 3 [Where did the hours fly to with such speed?]), despite all that has been lost, the poet still has life: 'Und so das Herz erleichtert merkt behende | Daß es noch lebt und schlägt und möchte schlagen'. (ll. 13–14) [And so the unburdened heart notices swiftly that it still lives, still beats and wishes to beat]. The most basic reality of the present moment — that his heart is still beating — suddenly becomes of overwhelming importance for the poet.

This is an abrupt return to physical immediacy after the ethereal metaphors of the previous stanza, but it is made not in despair, as in 'Elegie' ('Da bleibt kein Rat als grenzenlose Tränen' [No counsel remains but boundless tears]), but with hope. For not only does he have life, but he *chooses* life: 'möchte schlagen'. This is a new note of affirmation, indeed, given that the shadow of death has hung over the *Trilogie*, almost of defiance; and the continuing lines are anything but passive.[19] He offers up his heart in thanks for the 'überreiche Spende' (l. 15) [lavish gift]. The line 'Sich selbst erwiedernd willig darzutragen' (l. 16) [to offer up himself, willingly, in return] makes clear the real nature of the 'Aussöhnung' that is described here: namely, the poet's reconciliation with himself (and, perhaps, with his poetry). That terrible line in 'Elegie', 'Mir ist das All, ich bin mir selbst verloren', has been reversed. Now the poet's heart and, by extension, his self, is once again part of a reciprocal exchange ('erwiedernd'); what is more, the poet has sufficient self-respect to make such an offer. There is, moreover, a deliberately musical recapitulation in lines 12 and 18 ('Den Götter-Wert der Töne wie der Tränen', 'Das Doppel-Glück der Töne wie der Liebe'), which signifies the recognition of the possibility of harmony between emotion and its artistic expression. Poetry may not, in 'Aussöhnung', be endowed with the same conciliatory and revelatory qualities as music, but, through that formal intimation of harmony, the poem tiptoes away from the almost aggressive loss of faith in poetry expressed in 'An Werther' and 'Elegie'. The hope in the closing lines is cautious: in line 17, the subjunctive of 'fühlte' and the wistful 'o daß es ewig bliebe!' [could it but last forever!] are a reminder of the fragility of the happiness which has been found. But, in the echo of the last line of the second stanza in the last line of the third, 'Tränen' has been replaced with 'Liebe', resulting in the assertion (albeit a tentative one) that love, which had seemed so futile and tainted, is still possible. Moreover, the word 'Glück', which was only mentioned in order to emphasize its absence in 'An Werther', and not at all in 'Elegie', finally appears in this poem.[20] As the first strophe makes plain, 'Aussöhnung' has everything to do with the other two poems: and reconciliation is possible because of them, not in spite of them. In the final order which Goethe gave to the poems, reconciliation becomes the result of self-searching: for this (and, arguably, only this) makes the poet receptive to the call, the promise of something higher, that music seems to offer.[21] It is because the mood and preoccupations of 'An Werther' and 'Elegie' are not wholly dismissed from 'Aussöhnung' that the comfort which it offers is credible. In the final strophe, the past has not been forgotten; but the present moment, dismissed with such desperation in 'Elegie' — 'Nun bin ich fern! Der jetzigen Minute | Was ziemt den der? Ich wüßt' es nicht zu sagen' [Now I am far away! The present moment — what does it require? I could not say] (ll. 109–10)

— has been rehabilitated by the glimpse of transcendence, and by a new state of self-awareness which is content with a glimpse.

Chinesisch–deutsche Jahres- und Tageszeiten

The dialectic of memory and renewed attention to the present set up in the *Trilogie* paves the way for Goethe's last lyric cycle, the *Chinesisch–deutsche Jahres- und Tageszeiten*[22] (written 1827, published 1829). In his study of late style, Edward Said comments that: '[l]ateness is being at the end, fully conscious, full of memory, and also very (even preternaturally) aware of the present'.[23] Although Said's book is, for the most part, not concerned with Goethe, this particular observation lends itself very well to the *Jahres- und Tageszeiten*. They are timeless, concerned with timeless values; but they also display that peculiarly sharp sense of the present which Said emphasizes: '*Nun* weiß man *erst* was Rosenknospe sei | *Jetzt* da die Rosenzeit vorbei' [IX] [*Only now* can one know what a rosebud is: *now* that the season is past], 'Beschäftige dich *hier* und *heut* im Tüchtigen' [XIV] [Busy yourself, *here*, *today*, with good works] (emphasis mine in both cases). In each of these phrases, the sense of immediacy is increased by the doubling, even trebling, of terms used to indicate the present moment or present place. That 'preternatural awareness' of the present comes perhaps from the knowledge, more likely in old age than in youth, that every moment, every breath could be the last: and this makes possible what might be called an ultimate or heightened present, unimaginable earlier in life. This is certainly the implication of poem IX. Here, the last rose of summer is not lonely or pathetic, but is the summation of the floral world; its 'Glanz', its brilliance, represents a degree of knowledge, an understanding which he owes to the 'nahes Ende',[24] to being towards the end. There can, of course, be no 'nahes Ende' without all that has gone before ('Jetzt da die Rosenzeit vorbei'); in the first line of poem IX, the heaping of 'erst', which suggests the existence of a past, upon 'nun', which is more immediate, implies that the present invoked in these poems is one which is swelled by the past — 'full of memory'. Christine Wagner-Dittmar observes that the temporal structure of poem VII is achieved by the simple criss-crossing of different tenses.[25] Yet the effect is not confined to this poem. Although it is more explicitly retrospective than the others, past and present are woven together throughout in the cycle by the almost incessant (though always subtle) use of images and concepts familiar from earlier works. The delicate framework of these poems is formed from a philosophical and poetic idiolect developed over many years.

As with the *Trilogie der Leidenschaft*, this phenomenon operates on different levels. Sometimes the similarity with another work is on the surface. The affinity between poem XIII and 'Sitz ich allein' ['When I sit alone'] from the 'Schenkenbuch' ['Book of the Cupbearer'] in the *West-östlicher Divan*, for example, is quite open. Both express the poet's desire to be left alone with his glass of wine, and his quiet defiance of the opinions of others. Other poems are illuminated by Goethe's scientific thought. Poem III in particular embodies some of the principles of the *Farbenlehre*: Goethe's very particular conception of colour as set out in that text underscores the movement from the 'real' (the meadow) to the 'ideal' (Paradise), which is essential to the poem, indeed to the whole cycle.[26] Perhaps the richest example of poetic self-reference is poem XI: its last lines, 'Das Unvergängliche | Es ist das ewige Gesetz | Wonach die Ros' und Lilie blüht' [Intransience, that is the eternal law by which rose and lily bloom], resonate with at least two other major poems by Goethe. The notion of 'das ewige Gesetz' is, of course, the guiding principle of his morphology, and appears almost word for word in his theoretical poem, 'Die Metamorphose der Pflanzen' ['The Metamorphosis of Plants'] (1798): 'Jede Pflanze verkündet dir nun die ew'gen Gesetze' (l. 65) [Now every plant announces the eternal laws to you]. Moreover, the very last line of poem XI recalls the opening couplet of the *Divan*-poem 'Im Gegenwärtigen Vergangenes' ['Past in the Present']: 'Ros' und Lilie morgenthaulich | Blüht im Garten meiner Nähe' [Bathed in morning dew, the rose and the lily bloom in the garden near to me]. The relationship between poem XI and 'Im Gegenwärtigen Vergangenes' is the greatest clue that, notwithstanding their slight appearance, there are myriad pasts and presents layered upon one another in the *Jahres- und Tageszeiten*. The *Divan*-poem, in which, as its title tells us, the past shimmers through the present and the poetry of Hafiz is remembered in that of Goethe, is itself now taken up into a new present, and blossoms again through a new poem. We might call this practice, which can be detected throughout the cycle, poetic *Steigerung*.[27]

Of course, *Steigerung* in Goethe's conception does not mean simple repetition. It became clear in the poem 'Erinnerung' that remembering does not preclude moving on from the past — indeed, in some ways, it demands it; and the two poems just cited are both concerned with the principle of continuity in *change*. Although the *Jahres- und Tageszeiten* may look and sound like other works, they are uniquely themselves. Their character comes both from the memory of their poetic past, and from the ways in which they, consciously and deliberately, deviate or move on from that past. For all that it is so reminiscent of 'Sitz' ich allein', poem XIII is not the same. Whereas the priority of the poet in the 'Schenkenbuch' appears to be proving his individuality and breaking free of convention — 'Niemand setzt mir Schranken, | Ich hab' so meine eigne Gedanken' [No one sets me limits, I have thoughts of my own] — the principal voice of the Chinese poems is more concerned with the *type* of thinking that is being done. Poem XIII suggests that there is a difference between *Belehrung*, which suggests the accumulation of objective knowledge in the manner of the scientist, whereas *Begeisterung* suggests a higher level of self-consciousness, necessary for the writing of poetry, in which subject and object are fused. Another, strikingly deliberate, difference is that between poem VIII and its two main relatives, 'Anmutige Gegend' ['Pleasant Landscape'] from *Faust II* (composed at almost exactly the same time as the *Jahres- und Tageszeiten*[28]) and the early poem 'Auf dem See' ['On the Lake'] (1775, revised 1789). All three share the main theme of healing and nourishment, of being comforted in and through nature:

> Und durchs Auge schleicht die Kühle
> Sänftigend in's Herz hinein. (VIII)

> [And through the eye a soothing coolness slips into the heart]

> Die ihr dies Haupt umschwebt im luft'gen Kreise,
> Erzeigt euch hier nach edler Elfen Weise,
> Besänftiget des Herzens grimmen Strauß [...]
>   (*Faust*, ll. 4621–23)

[You who hover in a ring of air around this head, prove yourselves here in the noble elfin manner: soothe this heart's grim struggle]

> Und frische Nahrung, neues Blut
> Saug ich aus freier Welt;
> Wie ist Natur so hold und gut
> Die mich am Busen hält! ('Auf dem See')

[And from the free outdoors I suck fresh nourishment, new blood; how fair and good is nature, who holds me to her breast!]

Moreover, common to all three is the image of stars, and a lake; but whereas, in 'Anmutige Gegend' and 'Auf dem See', the stars are in abundance, and the wash of light and hope is reflected in the lake, in poem VIII, it is not starlight, not fruit, but 'Schwarzvertiefte Finsternisse' that the water reflects. The sudden appearance of this 'blind mirror', a symbol of death,[29] is the more of a shock because the positive version of the image is so familiar from the other examples; and it jars with the frequent perception of the older Goethe as the embodiment of serenity.[30] The poem does end on a note of consolation; verbs of play appear in relation to the willows and the shadows, and light is restored — indeed the 'Zauberschein' [magical shine] of moonlight appears. But it is a tentative, 'trembling' light, not the 'volle Pracht' [full splendour] of the moon which bursts on to the scene in 'Anmutige Gegend'. The 'Kühle' established at the end of the poem may be the precondition for the calm, apparently distanced reflections of the poems which follow: but for that brief moment in the first stanza, the intense personal difficulty of being close to the end, to dying, makes itself felt, and cannot quite be forgotten.

The dominant mode in the *Jahres- und Tageszeiten* is thus not just reflection, but self-reflection: the state of being 'fully conscious' which, for Said, defines 'lateness'. The role of self-reference in the cycle is both to reveal the continuing importance of the creative past of the poet, and, through the differences between these poems and earlier avatars, to open up new windows of insight, which are only possible from this new, very late, perspective.[31] Meredith Lee is quite right in her assertion that:

> it is through this process of 'Begeisterung' and 'geistig schreiben' that the poet has come to know the meaning of life in these later days. He has acquired the insight into his own autumn to answer the confused visitor in poem XII — that is, to pass one's time in neither longing nor remorse, but instead in satisfaction and quiet joy.[32]

The words '*his own* autumn' are crucial here, although Lee does not make as much of them as she might. For this state of 'Begeisterung' does not simply come from sitting quietly and having a good think; nor is it the guaranteed product of the 'wise distance of old age'.[33] Rather, as the poems themselves have shown us, it is the result of deep and sustained engagement with one's own history: for 'Begeisterung', like 'Aussöhnung', can come only from an understanding of the past which shapes and permeates it.

The Dornburg poems

The poems 'Dem aufgehenden Vollmonde'[34] ['To the rising full moon'] and 'Dornburg, September 1828'[35] were written the year after the *Chinesisch–deutsche Jahres- und Tageszeiten*, when Goethe had received another painful reminder of the approaching end, namely the death of Carl August, Grand Duke of Weimar and his dear friend. The poem progresses from the threat of desertion ('Willst du mich sogleich verlassen!', l. 1 [Would you leave me so soon!]) to ecstatic bliss ('So hinan denn! hell und heller', l. 9 [Onward then! bright and brighter]; 'Überselig ist die Nacht', l. 12 [ecstatic is the night]). Yet it is not just his 'Lebensgefühl',[36] his zest for life, which is restored and heightened here: for the poem is yet another example of *poetic* heightening. It is Goethe's last moon-poem, and exists in implicit dialogue with its predecessors. The most famous of these is 'An den Mond' ['To the Moon'] (first published in 1789, although the exact date of composition is unknown). Like 'Dem aufgehenden Vollmonde', the earlier poem is an intimate monologue addressed to the moon; but, despite this superficial similarity, it is strikingly different in other respects. Whereas, in 'An den Mond', the moon is addressed as a sympathetic guardian, by 1828 it has become much more like an alter ego, bound up in the poet's affairs. The quality of the light is also different: the earlier poem describes a gentle 'Nebelglanz' [shimmer of mist] being showered plentifully over 'Busch und Tal' [bushes and valley], yet, in 'Dem aufgehenden Vollmonde', the initially reluctant moonshine becomes ever brighter, more and more splendid. There is a corresponding difference in the progression of the poems: 'An den Mond' opens with a gift from the moon, but the tone gradually becomes more despondent, whereas the reverse is true of 'Dem aufgehenden Vollmonde'. The point of the later poem is not that the poet suddenly becomes ageless.[37] On the contrary, the disparity between this poem and 'An den Mond', the work of a much younger man, is evidence that the state which the poet describes is directly attributable to his age. For the old poet seems to have greater control. He cannot rid himself completely of pain: 'Schlägt mein Herz auch schmerzlich schneller' (l. 11) [Even though my heart beats more quickly, more painfully];[38] but in the ascent and increasing radiance of the moon is an image of his own life-force, which, though it seemed about to fade ('Dich umfinstern Wolkenmassen, | Und nun bist du gar nicht da', ll. 3–4 [Dark, cloudy masses surround you, and now you are not there at all]), now glows the more intensely for being threatened. Just as, in 'Aussöhnung', he realizes that he still has life, so here it is affirmed that, though the threat of departure and separation lurks, the present moment is still full of potential.

'Dem aufgehenden Vollmonde' displays that same 'preternatural awareness' of the present which could be detected in the *Jahres- und Tageszeiten*. The stages of the moon's ascent, and of the changing mood which accompanies its rise, are pressed into three brief stanzas. Each stage is quite distinct, yet the poem is so short that they all seem to flow into one another, to be part of the same 'Augenblick'. In the first verse in particular, the slippage between past, present, and future is greatly increased by the immediacy of the adverbs 'sogleich' and 'im Augenblick', which are juxtaposed with a moment that is yet to come ('Willst du mich sogleich verlassen!'), and with one which has already passed ('Warst im Augenblick so nah!' [You were so close but a moment since]). In the second stanza, that sense of simultaneity modulates from the temporal into the spatial. The poet is no closer to his beloved at the end of the verse — 'Sei das Liebchen noch so fern' (l. 8) [Be my darling ever so far from me]; but, aided and inspired by the ascent of the moon, he has found it within himself to overcome that distance, if only for a moment. The poem thus exemplifies both aspects of the very late perspective: an awareness of death's waiting, but also a certain security in one's own convictions. He has made certain not that the world is a rational place,[39] but that his life has meaning in the world, however fragile and, at times, embattled that sense of significance may be. It is arguably the ability to move in memory between the past and the present, and to use that experience of identification and differentiation (represented by poetic *Steigerung*) to understand the present, which gives the poet the confidence to say 'daß ich geliebt bin' (l. 7) [that I am loved], and which makes this night 'überselig'.

The poem 'Dornburg, September 1828', the partner to 'Dem aufgehenden Vollmonde', manipulates time in a similar way. It proceeds almost imperceptibly from the early morning to the setting of the sun, and the words 'wenn' [when] and 'dann' [then], which appear in the first two strophes and the third respectively, bind the different phases of the day together to give the impression of simultaneity. The juxtaposition of a human subject, the 'du' of the third strophe, with the sun, indicates that this image of the natural world is also the image of a human life; but the strange simultaneity of the phases suggests that the description of the advancing day is less 'Bild eines Lebenslaufs' [the image of a life's career][40] than the image of a particular stage of that career: a stage which, though evening approaches (the sunset is, after all, placed in the future tense), is nonetheless still full of the freshness of early morning and the brilliance of high noon. Moreover, the behaviour of the elements throughout speaks of completion: the subject of the first two lines is revelation, 'sich enthüllen', and the next two describe fulfilment, 'bunt sich füllen' [become full and colourful]. This is, arguably, long-awaited, for 'dem sehnlichsten Erwarten' (l. 3) suggests a longer period of anticipation than the span of a single night during which buds have closed. The second strophe moves briefly through strife, 'streitet' (l. 6) [quarrels], to resolution, 'verjagend' (l. 7) [chasing away], that brief turbulence framed on both sides by light and clarity: 'mit dem klaren Tage' (l. 6) [with the clear day], 'Blaue Sonnenbahn bereitet' (l. 8) [prepares a path of blue for the sun]. Thus the poem gives an image not of a whole life, but of a life as it nears completion, and has reached a certain level of *Erkenntnis* [recognition and understanding]. Yet the third stanza also expresses humility. The shimmering departure which it anticipates is that of the sun, not of the subject; indeed, the admiring gaze of the 'du' (ll. 9–10), together with his position of gratitude, 'Dankst du dann' (l. 9), distances him from the sun, 'der Großen, Holden' (l. 10) [the being both mighty and lovely]. The ease with which the gaze of the subject sweeps from one natural phenomenon to another in the poem reflects the level of insight which, in the evening of his own life, he has achieved; but the power of nature, of which the sun is the supreme example, will always outstrip his own.

Coda

We have now established the main features of Goethe's very late style: on the one hand, a preoccupation with the past, which manifests itself in frequent allusions to earlier works of his; and on the other, a heightened sense of the present, which is enriched by the past but also allows for, indeed demands, discoveries and innovations which move on from it. Whilst they for the most part avoid solipsism, these poems are evidently all concerned with the life of the self, with subjective experience. Yet earlier commentators in particular have tended to interpret Goethe's very late work as objective, generalizing. Erich Trunz, for example, argues in relation to the *Jahres- und Tageszeiten* that the self retreats behind the images of nature.[41] Hermann Korff likewise claims of 'Elegie' that all biographical reality has disappeared completely in the higher reality of the poem.[42]

Erich Heller offers a more sophisticated argument: he bolsters his claim that no serious connection can be made between 'Elegie' and the unfortunate episode in Marienbad by explaining that: 'das Ich des Gedichts [beginnt erst dort] als Subjekt *und* Objekt der lyrischen Betrachtung [...] zu sprechen [...], wo das 'nur'-menschliche Ich am Ende ist' [the self in the poem only begins to speak as the subject *and* the object of lyrical reflection at the point where the 'purely' human self has come an end].[43] His understanding of the self as both subject and object of poetic reflection is very helpful, as is his insistence that there is a split between the aesthetic, internal reality of the poem and the documented external circumstances which might have inspired it.[44] It is doubtful, though, whether poetry and life can be severed from one another as completely as Heller seems to think possible. It is, of course, important not to confuse the context and the content of Goethe's very late poems; but it is difficult to maintain that there is no correlation whatsoever, when so many of them refer overtly, or not very covertly, to the circumstances of his own life and poetry. The most explicit example of this is 'An Werther'; but the date and location of the composition of the second of the *Dornburg* poems are also given in its title. In the *Chinesisch–deutsche Jahres- und Tageszeiten*, moreover, the proximity of the garden world of the poems to Goethe's *Gartenhaus* and the surrounding park is not hard to divine;[45] the situation of the 'Mandarinen' described in poem I is a thinly veiled version of his own; and the symbolism of the changing seasons is arguably a reflection on the passing of his own life.

More importantly, what these critics, even Heller, fail to observe is that the 'personal' and the 'biographical' are not necessarily the same as the 'subjective'. Trunz asserts that the poet's priority in his late work is to portray life's common-places, which causes his style to appear more generalizing than in his more sponta-neous early work.[46] Yet a style which is more generalizing, more objective, can nonetheless contain a strong subjective element; and Goethe's poems do — that is his Kantianism. Elizabeth Wilkinson recognized this:

> Critics have noted the quality of objectivity in Goethe's poetry. I would prefer to speak of its subject-object-ivity. For only thus can we do justice to the personal element which is never absent from it. [...] [T]he essence of 'Gegen-ständlichkeit' [is] not that the observer, the subject, should be ruled out, but that he should not project on to the object.[47]

For Goethe, then, the subjective and the objective are inextricably linked; and his very late work is a particularly powerful demonstration of this. Contrary to Trunz's assertion, the *Ich* does not retreat behind the image of nature in the *Jahres- und Tageszeiten*. Though it may seem reticent in comparison with Goethe's earliest poems, the subject is essential throughout. The emphasis on colour in poems II and III, and on noise in IV, demand the presence of an *Ich*: for, as Goethe writes in the *Farbenlehre*, colours '[gehören] dem Auge, teils völlig, teils größtens [zu]' [belong to the eye, sometimes completely, sometimes just for the most part],[48] just as, if it is to be heard, sound requires an ear. The end of poem VIII is similar: 'Durchs Auge schleicht die Kühle | Sänftigend ins Herz hinein' (ll. 15–16). We can speculate *ad infinitum* on precisely whose eye or heart is meant here; the crucial point for now is that the subjective experience of *someone* is being described.[49] Moreover, the late poems are full of the emotions and beliefs of a self. We saw that 'Elegie' is not so much about Ulrike von Levetzow, or even a generic beloved, as about the experience of the one who is in love. The same is true of 'Dem aufgehenden Vollmonde', with the lines 'Zeugest mir, daß ich geliebt bin, | Sei das Liebchen noch so fern' (ll. 7–8). Thus the 'Naturbild' in these poems automatically implies an *Ich*. The two are inseparable for Goethe, as Karl Richter shows with his observation of the 'Umschlag von Naturerfahrung in Selbsterfahrung' [swing from the experience of nature into that of the self].[50] Indeed, as Goethe wrote in *Bedeutende Fördernis durch ein einziges geistreiches Wort*, a person can only know 'sich selbst, insofern er die Welt kennt, die er nur in sich und sich nur in ihr gewahr wird' [himself in so far as he knows the world, of which he only becomes aware through himself, and of himself through it].[51] Descriptions of the external world in the very late poetry are thus also attempts at self-knowledge on the part of the subject; and although in one sense, it is immaterial who the subject is, these poems are also, as we saw first in 'An Werther', about the experience of being *this* poet. Literary self-reference is the representation within the poems of the essential role of the subject in all experience.

It is important that that role be recognized, for it relates to another prominent theme in the very late work: that of the perennial search for understanding. Just as the *Ich* and the *Naturbild* are inextricably linked, so are self-knowledge and knowledge of the external or objective world.[52] Self-reflection, therefore, signifies that an advanced stage has been reached in the search for *Erkenntnis*. Yet the poet does not claim to have all the answers. 'An Werther' and 'Elegie' showed that delusion, self-deception, is a significant part of subjective experience; and, in poem X of the *Jahres- und Tageszeiten*, 'Forschung', untiring and ambitious though it is, is shown to be inferior in its achievements to the revelations which a symbol such as the rose can bring. It is significant too that, in poem IX, the gift of very-lateness is knowledge ('Nun weiß man erst'), specifically of the lesser rose*bud*. For, as the next poem goes on to explain, the rose itself is a manifestation of the absolute. Its significance can be *felt* unequivocally, 'unwidersprechlich', and faith is confirmed in perception as it blooms before the eyes of the subject ('In dir trifft Schau'n und Glauben überein' [In you, seeing and believing correspond]); but it cannot be named, it can still only appear to the human understanding as a 'wundersam Ereignis' — strange, sudden, inexplicable. That word, 'Ereignis' [event], along with the word 'Unvergänglich' in poem XI, links the rose-poems to the words of the Chorus Mysticus in the final scene of *Faust*:[53] 'Alles Vergängliche | Ist nur ein Gleichnis | Das Unzulängliche | Hier wird's Ereignis' [All that is transient is but a likeness; what was unreachable is here made manifest].[54] Moreover, the rose — 'Allerschönste', 'Königin' (X) [most beautiful, queen] — is without peers in its realm, just as the Mater Gloriosa is in hers: 'Du Ohnegleiche' [you who are without equals],[55] 'Jungfrau, Mutter, Königin, | Gottin' [Virgin, Mother, Queen, Goddess].[56] As we shall see in more detail in Chapter 4, *Faust* ends with a vision not of the incommensurable itself, but of being drawn towards it. The *Jahres- und Tageszeiten* likewise do not presume to expand too much on the details of 'das ewige Gesetz'; indeed, right at the end, they advise turning one's attention to more earthly matters: 'Sehnsucht ins Ferne, Künftige zu beschwichtigen | Beschäftige dich hier und heut im Tüchtigen' (XIV, ll. 3–4). Reflective engagement with and heightening of the patterns of life in poetry has brought the poet to the fullest understanding possible for him. But, as 'Aussöhnung' showed first, the reflective consciousness of the very late poems knows that it cannot transcend the ultimate present, which it has reached, to access the absolute; and that is perhaps its most powerful insight.

Notes to Chapter 1

1. See, for example, David Lindley: 'the emphasis on lyric poetry as image of the poet's mind is a very important aspect of the transformation and internalisation of the ode during the eighteenth century' (*Lyric* (London: Methuen, 1985), p. 63). Also David Wellbery: 'My genealogical analysis suggests [...] that lyric discourse is one in which subjectivity itself — its emergence, modulations and crises — is being elaborated, worked out and on' (*The Specular Moment*, p. 18).
2. *FA* II, 833–34.
3. *FA* II, 708.
4. In their commentary for Johann Wolfgang Goethe, *Sämtliche Werke nach Epochen seines Schaffens: Münchener Ausgabe*, ed. by Karl Richter and others, 21 vols (Munich: Hanser, 1985–98; hereafter MA), Gisela Henckmann and Dorothea Hölscher-Lohmeyer suggest that '[m]öglicherweise hat G. [sic] dieses Scherzgedicht speziell für Ottiliens Zeitschrift "Chaos" geschrieben' (*MA* XVIII.1, 456).
5. Meredith Lee, *Studies in Goethe's Lyric Cycles* (Chapel Hill: University of North Carolina, 1978), pp. 94–95.
6. Ibid., p. 95.
7. In Chapter 1 of his book *Jenseits des Unbehagens: 'Sublimierung' von Goethe bis Lacan* (Bielefeld: transcript, 2009), Eckart Goebel understands the *Trilogie* in terms of a process of sublimation, and concludes his analysis thus: 'Sublimierung heißt, dass in der Kunst erfahren werden kann, was im Leben vernichtend ist' (p. 57). Although I find the term 'sublimation' too fraught with complications to want to use it in my own readings, I agree with Goebel that the poems do something more with experience than simply describe it: they seek out the sublime, that which is awe-inspiring (which can be terrible or wonderful) and render it in aesthetic form.
8. Lee, *Goethe's Lyric Cycles*, p. 95.
9. *FA* II, 456–57.
10. Kaufmann, *Studien zu Goethes poetologischer Lyrik*, p. 418.
11. *FA* VII.1, 335.
12. Goebel, *Jenseits des Unbehagens*, p. 40.
13. Wild, *Goethes Versöhnungsbilder*, p. 53: 'Die Poesie vermag aus dem Labyrinth der Leidenschaften, der "ungewisse[n] Bahn" der Lebensbewegung [...] vorbildhaft den Ausweg zu weisen'.
14. Cf. Sebastian Kaufmann: 'Die Vorstellung von der heilenden Macht der Dichtkunst, wie Goethe selbst sie vielfach artikuliert und gestaltet hat, wird damit in Frage gestellt' (*Studien zu Goethes poetologischer Lyrik*, p. 427).
15. *FA* II, 457–62.
16. See Boyle, *Goethe: The Poet and the Age*, I, 294.

17. *Pace* Kaufmann, *Studien zu Goethes poetologischer Lyrik*, p. 447. The claim Kaufmann makes here derives, I think, from an erroneous association (and one surprising in a study of Goethe's self-reflexivity) of Schiller's dichotomy of the naive and the sentimental with Goethe's own poetic practice and ideals. The (I think equally mistaken) notion that Goethe saw human self-consciousness ('Reflektiertheit') as the cause of our sense of apartness from nature, and as the frustration of our hopes of 'Erfüllung', is a commonplace in writing on *Faust*, which I shall address in Chapter 4.

18. *FA* ii, 462.

19. *Pace* Meredith Lee, who writes of '[the] complete isolation and passivity [of the persona] in "Aussöhnung", where he is the grateful recipient of a grace proffered and affirmed, but not really understood' (*Goethe's Lyric Cycles*, p. 95).

20. See Goebel, *Jenseits des Unbehagens*, p. 53.

21. I agree broadly with Sebastian Kaufmann's conclusion that in 'Aussöhnung', 'Es geht nun nicht mehr darum, sich durch die göttliche Gabe der Poesie von dem zur Sprache gebrachten Leid zu befreien, vielmehr darum, dichterisch zu sagen, welche mit der Vergänglichkeit versöhnende Heilkraft von der Musik ausgeht' (*Studien zu Goethes poetologischer Lyrik*, p. 467). However, the notion of music as a *dea ex machina*, shared by Kaufmann (p. 457), by Elizabeth M. Wilkinson ('Goethes "Trilogie der Leidenschaft" als Beitrag zur Frage der Katharsis', *Freies Deutsches Hochstift: Reihe der Vorträge und Schriften*, 18 (1957), p. 17), and implicitly by Meredith Lee in her understanding of the poet as passive in 'Aussöhnung', requires some qualification. The moment described in that third poem is, I think, something more than one of 'jener scheinbar unmotivierten Auflösungen, die im Seelenleben wieder stattfinden' (Wilkinson, p. 17), and the role of music more than simply to effect '[ein völliger Bruch] mit allem, was vorangeganen ist' (ibid.). Rather, the self-searching of the previous two poems, and the fragments of self-knowledge that have been laboriously won in the process, have prepared the poet, have made him receptive to music. The dignity of 'Aussöhnung' is that the poet has crawled out of the indignity of 'Elegie'.

22. *FA* ii, 695–99.

23. Said, *On Late Style*, p. 14.

24. Werner Keller, *Goethes dichterische Bildlichkeit: Eine Grundlegung* (Munich: Fink, 1972), p. 224.

25. 'Die Zeitstruktur von Vergangenheit und Gegenwart wird durch die einfache Gegenüberstellung der Verbformen geschaffen [...] Erinnertes und Gegenwärtiges verknüpfen sich im Ablauf der Verse miteinander'. See 'Goethe und die chinesische Literatur', p. 201.

26. See Gisela Henckmann and Dorothea Hölscher-Lohmeyer: 'Im Sinne der "sinnlich-sittlichen Wirkung" der *Farbenlehre* ergänzt [das Grün] die durch das Rot erzeugte "ideale Befriedigung" (Bd. 10, S. 236, 22) durch die "reale Befriedigung" (ebenda, S. 238, 2)' (*MA* xviii.1, 417).

27. Elizabeth M. Wilkinson's article '"Tasso: ein gesteigerter Werther" in the Light of Goethe's Principle of Steigerung', *MLR*, 44 (1949), 305–28, offers a particularly full reflection on the sense of term *Steigerung*.

28. See, for example, Wolfgang Schadewaldt, 'Zur Entstehung der Elfenszene im 2. Teil des Faust', *DVjs*, 29 (1955), 227–36, or John R. Williams, *The Life of Goethe: A Critical Biography* (Oxford: Blackwell, 1998), pp. 129–30.

29. See Henckmann and Hölscher-Lohmeyer, *MA* xviii.1, 418.

30. Albrecht Schöne has exposed the pain that is in the background of much of Goethe's last poetic and scientific activity. This, Schöne suggests, was intended partly as a distraction from and an answer to his fear of death, present throughout his life and work, but which, unsurprisingly, became particularly acute in his final years. The letter which Goethe sent to Zelter from Dornburg on 10 July 1828, and which begins 'Bey dem schmerzlichsten Zustand des Innern mußte ich wenigstens meine äußern Sinne schonen', Schöne describes as 'die Antwort, die der alte Goethe auf den Tod seines fürstlichen Freundes gab, seine des eigenen Todes gewisse Antwort. Eine der großen Antworten des Menschen auf die menschliche Sterblichkeit'. '"Regenbogen auf schwarzgrauem Grunde": Goethes Dornburger Brief an Zelter zum Tod seines Großherzogs', *JWGV*, 81–83 (1977–79), 17–35 (p. 18).

31. Here I disagree with Karl Vietör, who argues that 'nur um den Preis des Verzichts auf jede hinzutretende Reflexion vermag es zu so tiefer Vermittlung von Stillewerden, von Frieden zu

gelangen, wie sie dieses friedevollste Altersgedicht Goethes vergönnt' (*Geist und Form: Aufsätze zur deutschen Literaturgeschichte* (Berne: Francke, 1952), p. 162). The reflective aspect of the *Jahres- und Tageszeiten* is subtle, but it is undeniably there; and I hope to have offered sufficient evidence by now that poem VIII is not as uniformly 'peaceful' as it may at first appear.

32. Lee, *Studies in Goethe's Lyric Cycles*, p. 135.

33. See Wagner-Dittmar, 'Goethe und die chinesische Literatur', p. 202.

34. *FA* II, 700.

35. Ibid., pp. 700–01.

36. See Günter Hess, 'Goethe und die poetische Mondsucht um 1828: DEM AUFGEHENDEN VOLLMONDE', in *Goethe Gedichte: Zweiunddreißig Interpretationen*, ed. by Gerhard Sauder (Munich: Hanser, 1996), pp. 357–67 (p. 357).

37. *Pace* ibid., p. 360.

38. The *Münchener Ausgabe* actually prints this line as 'Schlägt das Herz auch *schneller*, schneller' (*MA* XVIII.I, 27; my emphasis). According to Erich Trunz, Goethe replaced 'schmerzlich' with 'schneller' when he sent the poem to Marianne Willemer in October 1828 (See Trunz in his notes to the HA, I, 776), presumably to spare her the knowledge that he was suffering. 'Schmerzlich', though it doubtless also refers to emotional pain, can also be taken literally: Goethe is known to have had a heart condition and to have been suffering from angina. Since the poem was printed posthumously, and does not, therefore, appear in the *Ausgabe letzter Hand*, neither version can be said to be authoritative; but it seems likely that the version which includes 'schmerzlich', which he sent to Zelter soon after its composition, is truer to the complexity of his own feelings, and that he changed it out of consideration for Marianne.

39. *Pace* Reinhard Baumgart, 'Das erotische Gestirn', in *Johann Wolfgang Goethe, Verweile doch: 111 Gedichte mit Interpretationen*, ed. by Marcel Reich-Ranicki (Frankfurt am Main: Insel, 1992), pp. 461–62 (p. 462).

40. Baumgart, 'Magie und Vernunft', ibid., pp. 469–70 (p. 470).

41. Erich Trunz, 'Goethes späte Lyrik', *DVjs*, 23 (1949), 409–32 (p. 419).

42. 'die hinter [dem Gedicht] stehende Wirklichkeit ist von dem Dichter in solche ideale Höhe emporgehoben worden, daß sich die biographische Wirklichkeit darin ganz verflüchtigt hat' (Hermann Korff, *Goethe im Bildwandel seiner Lyrik*, II (Hanau: Dausien, 1958), p. 314).

43. Erich Heller, *Essays über Goethe* (Frankfurt am Main: Insel, 1970), p. 144.

44. Ibid., p. 145.

45. Compare the commentary by Henckmann and Lohmeyer, *MA*, XVIII.I, who point to the similarity of the poems with the Weimar 'Gartenlandschaft' described by Eckermann in the entry for 22 March 1824.

46. See Trunz, 'Altersstil', in *Goethe Handbuch*, p. 180.

47. E. M. Wilkinson and L. A. Willoughby, *Goethe: Poet and Thinker* (London: Arnold, 1962), pp. 27–28.

48. *MA* x, 27.

49. *Pace* Jane K. Brown:

> Reflection [of the stars in the lake in *Faust II*, 'Anmutige Gegend'] is of the object by the object — no subjects involved, just as in the late poem 'Dämmerung senkte sich von oben' [...] The subject has apparently no engagement in this process; instead, the reflection penetrates the viewer from outside his self. (Brown, 'Theatricality and Experiment', pp. 247–48)

50. Karl Richter, 'Naturwissenschaftliche Voraussetzungen der Symbolik am Beispiel von Goethes Alterslyrik', *JWGV*, 92–93 (1988–89), 9–24 (p. 15).

51. Quoted in Richter, 'Naturwissenschaftliche Voraussetzungen', p. 13.

52. 'Das forschende Subjekt wird seiner im Vorgang des Erkennens selbst gewahr' (ibid.).

53. Most of 'Bergschluchten', including the parts quoted here, was composed in 1830, though Goethe began work on it in 1826. It is, therefore, a product of the same creative period as the 'Jahres- und Tageszeiten'.

54. *FA* VII.I, 464.

55. Ibid., p. 463.

56. Ibid., p. 464.

CHAPTER 2

Autobiography

'Autobiography is [...] an interplay, a collusion, between past and present; its significance is indeed more the revelation of the present situation than the uncovering of the past' (Roy Pascal).[1] This certainly applies to Goethe, and the very late perspective needs to be borne in mind constantly when reading the *Zweiter Römischer Aufenthalt* (Part III of the *Italienische Reise*, composed in 1829) and *Dichtung und Wahrheit. Vierter Teil* (composed largely, though not exclusively, in 1830–31). They have as much in common with the other works of this phase of Goethe's life, especially *Wilhelm Meisters Wanderjahre*, as with the earlier instalments of the respective autobiographies — perhaps more.[2] The importance of the perspective from which Goethe's autobiographies were written (as opposed to that which they describe) is often acknowledged, but not taken any further. In his commentary on *Dichtung und Wahrheit* for the edition published by *Deutscher Klassiker Verlag* (Frankfurter Ausgabe), Klaus-Detlef Müller writes:

> Goethe [...] wußte, daß er nicht so sehr sein Leben selbst rekonstruierte als ein Bild seiner Persönlichkeit aus der Perspektive der Rückschau entwarf, und er wußte auch, daß die Wahrheit der Autobiographie [...] die des Selbstbewußtseins zum Schreibzeitpunkt ist.[3]

> [Goethe knew that he was not so much reconstructing his life itself as drawing up a retrospective image of his personality, and he also knew that the truth of autobiography is the truth of one's self-awareness at the time of writing.]

Although Müller's point is uncontroversial, it is striking how few analyses of Goethe's autobiographies give sustained attention to the perspective of the older man; most become absorbed in the portrait of the younger Goethe, whose story is the more prominent because it is the explicit focus of the narrative.[4] Yet, as both Müller and Pascal imply, that story owes as much of its character to the mature mind which has reconstructed it as to the youth on whose experiences it is based. Both are hesitant about the possibility of 'uncovering the past' in autobiography. Even if the aim is an entirely accurate reconstruction of the past (and that may not be at all what the autobiographer has in mind), the many intervening layers in the writer's personality and experience through which memory must work cannot but moderate the past which emerges in writing — especially when that past is as distant as it was for Goethe when he was writing his last autobiographical works. These are attempts at self-understanding by the mature mind, which reflects self-consciously on its earlier activity, but also on its present situation. In what follows I shall trace, as far as possible, the influence of the very late perspective.

The sculpting of the self's history necessarily results in an element of fiction. The degree of fictionality varies greatly from autobiography to autobiography, and from author to author. It may be as simple as the omission or invention of a few details for the sake of the narrative; or it may be deliberate, sometimes even explicit, storytelling (in every sense of the word). Accordingly, Goethe's *Italienische Reise* consists of correspondence which has been rewritten years after the event; indeed, in the case of Parts II and III, Goethe destroyed the original diaries and letters after he had worked them up, so that we only know them in their deliberately modified form. Moreover, *Dichtung und Wahrheit* does indeed turn on the interplay of fact and fiction, of poetry and truth which its title announces. The letter which Goethe mentions in the preface, the alleged trigger or inspiration for the whole undertaking, is in fact a fabrication;[5] and no small amount of what has been called 'the verifiable data of [Goethe's] life'[6] had to be reawakened in his own mind by stories which his mother had told to Bettina von Arnim. Indeed, as Goethe admits on the opening page of Book I:

> Wenn man sich erinnern will, was uns in der frühsten Zeit der Jugend begegnet ist, so kommt man oft in den Fall, dasjenige was wir von anderen gehört, mit dem zu verwechseln, was wir wirklich aus eigener anschauender Erfahrung besitzen.[7]
>
> [When we try to remember the events of our earliest youth, it often happens that we confuse what we have heard from other people with that which is truly the possession of our own reflective experience.]

Acknowledging that fictional (or not quite factual) dimension of an autobiography is not necessarily the same as making a charge of insincerity. On the contrary, it helps us to remain alive to the '*bewußte* Gestaltung der [...] Erfahrungen' [*conscious shaping of experience*][8] (my emphasis), that self-consciousness which is the defining activity in both the *Zweiter Römischer Aufenthalt* and *Dichtung und Wahrheit IV.*

Both aspects of autobiography highlighted so far — the juxtaposition of different perspectives and periods of a single life, and the interplay of fact and fiction — form part of a larger, more complex question: namely, that of the unity of the self. The creative manipulation in retrospective writing of the discrete events of a life can suggest a certain developmental logic — a sense that the self, for all the changes which it undergoes, is, at the deepest level, a unified phenomenon.[9] Poetic *Steigerung*, discussed in the previous chapter, is an aesthetic manifestation of this process, of old material being both upheld and transcended as it turns into something new; and that is part of the work of autobiography, too.[10] Yet the difficulty of uncovering the past fully may also lead to a sense of alienation from it. As we shall see, there is evidence, in both *Dichtung und Wahrheit IV* and the *Zweiter Römischer Aufenthalt*, of significant doubt on Goethe's part about the possibility of 'integration', indeed, of an 'ontologically secure historical origin'[11] for the self. The voice of the older Goethe is much more audible here than in the earlier instalments of the two autobiographies, as if to remind the reader of the distance between his present and former selves. Paul de Man contends that:

> [t]he interest of autobiography [...] is not that it reveals reliable self-knowledge
> — it does not — but that it demonstrates in a striking way the impossibility of
> closure and of totalization [...] of all textual systems made up of tropological
> substitutions.[12]

The 'impossibility of closure' is not only a feature but a theme of the later instalments of Goethe's autobiographical writings; yet the implied cause is less the inadequacy of 'tropological' structures than the mass of time that has settled between the original event and the moment of its recollection, and the potential block to self-knowledge which it represents. Memory, the faculty on which we rely for our sense of self, is porous; and if there is a unity of self, these works suggest, then it is at best an 'offenbares Geheimnis' [open secret].

Zweiter Römischer Aufenthalt

Preparations for the *Ausgabe letzter Hand* meant that the editing of his own life's material dominated Goethe's activity in the second half of the 1820s; and the *Zweiter Römischer Aufenthalt* is certainly composed in that editorial vein. Peter Boerner describes the work as a conglomerate of different literary forms, and of fragments from throughout Goethe's career.[13] Unlike the first two parts of the *Italienische Reise*, the rewritten correspondence from his second stay in Rome is juxtaposed with reports which are overtly retrospective; and self-contained pieces of writing are embedded within the whole, such as Karl Philipp Moritz's 1788 essay *Über die bildende Nachahmung des Schönen* [*On the Formative Imitation of Beauty*], or Goethe's own piece *Das Römische Carneval* [*The Roman Carnival*], first published in 1789. There is a curious dynamic at work here: for whilst details of his life appear to have been recorded definitively and for public consumption (that is, after all, the point of autobiography), the alteration of his correspondence and subsequent destruction of the originals ensured that *something* about his life would always remain private. We are presented here not with the Goethe of 1787–88, but with that man as the old Goethe wishes him to be remembered — however hard he might try to hoodwink us into believing otherwise: 'ich [möchte] nun meine Mitteilungen den damaligen Zuständen, Eindrücken und Gefühlen gemäß einrichten' [Now I would like to arrange what I have to say here in accordance with the circumstances, impressions, and feelings of the time].[14]

There is subtle, but insistent, emphasis throughout the *Zweiter Römischer Aufenthalt* on the inevitability of change with the passing of time. This works on two levels: it is evident within the letters themselves, and it becomes an issue in the interaction of the different time frames and perspectives which are rolled into the text. Goethe's manipulation of his archive by destroying the original letters from this period makes it impossible to know how much of the correspondence in the *Zweiter Römischer Aufenthalt* is 'authentic', and how much the work of the late 1820s. It is not unlikely that they underwent substantial alteration. But they still *purport* to represent the younger man, regardless of whether they actually do or not; and in that function they differ from the reports, which are explicitly the thoughts of the older man. The letter of 1 March 1788 conveys Goethe's intention to return to the early draft of *Faust* which he had written whilst still in Frankfurt:

> Natürlich ist es ein ander Ding das Stück jetzt oder vor funfzehn [sic] Jahren ausschreiben, ich denke es soll nichts dabei verlieren, besonders da ich jetzt glaube den Faden wieder gefunden zu haben. Auch was den Ton des Ganzen betrifft, bin ich getröstet; ich habe schon eine neue Szene ausgeführt, und wenn ich das Papier räuchere, so dächt' ich sollte sie mir niemand aus den alten herausfinden. (*FA* xv.1, 563)

> [Of course, it is not the same thing writing the piece out now as writing it fifteen years ago, but I think that it need not lose anything in the process, especially since I believe that I have now found my train of thought again. I feel consoled in respect of the tone of the whole piece, too; I have already added a new scene, and I fancy that, if I smoke the paper, no one will be able to detect my addition to the older pages.]

This must have been an interesting letter for the elderly Goethe, working on *Faust II*, to have found (or invented). He claims in this letter to see no difficulty in smoothing out the differences in style which fifteen years have brought; yet the sense of being sly or underhand, conveyed in the verb 'herausfinden', together with the amusing suggestion that he smoke-stain the newer pages, suggests that the passing of time brings changes which are only partly surmountable, and that the continuity between different parts of his work, and of his life, is an illusion which he would like to create. The perspective of the Goethe of 1787–88 (or, at any rate, the perspective which is recreated for him by his older self) is that of one struggling to maintain unity.

The Goethe of the 1820s, however, accepts that change is relentless, and the *Zweiter Römischer Aufenthalt* is structured in such a way as to make this apparent. The juxtaposition of the supposedly authentic letters and the retrospective reports introduces two perspectives, those of the younger and the older Goethe, into the work. These do not always sit comfortably together: although they correspond at certain points, they pull away from each other just as often. If, for example, some of the letters express the desire to resist change, the overall structure of the work does precisely the opposite. The slippage between the correspondence and the reports, and the perspectives which they represent, is often so subtle that it is easily overlooked; but it is finally made explicit in the April section that the purpose of the reports is to complete and add to the letters:

> Meine Korrespondenz der letzten Wochen bietet wenig Bedeutendes [...] Ich fasse daher in gegenwärtigen nachträglichen Bericht manches zusammen und nehme nur das auf, was aus jener Zeit mir, teils durch andere Papiere und Denkmale bewahrt, teils in der Erinnerung wieder hervorzurufen ist. (*FA* xv.1, 583)

> [My correspondence from the final weeks offers little of significance [...] So in the present, retrospective report, I shall summarize a good deal, and only incorporate things from that time which have either been preserved through papers and keepsakes, or can readily be called forth in memory.]

The words 'gegenwärtig' and 'nachträglich' draw attention to the very late perspective; and the notion of summarizing, editing, bringing out patterns which have become significant with hindsight, and suppressing those which have not, indicates that the purpose of this autobiographical undertaking is as much to interpret earlier experiences as it is simply to recall and invoke them. The 'present' of the *Zweiter Römischer Aufenthalt*, then, is the late 1820s.

The report for April, in keeping with so much of this period of Goethe's output, is full of memory. The account roams over a whole life, reaching into a past deeper even than the Italian experience:

> Indem ich dieses niederschreibe, werden meine Gedanken in die frühsten Zeiten hingeführt und die Gelegenheiten hervorgerufen, die mich anfänglich mit solchen Gegenständen [i.e. sculptures] bekannt machten, meinen Anteil erregten, bei einem völlig ungenügenden Denken einen überschwenglichen Enthusiasmus hervorriefen, und die grenzenlose Sehnsucht nach Italien zur Folge hatten. (*FA* xv.1, 587)

> [As I write this, my thoughts travel back to the earliest times. I am reminded of the circumstances which first made me acquainted with such objects, which aroused my interest and gushing enthusiasm, though my understanding was wholly insufficient, and which led to my boundless longing for Italy.]

In the lines which follow this brief paragraph, Goethe gives details of the first sculpture which made an impression on him, the cymbal-playing faun in Leipzig; he describes the Mannheim collection, which was, in his early youth, the only major collection of classical sculptures in Germany; and he describes the first plaster copies which, having had his eyes opened in Mannheim, he bought in Frankfurt. This brief foray into his very early experiences of classical art endows the Italian period with greater significance than simply a 'Hegire von Carlsbad' (*FA* xv.1, 430), a reaction to the pressures which had built up in Weimar: for the words 'einen überschwenglichen Enthusiasmus' and 'die grenzenlose Sehnsucht' imply that the trip was the culmination of many years of passionate anticipation, the seed of which had been planted 'in [den] frühsten Zeiten'. Yet, at the same time, the Italian journey is also given the status of an episode in a long and varied life: for the shift to the early years is framed on either side by the preoccupations of one who is 'somewhere towards the end'.

The preceding paragraph, concerned with the collection of works which stood in the last lodgings which he took in Rome, contains the striking sentence:

> Ich spreche von diesen Schätzen, welche nur wenige Wochen in die neue Wohnung gereiht standen, wie einer, der sein Testament überdenkt, den ihn umgebenden Besitz mit Fassung, aber doch gerührt ansehen wird. (*FA* xv.1, 587)

> [I speak of those treasures which only stood for a few weeks in the lodging, and I speak in the manner of one considering his testament and surveying the poss-essions which surround him with composure, but nonetheless with feeling.]

Although the word 'Testament' and the concomitant notion of departure nominally refer to the regret which Goethe felt at being unable to transport those treasures back to Germany, the words 'ich spreche' resound in the present tense — and, as was made very clear at the beginning of the report, that present is the late 1820s. The 'Besitz' which this speaker contemplates is not just the Roman art collection, but *all* his possessions, including (perhaps especially) his memories. He is resigned, but not without emotion: the words 'mit Fassung' [with composure] are particularly apposite to someone contemplating their own mortality. The report returns to this theme in the next section. Writing of a few date-palms which he had given to a friend in Rome, and which were still alive as he wrote the report, Goethe comments: 'Mögen sie den Besitzern nicht unbequem werden und fernerhin zu meinem Andenken grünen, wachsen und gedeihen' [May they not become an inconvenience to their owners, and furthermore may they grow and flourish in my memory] (*FA* xv.1, p. 589). These, too, are the words of one preoccupied with his legacy: for the curiosity, natural earlier in life, about the future course of one's own development, has shifted to a concern with how the traces which he leaves behind will fare. This anecdote is preceded by another, concerning the pine tree which he had planted in Angelika's garden: 'Späterhin fanden wohlwollende darnach forschende Reisende die Stelle leer und hier wenigstens die Spur eines anmutigen Daseins ausgelöscht' [Later, kindly travellers who searched for it on my behalf found the spot empty and here, at least, every trace of a previous, charming existence erased] (*FA* xv.1, 588). In the April report, then, as in so much of the very late writing, death and loss is a significant preoccupation, met by turns with composure and despondence.

A central, if implicit, theme of the *Zweiter Römischer Aufenthalt* is that of absence.[15] The two dominant modes in the work are retrospective writing and ekphrasis,[16] and absence is inherent in both. On the one hand, they are not just descriptive, but creative, seeking to make something present in a new prose which both describes and interprets: 'Ekphrasis [...] is an example both of the creative act itself — through the Greek *mimesis*, imitating, copying — and of the secondary critical act of commentary, description, revelation'.[17] Retrospective writing likewise both imitates and comments upon past experience. Yet, on the other hand, both modes are necessitated by the absence of what they describe: experiences which have passed, or images to which the reader has no direct access, must be remade in words for the benefit of the reader. Language also has its limitations for Goethe. In his letter of 29 July 1788, he writes of the Medusa in the Palast Rondini:

> Wie gern sagt' ich etwas darüber, wenn nicht alles was man über so ein Werk sagen kann, leerer Windhauch wäre. Die Kunst ist deshalb da, daß man sie sehe, nicht davon spräche, als höchstens in ihrer Gegenwart. (*FA* xv.1, 399)

> [How much I would like to say something about it, if everything which one could say about such a work were not empty puffs of air. Art is there to be seen, not to be spoken of, or spoken of at most in its presence.]

The distance which obtains between an original and the exposition of it is reminiscent of that opened up between different stages of a life by change and development. It is somewhat unjust to say that any description of art must be 'leerer Windhauch': the skilful use of language can make an object, even an atmosphere, vividly present. But that textual presence will necessarily differ from the empirical presence of the original; similarly, as will become clearer still in *Dichtung und Wahrheit*, a past which is written about cannot but be different from the past as it was experienced. Indeed, there is a sense in which no past is real, or, at least, every past is a mental construct. As soon as experience passes into memory, into reflection, it takes on a different aspect; and writing the past simply intensifies this process. Thus in both its major activities — the praise of great works of art and the evocation of past experiences — the whole of the *Zweiter Römischer Aufenthalt* is poised somewhere in the continuous flux between presence and absence, between renewal and loss.

Once again, the April report is characteristic of this tendency. One of the lengthiest anecdotes concerns a transaction which was not made, a statue which he did not buy. The emphasis on what he left behind, rather than what he took away, creates a certain emptiness at the centre of the report. There is, moreover, a strong element of suppression, of leaving things unsaid. Goethe begins to record his last meeting with the Milanese lady, but breaks off after a page and a half, remarking:

> Was sie darauf erwiderte, was ich versetzte, den Gang des anmutigsten Gespräches, das von allen Fesseln frei, das Innere zweier sich nur halbbewußt Liebenden offenbarte, will ich nicht entweihen durch Wiederholung und Erzählung; es war ein wunderbares zufällig eingeleitetes, durch inneren Drang abgenötigtes lakonisches Schlußbekenntnis der unschuldigsten und zartesten wechselseitigen Gewogenheit, das mir auch deshalb nie aus Sinn und Seele gekommen ist. (*FA* xv.1, 595)

> [What she replied, what I said next, indeed the course of that most lovely conversation, which proceeded wholly unfettered, and in which the inner selves of two people, only half aware that they loved, were revealed — I do not wish to desecrate all this with repetition and narration. It was a wonderful, laconic closing declaration, brought about by coincidence, yet made necessary by an internal urge, a declaration of the most innocent and most tender reciprocal inclination, which for that reason I have never forgotten.]

This paragraph tantalizes the reader by referring to an exchange in which the innermost selves of the interlocutors briefly come to light, and which has remained with Goethe ever since — and by stubbornly refusing to reveal any of the details. Here as elsewhere in the work, the inadequacies of language are highlighted: for the suggestion is that 'repetition and narration' would trivialize the delicate, but untrammelled, passion of the exchange. The refusal to divulge certain details is also characteristic of Goethe's autobiographical writing, which, even as it appears to be putting his life on public record, upholds a commitment to privacy. The uncertain biographical status of the relationship with the Milanese lady reinforces that privacy. The description of their encounter in the October report was overtly literary, expanding the event (a detail glossed over in the letters) almost into a novella; aspects of the tale are deliberately reminiscent of *Werther*, and with the ironic expression 'ein wertherähnliches Schicksal', the text reveals its own game. This literary manoeuvre raises the possibility that the version which we have of the relationship might be a fiction, and that the feelings attributed to it in the April report might be displaced from another.[18] But Goethe's evasiveness at times like this is such that we will never be able to do more than speculate. What he has put into words is that some part of personal experience will always remain inexpressible (or at least unexpressed) in words.

The two dominant tensions in the work — between what was and what is, and between absence and presence — are brought together in the final paragraphs, in Goethe's recollection of an experience three nights before his departure from Rome. The work is brought to an end in a way that is both rich in reflection, but also melancholy and surprisingly empty. For a writer so committed to colour, the scene is strikingly monochrome. It is illuminated by 'der volle Mond am klarsten Himmel' [the full moon in the clearest sky], which shows off the Capitol and the Colosseum to remarkable effect; yet that bright light also generates stronger shadows: 'Ganz finster, finstern Schatten werfend, stand mir der Triumphbogen des Septimus Severus entgegen' [The triumphal arch of Septimus Severus, quite dark, casting dark shadows, stood in my way] (*FA* xv.i, 596). The repetition of 'finster' evokes an atmosphere of apprehension, which is intensified in the second part of the sentence: 'in der Einsamkeit der Via Sacra erschienen die sonst so bekannten Gegenstände fremdartig und geisterhaft' [in the loneliness of the Via Sacra, the objects, otherwise so familiar, seemed strange and ghastly] (*FA* xv.i, 596). Eventually, the effect is so overwhelming 'daß mich ein Schauer überfiel und meine Rückkehr beschleunigte' [that horror overcame me and accelerated my return] (*FA* xv.i, 596). This fearfulness and forced departure is not at all how we would expect the journey so often referred to as Goethe's 'rebirth' to end. The attitude to memory and the preservation of experience is similarly ambivalent. On the one hand, Goethe remarks:

> Alles Massenhafte macht einen eignen Eindruck zugleich als erhaben und faßlich, und in solchen Umgängen zog ich gleichsam ein unübersehbares Summa Summarum meines ganzen Aufenthaltes. Dieses in aufgeregter Seele tief und groß empfunden, erregte eine Stimmung, die ich heroisch elegisch nennen darf [...] (*FA* xv.i, 596)

> [Everything which is massive makes a singular impression, as at once sublime and comprehensible, and in such surroundings I drew as it were an inestimable summary of my entire sojourn. I felt this deeply and intensely in my disquieted soul, and it gave rise to a mood which could be called heroic and elegiac.]

The words 'erhaben', 'tief und groß empfunden', and 'heroisch' suggest that his experience is full of sublime meaning, and the notion 'Summa Summarum' implies confidence in his ability to preserve and keep what is past. The insertion of Ovid's poem in the *Tristia*,[19] 'Cum subit illius tristissima noctis imago', at the end would seem to reinforce that assurance. It has stood the test of time as well as any Roman monument, and its inclusion here creates, as it were, a hall of mirrors of memory: Goethe, looking back over his stay in Rome, is reminded suddenly of the 'Rückerinnerung' of another writer, long ago. Yet, although the almost ghoulish shades of the earlier paragraph seem to have passed, the mood is still extremely sombre: the poem itself is the work of an Ovid 'im trauer- und jammervollen Zustande', and the 'Summa Summarum' which Goethe draws gives little cause, apparently, for celebration. Moreover, even as he celebrates memory through the allusion to Ovid, Goethe casts doubt on its usefulness: 'ich wiederholte das Gedicht, das mir teilweise genau im Gedächtnis hervorstieg, aber mich wirklich an eigner Produktion irre werden ließ und hinderte; die auch später unternommen, niemals zu Stande kommen konnte.' (*FA* xv.i, 596) [I recited the poem, parts of which rose up word-perfect in my memory, but which in fact made me stray from my own work and held me back; work which, even when resumed later, could never be realized]. Whereas, elsewhere in Goethe's work, memory has been creative and productive, here its ability to paralyse as well as inspire is highlighted.

Part of the reason for the strangely hollow quality of the scene, despite its intensity, is the sense that, again, there is much that is left unsaid. For once, there is a source to corroborate that suspicion, namely the original description of his last days in Italy, which Goethe wrote as early as 1817.[20] There, rather than relying on a mood or atmosphere to suggest painful emotions, he is much more explicit: 'Bei meinem Abschied aus Rom empfand ich Schmerzen einer eignen Art' [Upon my departure from Rome, I experienced pain of a singular kind].[21] He remembers spending the return journey at work on *Torquato Tasso*, and compares his fate with that of the eponymous character: 'Der schmerzliche Zug einer leidenschaftlichen Seele, die unwiderstehlich zu einer unwiderruflichen Verbannung hingezogen wird, geht durch das ganze Stück'[22] [The painful streak of a passionate soul, which is drawn irresistibly to irrevocable exile, runs through the entire play] The suggestion of this passage is slightly different from the received version of the ending. Rather than some internal urge taking hold and pushing him away from Rome because his time there is up, here we are told of a *pull* back into 'exile', which is against his will but beyond his control. What is strongly implied here, but suppressed in the later version, is his ambivalence towards the court life to which he had to return, but which, as for Tasso, was often profoundly at odds with his own nature. There are a number of possible motivations for the decision to remove those feelings from display in the later version. It doubtless seemed better, in the interest of the image which would be put out to posterity, to remove hints of conflict; Goethe's sorrow at the recent death of Carl August might also have tempered his criticism of life in Weimar. But it could also be that, once again, he is preoccupied as much with the present as with the past, and that the pain at quitting Rome, once so raw, has become less relevant than the final departure which he now faces. For it is noticeable that this later version has no destination. The original relates, albeit briefly, his itinerary back through Italy, even if his destination is 'Verbannung'; the final version, by contrast, stops in Rome, looks deep into the past in its final lines, and gives the sense that a cliff-edge has been reached. If this is also a reflection of the present of the old man for whom the end is near, then it is a much more fragile present than was suggested in the *Chinesisch-deutsche Jahres- und Tageszeiten* or the *Dornburg* poems.

Dichtung und Wahrheit. Vierter Teil

Dichtung und Wahrheit is a self-conscious work throughout. It is written in the expectation that the reader will know Goethe's works; and, in the earlier parts, a particular public image is carefully constructed. The letter (of Goethe's own writing), which he pretends in the preface to have received from friends, asks to know 'die Lebens- und Gemütszustände, die den Stoff [zu den Dichtwerken] hergegeben'[23] — that is, to know where the poetry came from. Throughout Parts One to Three, accordingly, moments from his own experience are deliberately made to resonate with scenes from his writing. In Book X, for example, there is a scene which is reminiscent of 'Marthens Garten' in *Faust I*: two couples, one slightly older, one younger, walking arm in arm, each pair accompanying the other, yet enjoying a private dialogue with the immediate partner.[24] There is much in the characterization of Friederike here to remind us of Gretchen[25] — more, in fact, than in the figure in *Dichtung und Wahrheit* who is known as Gretchen. Poetry is woven into the fabric of life just as much as it was (it is implied) originally drawn out of it;[26] yet, in the first three parts, this is kept implicit in the interest of creating a smooth structure and sovereign narrative that will convince the reader of the 'truth' of the account. In Part IV, by contrast, the disparity between the narrating and experiencing selves is no longer concealed, and the voice and preoccupations of the narrator (as well as the narrated) can be heard much more clearly. This work, like the *Zweiter Römischer Aufenthalt*, juxtaposes multiple stages, early and late, of the experience and work of its author, and no longer tries to create an illusion of complete continuity between them. The structure of Part IV is, arguably, analogous to the self, or the sense of self, of an older person: for in the course of a life, new developments build on, surpass, sometimes even contradict, earlier ones, so that the personality eventually comes to consist of layers of the same 'I'. Development is, of course, not always entirely smooth and logical, and Part IV also lays bare the differences between the stages to which it bears witness.

In addition to the experiences and events of 1775, *Dichtung und Wahrheit IV* also records what (from the perspective of 1830–31) are more recent turns in Goethe's thought. The opening and closing sections, for example, belong to the earliest stratum of work (in 1813) on Part IV,[27] and they invoke concepts which were as characteristic of that period of his life as of his mid-twenties. Towards the beginning of Book XVI, the concept of 'Entsagung' [renunciation] is introduced.[28] Its mention here is fleeting, compared to the detailed treatment it was to receive later, especially in *Wilhelm Meisters Wanderjahre*; and the decision to leave the reference as it was in 1813, rather than work it up further in the light of related thoughts in the *Wanderjahre*, perhaps reflects an interest in preserving some trace not just of the Goethe of 1775 or 1830–31, but of some of the intervening parts of his life also. The conception in Book XX of 'das Dämonische' [the daemonic], likewise, is distinct from earlier and later uses of it. H. B. Nisbet shows that 'Dämon' had many senses for Goethe, and that '[t]here is no one definition to which they can all be reduced';[29] the passage in *Dichtung und Wahrheit*, he argues, is the point at which Goethe 'worked out his doctrine of "das Dämonische"',[30] and began to consolidate a set of ideas and associations surrounding the word 'Dämon', which he had up until then been reluctant to rationalize.[31] Although, if we can judge by his conversations with Eckermann, the notion modulated further in his usage in the last decade of his life,[32] the version from 1813 reflects a cast of mind which becomes increasingly characteristic of the late and very late phases: a sense, as we saw in the *Zweiter Römischer Aufenthalt*, of the limitations of human understanding, and a concern 'not to remove mystery, but to preserve it'.[33] Benedikt Jeßing writes that 'das Dämonische' is an expression of '[d]as Unbegreifliche der Konstitution von Welt und Leben' [the element of the incomprehensible in the constitution of the world and of life],[34] and Angus Nicholls shows that, for Goethe, 'the daemonic is fundamentally excessive in terms of both conceptual and linguistic representation'.[35] The mentions of 'Entsagung' and 'das Dämonische' are, therefore, witnesses both to the specific period from which they date, and evidence of new directions in Goethe's thought which were to become more explicit in the decade leading up to the final phase of work on *Dichtung und Wahrheit IV*.

Where the theme of the limitations of knowledge and understanding appears in *Dichtung und Wahrheit IV*, it provides evidence that the very late perspective is at work. A particularly striking example is the account of Jung-Stilling's failed attempt to cure a new patient, a Herr von Lersner. The significance of the episode is indicated by the amount of space dedicated to it, given that, apart from the fact of his friendship with Jung, it is not drawn directly from Goethe's experience. The theme of blindness and its recalcitrance to treatment is woven tightly together with that of the loss of confidence and the onset of self-doubt in an individual: 'Der Zustand in den unser Freund dadurch geriet läßt keine Schilderung zu; er wehrte sich gegen die innerste tiefste Verzweiflung von der schlimmsten Art' [The state in which our friend found himself as a result permits no description; he fought against the innermost, deepest despair of the worst kind] (*FA* xiv, 744). The failure to restore Lersner's sight is all the more bitter because Jung-Stilling's (almost) spotless record of success in treating cataracts had conferred on him the aura of an expert. In previous cases, the removal of the 'cloudy lens' had led to the revelation of the world for the patient: 'Nach vollbrachtem schmerzlosen Schnitt durch die empfindliche Hornhaut sprang bei dem gelindesten Druck die trübe Linse von selbst heraus' [After a painless, successful cut through the sensitive cornea, and with the gentlest pressure, the cloudy lens would spring out of its own accord] (*FA* xiv, 741). In Lersner's case, however, the lenses have to be forced out, and still clarity of vision is not restored. The persistence of blindness defies the scientific methods developed to combat it, and exposes their limitations. The painful irony of the case is that, even where human activity is at its most visionary, it is still confronted at every turn by its blindness. This theme is not incidental, but is at the very core of the autobiographical enterprise: for our self-understanding is equally limited. The accumulation of experience can help. The younger Goethe is presented at times as understanding less about his situation than the older, who has the benefit both of hindsight and of the increased capacity for reflection which comes with maturity: 'Dergleichen Betrachtungen jedoch waren gänzlich außer dem Gesichtskreis jener Jünglinge' [However, reflections of that kind lay quite beyond those youngsters] (*FA* xiv, 805). Yet *Dichtung und Wahrheit IV* makes plain that the passing of time also entails loss: for the pores of memory render it inevitable that some aspect of our development will always trickle away and remain out of sight.

Although it is central to the *Zweiter Römischer Aufenthalt*, the notion of absence there remains implicit, a disquieting sense rather than an explicit theme. But it is drawn out much more in *Dichtung und Wahrheit IV*, which is full of references — some overt, some more subtle — to the difficulty of directly uncovering the past. Goethe alludes at points to the insufficiencies of his memory: 'Das einzige was ich mir zwischen da und Zürch noch deutlich erinnere ist der Rheinfall bei

Schafhausen' [The only thing between there and Zurich that I can still remember clearly is the Rhine Falls near Schaffhausen] (*FA* XIV, 793). The brief aside which follows the description in Book XVIII of the noisy debate in his parents' house on tyrants and wine is particularly revealing:

> Wenn ich hier, wie die besten Historiker getan, eine fingierte Rede jener Unterhaltung einzuschieben in Verdacht geraten könnte, so darf ich den Wunsch aussprechen es möchte gleich ein Geschwindschreiber diese Peroration aufgefaßt und uns überliefert haben. Man würde die Motive genau dieselbigen und den Fluß der Rede vielleicht anmutiger und einladender finden. Überhaupt fehlt dieser gegenwärtigen Darstellung im Ganzen die weitläufige Redseligkeit und Fülle einer Jugend, die sich fühlt und nicht weiß wo sie mit Kraft und Vermögen hinaus soll. (*FA* XIV, 785)

> [At this point, there might be suspicion that I have inserted a fabricated speech into the conversation, just as the best historians did; but if so, I could be forgiven for wishing that a notary had taken down this peroration and handed it on to us. The reader would find the motifs just the same, and the flow of speech perhaps more graceful, more inviting. What is missing entirely from this present depiction is the youthful propensity to talk at length and with great energy, a youthfulness full of pride, yet unsure what to do with its strength and potential.]

Here, Goethe openly acknowledges that the words which he puts into the mouth of his younger self are not his as he spoke them then, and that the version in the autobiography is, in some respects, an unsatisfactory one ('Überhaupt fehlt dieser gegenwärtigen Darstellung [...]') — although, as he implies, he is in the company of the great historians of antiquity, notably Thucydides and Livy, for whom it was common practice to invent speeches for the protagonists of their histories. Significantly, though, it is not only the absence of a means of recording, however primitive ('Geschwindschreiber'), which makes this inevitable. It is also the fact that the perspective of youth cannot be fully recaptured by an old man. The subject matter ('Motive') may be the same, but the style ('anmutiger und einladender') and mood ('weitläufige Redseligkeit und Fülle') of the young man's speech cannot but differ profoundly from the equivalent which the elderly writer has to offer. The phrase 'uns überliefert' (in connection with the wish that the speech had been recorded at the time) imply that his younger self has become almost foreign to him, that it is as if his own words had been spoken by someone else. Yet it is noticeable that Goethe evades the anticipated charge of inauthenticity ('fingiert'). He does not deny that the monologue differs significantly from the 'original', but nor does he explicitly concede that it is a fake. The implication is that it would be less genuine if he had tried to emulate the style and syntax of a younger man, which would at best have resulted in an awkward piece of self-imitation. The speech in the text has its own authenticity as a memory: necessarily different from the original event, but bearing traits of both the experiencing and the reflective selves. What we have here is 'the past as it appears in [the autobiographer's] mind, his present mind'.[36] Whether this constitutes a satisfactory unity of present and former selves, however, is another question.

Even where Goethe is able to draw on a record such as a diary, the same difficulties confront him. Goethe uses his diary in part of the reconstruction of the

Swiss journey, but Robert Gould comments that:

> experience [...] largely defies retrospective narrative, and this is brought to the
> reader's attention by the commentary and the recourse to the source text (the
> diary) which is quoted to cover the remainder of the upward journey to the
> watershed overlooking Italy.[37]

Klaus-Detlef Müller, for his part, notes that Goethe alters the style of the notes
he had made as a young man.[38] These changes vary in kind. They may be simple
orthographic changes: hence the 'jetzo' [now] in the diary, old-fashioned by the
time *Dichtung und Wahrheit* was being written, becomes 'jetzt' in the final text
(*FA* XIV, 925 and 804). Sentences are often (though not always) filled out, so that
the fragmentary diary form is replaced by a narrative with an easier flow; and
descriptions are frequently extended, with more detail supplied. An emotional
coloration not present in the diary is sometimes added. In the passage about 'den
18. Sonntags', for example, more is made than in the original notes of the clouds
which surround the climbers at the summit: first the narrator bemoans their
unpleasantness, then he expatiates on the remarkable views which they reveal when
they do finally part. Most significantly, however, Goethe makes overt reference to
his own interference. He admits at one point that he would not have known how to
describe his mood and that of his fellows at the time without the prompt from his
diary, 'Lachen und Jauchzen dauerte bis Mitternacht' [Our laughter and high spirits
lasted till midnight] (*FA* XIV, 804). Elsewhere, the narrative jerks suddenly into the
present. A passage comparing the cliffs to the backdrop in a theatre, indifferent
to the fates and fortunes of the players before them, is followed by this assertion:
'Dergleichen Betrachtungen jedoch waren gänzlich außer dem Gesichtskreis
jener Jünglinge, das Kurzvergangene hatten sie aus dem Sinne geschlagen und
die Zukunft lag so wunderbar unerforschlich vor ihnen wie das Gebirg in das sie
hineinstreben' (*FA* XIV, 805–06) [However, reflections of that kind lay quite beyond
those youngsters; they had put what had recently passed out of their minds, and
the future lay before them, as wonderfully inscrutable as the mountain range into
which their ambition now led them]. The absence from the original diary of the
theatrical metaphor indicates that Goethe includes himself in 'jener Jünglinge'. Both
these interventions imply that the older Goethe sees cheerfulness and spontaneous
energy as characteristic of youth; and this begs the question whether other, similar
depictions not present in the diary — for example, 'frisch und mit mutwilliger
Behendigkeit' [fresh and with mischievous agility] (*FA* XIV, 803) — might be efforts
on the part of the elderly writer to convey what youth is like, as much as memories
of how he actually felt. Indeed, memory appears in all its contradictoriness here.
Its importance is highlighted in the contrastive example of the young men, whose
future, it is suggested, is so inscrutable partly because they are unreflective and
forget ('das Kurzvergangene hatten sie aus dem Sinne geschlagen'). It is, of course, as
impossible in old age as in youth to predict the future, but the capacity to recognize
patterns from past experience can at least provide a guiding torch for the present and
the future, and this is as yet underdeveloped in the young men. Yet the unconcealed
interference of the older voice in these passages also marks a refusal to pretend
that recollections can be written as if nothing had changed in the meantime, or to

ignore the loss of one type of self-knowledge (that is, quite how one was), despite the gain of another (a better idea of who one is), with the passing of time.

A related conundrum arises with the habit, peculiar to Part IV (but, as has frequently been noted, reminiscent of the *Wanderjahre* with its many inserted texts), of substituting poems written in 1775 for prose description, in order to give a more 'authentic' or immediate sense of the situation or atmosphere rendered in the narrative. On the one hand, these poems supply what was lacking in the paragraph quoted above, namely written material which is genuinely an expression of that younger self. They appear to compensate for the deficiencies of memory by their status as surviving pieces from Goethe's youth, and for the deficiencies of language because they belong to the most expressive and suggestive of genres. Yet, on closer inspection, there is an element of hesitation as each poem is introduced. Goethe introduces 'Herz, mein Herz' and 'Warum ziehst du mich unwiderstehlich' (known elsewhere as 'Neue Liebe, Neues Leben' and 'An Belinden' respectively) with the words: 'Um aber doch diese betrachtende Darstellung, einer lebendigen Anschauung, einem jugendlichen Gefühl *anzunähern*' [But in order to *bring* this description *closer* to lively contemplation, to youthful feeling] (*FA* XIV, 749; my emphasis). Even with the help of these poems, then, the reflective ('betrachtend') writing of the older man can only *approximate* the spontaneous, 'lebendig' feeling of youth. Similarly, after the poems, Goethe writes: 'Hat man sich diese Lieder aufmerksam vorgelesen lieber noch mit Gefühl vorgesungen, so wird ein Hauch jener Fülle glücklicher Stunden gewiß vorüber wehen' [If these songs have been read aloud with care, or preferably sung with feeling, then a hint of the fullness of those happy hours will certainly waft by] (*FA* XIV, 751). The wording here might be purely ornamental, but it is nonetheless significant that the access to the past which these poems are supposed to have brought is described not in terms of immersion or a profound shift in feeling, but rather as a 'breath', a 'hint', which is no sooner felt than gone ('vorüber'). Moreover, some of the inserted poems were known in their own right long before *Dichtung und Wahrheit* was written. They may already have particular personal significance for the reader of the autobiography, which further reduces the likelihood of their providing access to Goethe's past without any interference. His awareness of this is signalled by the phrase 'vorgesungen' in the quotation above. This implies the intervention of a composer, and, perhaps, a private concert setting: that is, a wholly different temporal and cultural context from the events in 1775 which occasioned these poems. The poems contribute, therefore, to the theme of the elusiveness of the past, even though, on the surface, Goethe claims the opposite role for them.

This point is subtly but deliberately reinforced by the fact that the poems, included ostensibly in order 'von jenen glücklichen Momenten einige Ahnung herüber[zu]bringen' [to convey some idea of those happy moments] (*FA* XIV, 799), were *not* always written at the exact time or for the occasion which is the focus of the narrative at that point. Goethe openly rejects a poem, 'Lilis Park', which was directly about his relationship with Lili Schönemann, in favour of 'Ihr verblühet, süße Rosen' ['You are fading, sweet roses'], in his view a better poem, but from a different context (the play *Erwin und Elmire*); and 'Auf dem See', though originally composed in Switzerland in 1775, is actually included here in its revised form from 1789. Thus, even without the qualifications and hesitations which surround them, the poems in *Dichtung und Wahrheit IV* often stand at a clear distance from the 'glückliche[n] Momente[n]' which they are supposed to represent. Of course, poetry is never the straightforward transformation of experience: life is manipulated and reflected upon before it becomes a poem. This is not contradicted by Goethe's contention that his poems from that period expressed 'durchaus nichts überspanntes, sondern immer das Gefühl des Augenblicks' [absolutely nothing exaggerated, but always the feeling of the moment] (*FA* XIV, 833). Their subject matter is indeed nothing out of the ordinary ('nichts überspanntes'), and it is not unreasonable to assume that they genuinely did have something to do with a particular feeling at a particular moment. But this is not to say that they are records of unmediated experience. That is impossible in any form of discourse, and poetry, as we saw in the previous chapter, is the most self-conscious of genres. Goethe's claim is a little misleading, though, and probably disingenuous: it fits in with his portrayal (for those who would believe it) of himself as a spontaneous poet, unaware of the workings of his own creative mind — at the beginning of Part IV, for example, he compares himself to the sleepwalker ('mein [...] nachtwandlerische[s] Dichten', *FA* XIV, 733). Poetry has its own immediacy, but that is *not* the same as the immediacy of empirical experience. What it *does* offer is a sense of the possible significance underlying each experience: for the power of poetry is to give expression to feelings barely felt, to bring out an essence not apparent to the everyday level of awareness. This is particularly true of 'Auf dem See'. Even in 1775 'Auf dem See' was more than a simple record of the events and environment of a particular day in Goethe's life; rather, it was already an act of self-interpretation.[39] What Goethe really puts on display with these poems is his self-understanding of long ago. That self-understanding is necessarily different from the one which is being exercised in the writing of *Dichtung und Wahrheit*, which tells a 'life-story' much nearer to completion. The distance detected earlier between the poems and the 'present' perspective can be attributed partly to the inaccessibility of the past, but also to the sense that, in his earlier writing about himself, he both is and is not yet the person he becomes, just as, in his later writing, he both is and is no longer the person he once was. The poems are modified by their inclusion in this larger autobiographical framework. Where they were once active in the development of the poet's sense of self, now they serve as memories of earlier moments of his inner life within the context of a new piece of self-interpretation.

Where Goethe does find new words for past experiences, the predominance of the very late perspective is clear: as, for example, in a peculiarly self-referential passage in Book XVII. The section of Goethe's account of his blossoming relationship with Lili Schönemann, beginning 'Es war ein Zustand von welchem geschrieben steht: "ich schlafe aber mein Herz wacht"' [This was a state about which has been written: 'I sleep, but my heart waketh'] (*FA* XIV, 762), is remarkably similar to the poem 'Der Bräutigam' ['The Bridegroom'].[40] There is some disagreement about precisely when 'Der Bräutigam' was written, but the general feeling is that it dates from 1824–25.[41] It belongs to the same stratum of composition as the corresponding part of *Dichtung und Wahrheit IV*, for which Goethe produced a rough schema in 1825,[42] and which he finally worked up in full in 1830:[43] firmly within the very late phase, in other words. Both it and the poem do have resonances with the events of 1775: not just (or even so much) through their subject matter as through the quotation from the Song of Songs ('ich schlafe aber mein Herz wacht', echoed in the first stanza of 'Der Bräutigam'), which Goethe was translating in 1775.[44] Yet, in its mood and tone, the poem (and, by implication, the related prose passage) bears the hallmarks of the older Goethe. 'Der Bräutigam' is the work of an old man remembering or imagining what it is like to be a young man betrothed and in love, not the rhapsodic self-expression of that young man himself.

Those two selves are linked (though not merged) by the words 'Um Mitternacht' [at midnight] with which the poem opens, referring to the past, and which are repeated in the fourth stanza as the poem shifts into the present. The first three stanzas are marked by restlessness: 'ich schlief, im Busen wachte | Das liebevolle Herz' [I slept, but in my bosom my loving heart was awake], or 'mein emsig Tun und Streben' [my diligent activity and striving]; even the hope in line 12 has a certain urgency about it. In the final stanza, by contrast, the dominant theme is rest. The night has taken on a different significance. Unlike the younger man, whose ardent heart defies it, the older man is sunk in a dream of a deeper night still, for the final three lines are unmistakably, though not morbidly, preoccupied with death. Whereas the inner light of the younger man is almost always at odds with the phases of the natural light, the two appear to have been reconciled by the fourth stanza. The heart whose love was as bright as day may now anticipate slipping into the last obscurity, but with that comes rest, and some reconciliation with the trials of life: 'O sei auch mir dort auszuruhn bereitet, | Wie es auch sei das Leben, es ist gut' [O let that place be ready for me to rest there, for however life is, it is good] (l. 16). The role of the stars as the poet's guide, 'Um Mitternacht der Sterne Glanz geleitet' [led at midnight by the brilliance of the stars] (l. 13), is similar to that of the moon in 'Dornburg, September 1828' and the sun in 'Früh, wenn Tal, Gebirg und Garten'. Yet the ending is bittersweet. The poet and his beloved have been separated, otherwise he would not need to wish for reunion; and the modification of the story of the Magi, so that 'der Sterne Glanz' leads not to a birthplace but to a tomb, serves as an additional, jarring reminder that this reunion can only occur in death, without the promise of living contact for which the younger man could live in hope. Despite the mirroring of earlier elements of the poem in the final stanza, it is once again the difference between the perspective of the older man and the younger which ultimately receives emphasis.

Given that it comes later in the chronology of Goethe's work in the 1820s, the corresponding passage of *Dichtung und Wahrheit* can be read as a reworking of 'Der Bräutigam'. All the major features of the poem — the wakefulness of the young man, the theme of love being brighter than day, the starry night — are, superficially, reproduced. In other words, Goethe has used the text of a poem that he wrote as an old man to help portray his experiences as a young man. The implications of this for our theme of 'uncovering the past' are clear; and it is abundantly clear from this case that, in the 1820s, Goethe was constantly reflecting on and revisiting his works, even those which he had written relatively recently. But he has done what, as we shall see, he does in Book III of the *Wanderjahre*: namely, to produce a prose epigone of an exquisite poem of his own.[45] For, between the parallels with 'Der Bräutigam', there are marked touches of bathos. The poem describes the absorption of the couple in one another, to the extent that they are each other's world: in the third stanza, the description of their reciprocal gaze is preceded and followed by the movements of the sun, as if that gaze were so deep that it could be wrapped around the world. In the prose version, however, the end of their evening together involves taking Lili's chaperone home rather than gazing 'Hand in Hand' at the setting sun: 'nachdem ich sie und die Gesellschaft von Türe zu Türe nach Hause begleitet' [after I had taken her and her companion home from door to door] (*FA* XIV, 762). Moreover, the absence of the beloved is described in the poem in terms of insufferable heat, which the younger self only survives because of the promise of refreshment in the 'cool evening' of her company. In *Dichtung und Wahrheit*, by contrast, Goethe wanders about after he and Lili have parted, full of thoughts and hopes of her ('ich setzte mich auf eine Bank, in der reinsten Nachtstille, unter dem blendenden Sternenhimmel, mir selbst und ihr anzugehören' [I sat down on a bench, in the purest silence of night, under the dazzling firmament, in order to belong wholly to myself and to her]), but is quickly distracted by the shufflings of nocturnal animals: 'Bemerkenswert schien mir ein schwer zu erklärender Ton [...]. Es mochten Ygel oder Wieseln sein, oder was in solcher Stunde dergleichen Geschäft vornimmt' [I was captivated by a sound difficult to explain [...] It was likely hedgehogs or weasels, or whatever else goes about similar business at that hour] (*FA* XIV, 763).

There are a number of possible reasons for the decision to produce this ironic 'alternative version'. The prose version gives us, fittingly, a more prosaic reality than 'Der Bräutigam', and this could constitute a discreet reflection on the *difference* between life and poetry, notwithstanding their interdependence. This is borne out in the narrative: for Goethe comes to realize, soon after his betrothal, that what is true in feelings and in poetry may not be supported by external circumstances, and is led by his lack of means to the decision (rather pompously expressed) to see 'ob man Lili entbehren könnte' [to see if one could do without Lili] (*FA* XIV, 785). Moreover, perhaps the most significant difference between his life and the poem is that he never really was a 'Bräutigam': when he did finally marry Christiane Vulpius, the ceremony was perfunctory, and he was too mature to fit the topos of the bridegroom which we find in poetry. Despite his love for Christiane, the wound inflicted by the parting from Lili remained with Goethe for his whole life; it is perhaps the bitterness of this enduring sense of a lost opportunity which led him to infuse with irony a description which, as its poetic counterpart makes clear, had so much resonance for him.

The tendencies discussed in relation to both autobiographies converge in the final paragraph of *Dichtung und Wahrheit IV*. Once again, Goethe quotes an earlier work of his own:

> Kind, Kind! nicht weiter! Wie von unsichtbaren Geistern gepeitscht gehen die
> Sonnenpferde der Zeit mit unsers Schicksals leichtem Wagen durch, und uns

bleibt nichts, als mutig gefaßt, die Zügel festzuhalten, und bald rechts, bald links, vom Steine hier, vom Sturze da die Räder abzulenken. Wohin es geht, wer weiß es? Erinnert er sich doch kaum, woher er kam. (*FA* xiv, 852)

[Child, child! no further! As if whipped by invisible spirits, the sun-horses of time run away with the light carriage of our fate, and there is nothing left for us but to hold the reins tight, courageous and composed, and to steer the wheels first right, then left, away from stones here, from the precipice there. Where this will lead, who knows? For he can scarce remember whence he came.]

But these words from *Egmont* take on a different aspect in the new context into which they have been inserted. A certain dramatic irony has run throughout *Dichtung und Wahrheit*: for it is written in the full knowledge of the developments of the intervening years, that is, of the future of which the narrated subject has as yet but the vaguest inkling. The strangeness of the undertaking to recreate the earlier perspective is heightened here. Whilst the imagery of being tossed about by the ineffable forces of fate gives a vivid sense of the nervous anticipation of the young man, the narrator's knowledge and ours that the 'Wagen' in which young Goethe is sitting is taking him to a life not just of poetry, but of the court and bureaucracy, makes the rhetoric seem somewhat inflated. The passage can, however, be read on another level: namely, as a reflection once again of the very late perspective. As we saw earlier, the ending of the *Zweiter Römischer Aufenthalt* can be interpreted as anticipating a much more final departure than simply leaving Italy. Here, likewise, the words 'Wohin es geht, wer weiß es?' could refer to a much deeper unknown — that of the end of life — than the personal fate and future of the young man, which has in the meantime become known. Similarly, the final sentence could refer to that forgetfulness of the young man, to which Goethe alludes in the context of the Swiss journey, as he rushes from experience to experience. But it could also encapsulate that sense which builds up through repeated references in the two autobiographies: the sense, namely, that our knowledge of ourselves, like our knowledge of everything else, remains essentially limited, however much our understanding is enhanced by experience. The elusiveness of the past, and the inability of even the most reflective consciousness to keep hold of all the different stages of its selfhood, are highlighted once more in the ironic decision to end as long and detailed an autobiography as *Dichtung und Wahrheit* with the words 'Erinnert er sich doch kaum, woher er kam.'

Notes to Chapter 2

1. Roy Pascal, *Design and Truth in Autobiography* (London: Routledge and Kegan Paul, 1960), p. 11.
2. Several critics have recognized the affinity between the *Zweiter Römischer Aufenthalt* and *Wilhelm Meisters Wanderjahre*: Gerhard Schulz observes that, in both works, 'the most heterogeneous literary forms are colorfully combined', and Stefan Oswald hints at a similarity in the prevailing mood of the two works with his subheading '*Zweiter Römischer Aufenthalt: der Entsagende*'. Schulz, 'Goethe's *Italienische Reise*', in *Goethe in Italy, 1786–1986*, ed. by Gerhart Hoffmeister (Amsterdam: Rodopi, 1988), p. 7; Oswald, *Italienbilder: Beiträge zur Wandlung der deutschen Italienauffassung 1770–1840* (Heidelberg: Winter, 1985), p. 98. Similarly, Dennis Mahoney notes that '[b]y Part IV of *Dichtung und Wahrheit*, the narrator has become more like the "editor" of the 1829 version of *Wilhelm Meisters Wanderjahre*'; and Erich Trunz draws attention to the striking

similarity between the 'Josephsnovelle' in the *Wanderjahre* and the description in *Dichtung und Wahrheit*, Book XVIII, of the encounter with the pilgrims shortly before arriving at Maria Einsiedeln in Schwyz, Switzerland — an episode, moreover, of which there is no mention in Goethe's diary from 1775. Mahoney, 'Autobiographical Writings', in *The Cambridge Companion to Goethe*, ed. by Lesley Sharpe (Cambridge: Cambridge University Press, 2002), pp. 147–59 (p. 150); Trunz, commentary for the *Hamburger Ausgabe*, x, 627.

3. *FA* xiv, 1059.

4. Robert Gould's article 'The Functions of the Non-Literary Quotations in Part 4 of *Dichtung und Wahrheit*', *GLL*, 44 (1991), 291–305, is an important exception.

5. See notes to the MA, xvi, 922.

6. Derek Bowman, *Life into Autobiography: A Study of Goethe's 'Dichtung und Wahrheit'* (Berne: Herbert Lang, 1971), p. 21.

7. *FA* xiv, 15.

8. Oswald, *Italienbilder*, p. 94.

9. See, for example, Harald Schnur: 'Integration ist der basale Begriff zur Analyse [der Autobiographie] — und zugleich von personaler Identität' ('Identität und autobiographische Darstellung in Goethes "Dichtung und Wahrheit"', *JFDH* (1990), 28–93 (p. 29)).

10. See Klaus-Detlef Müller: 'der Sinn des Lebens ist nicht in seiner Ereignisfolge vorgegeben, sondern muß in der Reflexion gewonnen und in der Darstellung erzählerisch vermittelt werden' (*FA* xiv, 1058).

11. Nicholls, 'Goethe and Twentieth-Century Theory', p. 169.

12. Paul de Man, 'Autobiography as De-facement', *MLN*, 94 (1979), 919–30 (p. 922).

13. Peter Boerner, 'Italienische Reise (1816–29)', in *Interpretationen: Goethes Erzählwerk*, ed. by Paul Michel Lützeler and James E. McLeod (Stuttgart: Reclam, 1985), pp. 344–62 (p. 351).

14. *FA* xv.1, 380. Further references to this volume are given after quotations in the text.

15. Richard Block also recognizes it, but his argument has a different focus. He contends that, in Italy, Goethe experiences the absence of those, namely Winckelmann and his own father, who made Italy what it is for him, even as his presence there revives their memory. Indeed, the journey itself enacts a kind of absence: 'This is the magic of his Italian journey: he assumes the ideal character of absence only to turn up later without having truly disappeared' (*Spell of Italy: Vacation, Magic and the Attraction of Goethe* (Detroit: Wayne State University Press, 2006), p. 62). Block is concerned, then, with the Italian *experience*; but absence is also fundamental to the *writing* of the *Zweiter Römischer Aufenthalt*.

16. Much of the work consists of descriptions of works of art which, unless we happen to be in Rome ourselves, we do not have in front of us.

17. Stephen Cheeke, *Writing for Art: The Aesthetics of Ekphrasis* (Manchester: Manchester University Press, 2008), p. 185.

18. The exact nature of the feelings between Goethe and Angelika Kauffmann, for example, remains unknown, but it is likely that they were more than simple friendly regard, though not necessarily sexually amorous either: 'there was enough of the maternal in her warm affection for him to maintain, if in a milder climate, that aura of sexually neutralized emotion in which he had chosen to live for the past twelve years' (Boyle, *Goethe: The Poet and the Age*, I, 488).

19. *Tristia*, III.3.1.

20. See *FA* xv.2, 1155–57.

21. Ibid., p. 1156.

22. Ibid., p. 1157.

23. *FA* xiv, 12. Further references to this volume are given after quotations in the text.

24. Ibid., pp. 473–74.

25. For example, the words 'durch die Klarheit, womit sie sprach, machte sie die Nacht zum Tage', or 'Es war mir sehr angenehm, stillschweigend der Schilderung zuzuhören, die sie von der kleinen Welt machte, in der sie sich bewegte' (*FA* xiv, 474)

26. The guiding idea of Gabriele Blod's analysis is Goethe's own description, in 1811, of his autobiography as a 'Lebensmärchen':

    Sein 'Lebensmärchen' setzt Goethe aus mehreren Märchen zusammen: Knaben-, Jünglings- und Familienmärchen [...] [Es] ist eher eine Ramenhandlung denn eine einzelne Geschichte. Auch das klingt in einer Wendung an: Als 'Tausend und eine Nacht meines wunderlichen Lebens' bezeichnet er *Dichtung und Wahrheit* von Trebra und Zelter gegenüber. (Gabriele Blod, *'Lebensmärchen': Goethes Dichtung und Wahrheit als poetischer und poetologischer Text* (Würzburg: Königshausen und Neumann, 2003), pp. 52–53)

27. I rely here on Siegfried Scheibe's article 'Der vierte Teil von "Dichtung und Wahrheit": Zur Entstehungsgeschichte und Textgestalt', *JGG*, 30 (1968), 87–115, in which he charts the development of Part IV, identifying five main 'Arbeitsphasen': 1813, 1816, 1821, 1825, and 1830/31 (the last being by far the most concentrated period of work). The major commentaries tend also to take their lead from Scheibe's work.

28. *FA* XIV, 729.

29. H. B. Nisbet, '*Das Dämonische*: On the Logic of Goethe's Demonology', *Forum for Modern Language Studies*, 7 (1971), 259–81 (p. 265).

30. Ibid.

31. See also Angus Nicholls: 'the daemonic is something that can only be cognized in retrospect, and in this regard its function [in *Dichtung und Wahrheit IV*] is to enable a recognition of previous strivings, efforts and desires' (*Goethe's Concept of the Daemonic*, p. 228).

32. Nisbet, '*Das Dämonische*', p. 261.

33. Ibid., p. 270.

34. Benedikt Jeßing, 'Dichtung und Wahrheit', in *Goethe Handbuch*, III, ed. by Bernd Witte and Peter Schmidt (Stuttgart: Metzler, 1997), pp. 278–330 (p. 329).

35. Nicholls, *Goethe's Concept of the Daemonic*, p. 228.

36. Pascal, *Design and Truth*, p. 71.

37. Gould, 'The Functions of Non-literary Quotations in *Dichtung und Wahrheit*', p. 295.

38. *FA* XIV, 1282. The diary is included in the 'Paralipomena' section of this edition, pp. 925–26.

39. Nicholas Boyle observes that,

   although 'On the Lake' contains autobiographical elements, it is an autobiographical poem only in a rather complex sense. It is essentially a poem about having an autobio- graphy, about being in a landscape when you have a life-story that you tell yourself, an incomplete life-story of your own. (*Goethe: The Poet and the Age*, I, 206)

40. *FA* II, 702.

41. See *FA* II, 1221; *MA* XIII.1, 688.

42. See *FA* II, 1222.

43. See Scheibe, 'Der vierte Teil von "Dichtung und Wahrheit"', p. 96.

44. See Boyle, *Goethe: The Poet and the Age*, I, 210.

45. See Chapter 3 for a fuller discussion of this.

CHAPTER 3

Prose Fiction

Wilhelm Meisters Wanderjahre is the summation of all Goethe's prose writing, and the most overtly and radically experimental piece in any genre from this period of his output. In the months of 1828–29 when he completed the second version of the novel, he was working as editor and arbiter not only of the 1821 edition of the piece, but of a lifetime of work. The original version was reviewed, expanded, and worked up into something quite different.[1] We saw in Chapter 1 that the simple regrouping of three poems in 1826 to form *Trilogie der Leidenschaft* constituted a significant intervention in the semantics of each one; and the 1829 edition of the *Wanderjahre* was the product of reworking on a much larger scale. The novel contains elements of all Goethe's previous prose works: the alternation between novella and frame narrative is reminiscent of the *Unterhaltungen deutscher Ausgewanderten* [*Conversations of German Emigrés*]; the preoccupation with relationships and rivalries in many of the inserted pieces recalls *Die Wahlverwandtschaften* (which, of course, began life as a novella for the *Wanderjahre*); and certain characters are carried over from the *Lehrjahre*, although not as many as might be expected in a regular sequel, and there are a number of parallel scenes. Yet, as with other very late works, these echoes sound in a piece which is markedly different from all that has gone before. *Novelle*, too, though it was originally conceived in 1797, was not worked up fully until 1826–27, and bears the hallmarks of the very late perspective. Both pieces are remarkable for their literariness, the awareness which they demonstrate of the world, of life, as made or shaped by texts, and of those texts themselves as inherently intertextual; but both also put their literariness to work. *Novelle* poses a problem and resolves it by self-conscious means; and, in the *Wanderjahre*, literariness is the means chosen to meet the challenges both of very-lateness and of modernity.

Novelle

The story of *Novelle* is that of an ascent towards an ideal. The characters climb a mountain, driven by the desire of the Princess to see the old Stammburg, which represents the unknown, the inaccessible: 'Es ist eine Wildnis wie keine, ein zufällig-einziges Lokal' [It is a wilderness like no other, an arbitrary, singular place].[2] There are various stages to the ascent, which is unending: the 'disordered ambition'[3] of the Princess and the 'erhöhte Jagdlust' [heightened desire to hunt][4] of the Prince and his courtiers is soothed by the boy's song, and the violence of the previous scenes has yielded to 'eine vollkommene Stille' [consummate silence], the silence of harmony, before the Stammburg has been reached; and only the boy, the warden, and the boy's mother follow the lion into the old castle. Even then, though, there is a further stage, which no one completes. In his description of the castle, the Prince's uncle had mentioned a tower, with an obstruction in it:

> auf den Stufen die in den Hauptturm hinaufführen [hat] ein Ahorn Wurzel geschlagen und sich zu einem so tüchtigen Baume gebildet [...], daß man nur mit Not daran vorbeidringen kann um die Zinne, der unbegränzten Aussicht wegen, zu besteigen. (*FA* VIII, 536)

> [on the steps leading up to the main tower, a maple has put down roots and grown into so mighty a tree [...] that one can only pass by with great difficulty if one is to climb on to the battlements, which offer a boundless view.]

The tower and the tree represent a height which no character in the story will reach, and thus the potentially infinite nature of the search for truth.

Heightening is not confined to the imagery of *Novelle*, but extends to its style and structure. The model of poetic *Steigerung* is that of an ascent which incorporates depth: and that is precisely what happens in *Novelle*, which 'achieves its final miraculous reconciliation [...] by drawing into the present the primordial source of the Occidental literary, ethical and religious traditions'.[5] The range of its symbolic reference, from the biblical to the medieval, from antiquity to Goethe's own age, is out of all proportion to its slight span: the work is only about twenty pages long, and the action takes place within a single day. It is full of figures and structures from an altogether different time, themselves almost memories: the Stammburg, for example, now largely a ruin, and the animal keeper's family, whose almost primordial nature is indicated by the 'natürliche Sprache' [natural language] spoken by the mother. It is also full of *literary* memory. In the characterization of the boy are shades of Orpheus, Androcles, Daniel, and St Jerome,[6] and the lines of his song are highly allusive: the motif 'Blankes Schwert erstarrt im Hiebe' [the shining sword freezes in mid-blow], for example, is to be found in the *Arabian Nights*, as well as in medieval legends; and the words 'Und die Welle schwankt zurück' [And the wave draws back] echo both Exodus and Job.[7] Moreover, although *Novelle* is less overtly self-referential than some of Goethe's other works, it resounds, as we have come to expect of this phase, with echoes from elsewhere in his *œuvre*. The fire which haunts the Uncle is reminiscent of that which rages in the memories of the townsfolk in *Hermann und Dorothea*; in the propensity of the Princess to allow stories (the Uncle's tale about the fire in the marketplace) and images, *Schreckbilder* (the crude illustration of the tiger on the placard) to cloud her perceptions and judgement, we see shades of *Werther* and *Die Wahlverwandtschaften*; and both the form of the piece and its theme of reconciliation recall Goethe's *Märchen*. Yet, though the elements are familiar, they sit in a framework which is different, new, and utterly characteristic of this phase: for again and again in Goethe's very late works, we encounter both the motif and the practice of ascension, ascension to the new from and through the old.

Novelle undergoes yet another level of heightening, beyond this general allusiveness, at the end. Before the boy's song charms the lion, it tames the company, including the royal hunting party and the princess:

'Alles war still, hörte, horchte und nur erst als die Töne verhallten konnte man den Eindruck bemerken und allenfalls beobachten. Alles war beschwichtigt; jeder in seiner Art gerührt' (*FA* VIII, 552)

[All were still, listening, and only when the notes died away could they feel, and at best observe, the impression. All were soothed, each moved in his own way].

Many of the verbal elements of the boy's song are taken from the prose of *Novelle* itself, and transposed into a different form. His mother's grief at the killing of the tiger is modulated into a positive image, in which lions live intimately alongside 'dem Guten' [the good man], a humanity reconciled with nature rather than in competition with it. Indeed, the lines 'Löw' und Löwin, hin und wieder, | Schmiegen sich um ihn heran' [Lion and lioness, moving back and forth, nestle round him] (*FA* VIII, 551), resonate with 'Bergschluchten', the final scene of *Faust II*: 'Löwen sie schleichen stumm | Freundlich um uns herum' [Lions pad silently, fondly around us].[8] Similarly, he retains elements of his father's Old Testament-style paean — the references to 'Engel' [angels] and 'der Ewige' [the eternal being], for example — and works them into an altogether tauter linguistic framework, the euphonic and rhythmic power of which exceeds that of prose. Once the boy reaches the lion, the prose becomes increasingly drawn into the mood of the song (as indeed the narrator comments: 'sein beschwichtigendes Lied [...], dessen Wiederholung wir uns auch nicht entziehen können' [his soothing song [...] which we too cannot keep from repeating], *FA* VIII, 554), and the narration begins to take on its characteristics. Just as lines of the song are repeated, so are elements of the prose: for example, the words 'sang weiter' [continued to sing] recur, indeed begin almost to provide the rhythm and structure of the last paragraphs, and the notion of transfiguration occurs twice in as many pages — 'bis er sich [...] wie verklärt niedersetzte' [until he sat down, as if transfigured] (*FA* VIII, 554), 'und wirklich sah das Kind in seiner Verklärung aus wie ein mächtiger siegreicher Überwinder' [and truly, the transfigured child had the appearance of a powerful, victorious conqueror] (*FA* VIII, 555). The subject matter of prose and poem is harmonized: both relate the overcoming of violence and the peaceful communion of living things, and the text ends in a potentially infinite state of flux between the two types of text, as they echo, comment on, and make way for each other. The text not only describes, but actually becomes the vehicle of harmony, resolving the tensions of the story within itself and for itself.

Novelle does not end, exactly, but moves into transcendence. Just as the tower in the *Stammburg* suggests further stages to the ascent, so the text stops short of representing the whole revelation of the ideal. Although, as Nicholas Boyle observes, 'what was "Gleichnis" has now become "Ereignis"',[9] the text hints at the possibility that there is more to discover beyond this specific 'Ereignis'. When the boy and the lion emerge from the hollow within the castle, the lion settles 'in den letzten Strahlen der Sonne, die sich durch eine Ruinenlücke hereinsandte, [und setzte sich] wie verklärt nieder' [in the last rays of the sun, which penetrated through a hole in the wall of the ruin, and sat down as if transfigured] (*FA* VIII, 554). The quality of the light is important. It is not the strong light of the gold and precious stones which flashes through the Book of Revelation, or of the fire in which God appears to Moses in Exodus: it is a soft, modest light which filters through gaps in the ruin. The sun is setting on a significant 'Ereignis'; but the walls of the castle still block out much of its glow. Moreover, the element of hesitation in 'wie verklärt' (as opposed to just 'verklärt') is reiterated a few lines later:

> *Ist es möglich zu denken*, daß man in den Zügen eines so grimmigen Geschöpfes, des Tyrannen der Wälder, des Despoten des Tierreichs einen Ausdruck von Freundlichkeit von dankbarer Zufriedenheit, habe spüren können so geschah es hier [...]. (*FA* VIII, 555; my emphasis)

> [If it is possible to imagine that, in the features of so grim a creature, the tyrant of the forests, the despot of the animal kingdom, an expression of friendship, of grateful contentment could be discerned, then so it was here.]

Even in the middle of the glorious description, and textual enactment, of the complete restoration of harmony and understanding between nature and humankind, doubt is raised as to whether our minds are even equal to imagining that possibility; and, just as it was becoming a reality, the ideal becomes an ideal once more. The strategy of the text is to suggest rather than to show. This attitude to representation, which values openness and possibility above all, is in direct and deliberate contrast to that behind the marketplace image of the tiger, which was the trigger of tragedy: there, the tiger's characteristics are reduced to a crude, commercial (mis)representation, which compounds the lack of understanding already innate in those who see it, and adversely affects their perceptions afterwards.

Novelle ends, then, on a note of possibility rather than of absolute achievement: the *possibility* that we might be able to look beyond imperfect representations that have become ingrained in our minds (the pouncing tiger, or the lion as king of beasts, as 'Despot des Tierreichs') to a different, truer face of things. That movement towards truth is the ascension implicit both in the imagery of the text and in its own movements; but, in a tacit acknowledgement of the limitations even of this representation, it is left implicit. The characters and their situation melt away, until all we are left with is the text. The poem has the last word, and it has come into being literally through the prose, through its textual resources. This is the level of literariness, of self-consciousness, which will become the norm in *Wilhelm Meisters Wanderjahre*.

Wilhelm Meisters Wanderjahre

If *Novelle* can be likened to the poetry of this period, *Wilhelm Meisters Wanderjahre* has a good deal in common with the autobiographical works. We have seen that these express strong reservations about memory; and in the *Wanderjahre*, doubts about narrative (for autobiographical memory is, after all, a narrative faculty) are taken to their logical extreme. The most immediately striking feature of the novel is the lack of an overarching narrative voice, or even a strong narrative trajectory, and the proliferation instead of different voices and threads of story. The constitutive elements of the *Wanderjahre* exist in an intimate, but frequently obscure and always open relationship to one another. Steve Dowden observes of the words 'Ist fortzusetzen' [To be continued] with which the novel closes: '[Goethe's] bit of drollery at the end of the *Wanderjahre* gives us the measure of human contingency, and with it the contingency of his narrative. There are natural limitations to his control over it'.[10] 'Ist fortzusetzen' has, I think, greater implications than this, as we shall see later; but Dowden is right to emphasize contingency and limitation, for these issues are central to both the form and the content of the work. Goethe himself remarked in a letter to Rochlitz on 23 November 1829:

> Mit solchem Büchlein aber ist es wie mit dem Leben selbst: es findet sich in dem Komplex des Ganzen Notwendiges und Zufälliges, Vorgesetztes und Angeschlossenes, bald gelungen, bald vereitelt, wodurch es eine Art von Unendlichkeit erhält, die sich in verständige und vernünftige Worte nicht durchaus fassen und einschließen läßt.[11]

> [But this little book is comparable to life itself: in the complex whole can be found things which are necessary and things which are incidental, parts which have been moved forward and parts which have been added, successes here and failures there; and all this gives it a kind of infinity, which cannot quite be grasped and contained in sensible, rational words.]

As we saw in the previous chapter, the subtle implication of the autobiographical writings is that the unity of the self is an 'offenbares Geheimnis'; and Goethe's description of the *Wanderjahre* here as a work which, while it is by no means wholly arbitrary, can never be fully grasped, suggests that the unity of this novel likewise remains an open secret. Closer analysis of the novel will show just how significant the theme of the secret was for Goethe in his old age. It symbolizes the recognition of human limitations: an act of insight which is what I understand by *Entsagung*.

The (non-)narrative style of the *Wanderjahre* can be attributed in part to the influence of, among others, Diderot, Sterne, and Fielding, all of whom were familiar to Goethe (indeed, there are even references to Sterne in the collection of maxims at the end of Book II), and all of whom experimented with multi-perspectival and digressional narratives;[12] but the style is also symptomatic of Goethe's own situation and outlook in the later 1820s. It should be no surprise, given the degree of self-consciousness which we have encountered in other works of his from this period, that literariness should be a defining feature of the *Wanderjahre*: the understanding, that is, of life as shaped by a great shared textual past, one of symbols, poems, narratives, history, through which we are formed and have come to understand ourselves. Of course, this is not a new insight for Goethe; but, more than any other text of his, the *Wanderjahre* creates its own worded world of short stories, letters, aphorisms, poems. Text, or textuality, is itself a theme in this novel, which anticipates the self-reflexive prose generally held to be characteristic of modernism. This leads us directly to another major aspect of the work. Whereas, in the autobiographical writings, the issue is the fragility of memory, in the *Wanderjahre* it is modernity, and the confusion which it causes for the human subject.[13] One of the key motivating forces in the work is the question of how to find a form and style, and above all the subject matter, appropriate to the new situation. Günter Saße, among others, has shown that the fragmentary nature of the *Wanderjahre*, the proliferation of narrative voices and styles, is a tacit acknowledgement that conventional ideals of composition are no longer equal to the challenges of the day.[14]

The idea of modernity is no more a new issue for Goethe than the unreliability of memory. Where the conception in the *Wanderjahre* differs from that explored in the *Unterhaltungen*, say, or the *Lehrjahre*, is in its material and social emphasis, the sustained preoccupation with science, industry, and social existence. There had been major and rapid changes in all of these areas throughout Europe for some decades already (the beginnings of the first Industrial Revolution, after all, are in the early eighteenth century); but it was in the early part of the nineteenth century that disparate social, political, and technical developments began to converge into something like an image of modern — that is to say, late — Europe, and it is in the *Wanderjahre* that Goethe addresses this most directly. In respect of the transition between the editions of 1821 and 1829, Hans Reiss emphasizes the decisive nature of the shift from domestic travel to emigration;[15] and, as we shall see, the theme of emigration is intimately bound up with, indeed is explored as a partial (but only partial) response to, the challenges of modernity. Thus the concern with modernity becomes more pronounced in the second edition of the novel; but so, too, does the sense of reconciliation with this late Europe in which Goethe finds himself. For Wilhelm's decision in the 1829 version to stay in Europe implies a new acceptance of the restrictions of Europe, of its past but also of its confused present.

Dealing with modernity, therefore, involves compromise for Goethe: and this is the connecting arc to the theme of limitation. Book III of the *Wanderjahre* explores how developments in, for example, technology, often fail to translate unequivocally into happiness and progress for all people, thereby breeding limitations even as they promise new things. On the other hand, as the experimental nature of its composition attests, the novel does not clamour for an outright rejection of anything that is not tradition. In simple terms, two major questions underlying the novel are how to write about things adequately, and how to write about them now, in this modern era of European history, and in this very late phase of the writer's own life. They are not always addressed directly, at the surface (there are, for example, large parts of the novel which appear not to be concerned with contemporary Europe), but, at a deeper level, these questions are a strong motivating force in the composition of the *Wanderjahre*; and its self-reference — for constantly, if with varying degrees of explicitness, it makes a theme of its own composition — is intimately bound up in this. In what follows I shall concentrate mainly on those parts of the novel which are new in the second version,[16] although it would not be representative of the work as a whole to treat them in isolation. Where a section carried over from the first edition is particularly relevant it will be incorporated into the analysis.

Self-conscious prose

Rather than seeking to create the illusion of an overarching narrative, then, the text of the *Wanderjahre* deliberately lays open the process of writing. As the novel draws to a close in Book III, chapter 14, we find overt reference to the activity of the writer:

> Hier aber wird die Pflicht des Mitteilens, Darstellens, Ausführens und Zusam-
> menziehens immer schwieriger. Wer fühlt nicht daß wir uns diesmal dem Ende

nähern, wo die Furcht in Umständlichkeiten zu verweilen, mit dem Wunsche nichts völlig unerörtert zu lassen uns in Zwiespalt versetzt. (*FA* x, 720)

[Here, however, our duty to inform, depict, expound and draw together becomes ever more difficult. Who could doubt that, this time, we are reaching the end: and we are torn between the fear of lingering for too long on details and the desire not to leave anything wholly untouched.]

This could also be understood as a more general reflection on Goethe's own situation: for the dilemma described here of having to finish without having said everything, or having to say things without feeling that they are finished, is one which becomes particularly acute in the very late phase. On its own a comment such as this is not unusual. The final chapter of Jane Austen's *Mansfield Park* also gives direct expression to the writer's sense that it is time to dispatch her work, although here her pragmatic attitude seems a matter of choice rather than necessity:

Let other pens dwell on guilt and misery. I quit such odious subjects as soon as I can, impatient to restore everybody, not greatly in fault themselves, to tolerable comfort, and to have done with all the rest.[17]

It is, rather, the frequency with which the construction, or constructedness, of the text is exposed, which makes the *Wanderjahre* distinctive. In Book III, chapter 10, the narrator teases the reader by offering information, and then immediately withholding it:

[Der Astronom] fing nunmehr nach erhaltener Erlaubnis folgendermaßen zu lesen an. —
    Wenn wir aber uns bewogen finden diesen werten Mann nicht lesen zu lassen, so werden es unsere Gönner wahrscheinlich geneigt aufnehmen [...] Unsere Freunde haben einen Roman in die Hand genommen, und wenn dieser hie und da schon mehr als billig didaktisch geworden, so finden wir doch geraten, die Geduld unserer Wohlwollenden nicht noch weiter auf die Probe zu stellen. (*FA* x, 381)

[[The astronomer], having received permission, began to read as follows. —
    But if we feel moved not to let this worthy man read, our patrons will doubtless look favourably upon this action. [...] Our friends have picked up a novel, and if, here and there, it has already become more didactic than is appropriate, then we consider it advised not to try the patience of our kind readers any further.]

This raises the reader's awareness of the extent to which the material presented on the page has been manipulated, if allegedly in his or her interest: the reader is placed at one remove from the material, and is reminded that reading is not unmediated experience. It is also a very funny moment: if the narrator teases the reader, he also speaks teasingly of the writer of the novel (or the writer of the novel puts teasing words in his mouth): 'wenn dieser [Roman] hie und da schon mehr als billig didaktisch geworden'. This self-ironic gesture is more complex than it might seem. For, at the very same moment that the author appears to yield control over his material, by having one of his narrators laugh at his work, he also continues to assert his control, and in the most complete possible way. The refusal to divulge a detail to the reader is a pretence, the detail itself a fiction, and thus the author reveals himself once more to be the director of the illusions created by his narrative. This fine balance of retreat and assertion is a manifestation at the structural level — that is to say, right at the surface of the text — of a thought pattern which runs much deeper in the novel, and about which there will be much more to say later: namely, the tension between the limitations of human discourse and the pursuit of the ideal.

The narrative is also disrupted throughout the novel by the insertion of extraneous material. This had always been a feature of Goethe's prose: in *Die Leiden des jungen Werthers*, for example, large passages from Ossian are incorporated, and the description of Werther's death is calqued, sometimes word for word, on Kestner's report on the death of Jerusalem. It is, however, in the very late phase that disruptions to the narrative become the norm, and a theme in themselves. The most obvious example of such an insertion in the *Wanderjahre* is Lenardo's diary, which also contains many of the other reflexive features typical of the novel.[18] The material comes to us apparently unformed, and we must wait for the continuation of it: at the end of the first part (Book III, chapter 5), we are told that Makarie is reading the second part, which we are not given until chapter 13. The first part oscillates between Lenardo's subjective impressions of the Swiss weaving community (especially the allure of the pretty girls at their spinning wheels) and factual descriptions of the entire process of weaving, from carding to the manufacture of cloth. Again, the material for this report is borrowed from an external source, this time Heinrich Meyer on the production of cotton. Indeed, in an observation which strengthens the case for understanding these very late works as proto-modernist, Ehrhard Bahr notes a parallel with the highly technical description of the Dublin waterworks in James Joyce's *Ulysses*.[19] The continuation of Lenardo's diary is concerned with his reunion with Frau Susanne, the 'nut-brown maid' about whom we heard in Book I, although here too there is the insertion of some *Spruch*-like passages,[20] which would not be out of place in the collections of maxims at the end of Books II and III. Given that Makarie (who is closely associated with the maxims) is supposed to have had the second part in her possession before it reaches Wilhelm, and therefore the reader, those passages could be seen as insertions within an insertion, as if some of her papers had, deliberately or not, found their way into the leaves of the diary. Finally, both parts of the diary move unannounced from the first into the third-person, without any indication that the diary has come to an end. This is especially peculiar in the first part. After the entry for 18 September, about two pages of narration by an anonymous voice follow, in which the letter from 'Freund Wilhelm' which had so comforted Lenardo is mentioned; and this is followed by the words 'Hier endigte das Manuskript' [here the manuscript ended], and an indication that 'Freund Wilhelm' has in fact been reading it. If we are to take it that the pages by the anonymous author have been bundled together with Lenardo's diary, then this gives weight to the notion of the *Wanderjahre* as an 'archive', its material organized in layers as well as in chronological sequence.[21]

The concern with modernity central to the novel as a whole is also an overt preoccupation in Lenardo's diary. In the second instalment, Frau Susanne laments the onward march of industrialization: 'Das überhand nehmende Maschinenwesen quält und ängstigt mich, es wälzt sich heran wie ein Gewitter, langsam, langsam; aber es hat seine Richtung genommen, und es wird kommen und treffen' [The world of machinery, which is gaining the upper hand, torments and frightens me. It rolls on hither like a storm, slowly, slowly; but it has taken its course, and it will come and strike] (*FA* x, 713). The threat posed by mechanization is thrown into relief by the detailed descriptions in the first part of the diary both of the carefully preserved traditions of manufacture, and of the community that revolves around it. All the generations are involved in the practice and preservation of received knowledge. The motor for emigration is the sense that modern Europe has reached a difficult point in its development, and the desire to advance by implementing the best of its traditions in a new context. It becomes clear in this section that, in the world of the novel and the mind which created it, modernization renders established identities unstable. The form of the novel both captures that instability in the deliberate fragmentariness of its narrative and seeks to find some sort of equilibrium. The means for this is irony. Emigration is only a partial solution, and the novel also draws attention to its own unsatisfactoriness — as, for example, in the overtly contrived tying up of loose ends discussed above, or in the playful self-irony of the astronomer episode. But, as we shall see later, that very airing of limitations is also conceived as the necessary condition for greater understanding. Moreover, although some aspects of modernization pose a particular threat in the novel, it does not advocate conservatism for its own sake: the same Susanne who expresses her alarm at mechanization speaks of her caution when dealing with received structures, especially religion. The text of the *Wanderjahre* likewise, as we have already seen so often with the very late Goethe, draws on old resources, preserves them as any archive should, but also makes them work in new ways. It will be no surprise, then, that rewriting is a major element of the novel.

Rewriting in the Wanderjahre

Both versions of the novel open with Wilhelm and Felix climbing in a mountainous region. The view from atop a mountain, when so much more of life than could usually be seen is spread out below and around, is akin to that from towards the end of life, to the unprecedented diversity of questions which come into the field of vision of an elderly person. The opening scene of the *Wanderjahre* is — quite literally — a 'heightened' version of that of Book VIII of the *Lehrjahre*, in which Wilhelm and Felix are also exploring nature together. Whereas the earlier scene takes place on the flat, in a garden, the mountains in the *Wanderjahre* afford a much more wide-ranging view. This new setting, as well as being more dramatic than the other, is also more dangerous: 'The "fool's gold" of this opening scene symbolizes that these new wanderings take place in a stranger and more deceiving environment than we have previously encountered in the *Lehrjahre*'.[22] Here too, then, the very late perspective manifests itself in images which are both richer and more ambivalent than before. This broadening-out is not confined to the transition between much earlier and much later works; it can also be detected in the reworking of the 1821 edition into that of 1829. Accordingly, there is a slight but significant variation in the later version of that first scene. Whereas, in 1821, Felix's questions stop with the 'Katzengold', in 1829 he moves from geology to botany ('was ist das? Eine Frucht, versetzte der Vater' [what is that? A type of fruit, replied the boy's father], *FA* x, 263), and from there to the animal kingdom ('Ich will ein Jäger werden. Es ist gar zu schön den ganzen Tag im Walde zu sein und die Vögel zu hören, zu wissen wie sie heißen, wo ihre Nester sind', etc. [I want to be a hunter. It is such a wonderful thing to be in the forest all day and to hear the birds, to know what they are called, where their nests are], *FA* x, 264). In short, the scope of Felix's questions now extends from one area of the study of nature to all of it; and, given the increased emphasis on emigration in 1829, this expansion of perspective from the first to the second edition applies throughout the novel.

Although, for the most part, the differences between the versions of 1821 and 1829 result from the addition of material, there are a few cases of material being jettisoned — the seven poems, for example, which in 1821 precede 'Die Flucht nach Ägypten'. One particularly significant excision is the episode in chapter 13 of the 1821 edition, in which Wilhelm describes seeing Natalie, who is on the other side of a ravine, through a telescope. In 1829, the section in the 'pedagogical province' is extended, a letter from Hersilie added, and Natalie herself now only remembered in a letter which Wilhelm writes, and in which he remembers the distressing death of his childhood friend the fisher-lad. The original episode does not obviously demand to be eliminated. The playful scepticism with which it is introduced is wholly in keeping with the editor's acknowledgment of the instability of other sources in the novel (especially, in the 1829 edition, of documents relating to Makarie): 'die unwahrscheinlichste Erzählung [...] von der Art wie jene Märchen, durch welche man die Neugier des Hörers lange mit Wundern hinhält und zuletzt erklärt: es sei von einem Traum die Rede gewesen' [the most unlikely story [...] in the manner of those tales which hold the interest of the listener with reports of miracles, before finally declaring that it was all a dream] (*FA* x, 162). Similarly, Wilhelm's musings on the uncanny nature of the perspective which the telescope provides are echoed in his ambivalent reaction to the view from the observatory (1829, Book I, chapter 10) — although this time, unlike the episode with Natalie, there is no one gazing back at him. And, of course, there is the related scene in *Novelle*, which reduces reciprocity to imagination:

> Die schöne Dame richtete [...] das Fernrohr etwas tiefer nach einer öden, steinigen Fläche, über welche der Jagdzug weggehen mußte [...] [B]ei der Klarheit und Vergrößerungsfähigkeit des Instrumentes, erkannten ihre glänzenden Augen deutlich den Fürsten und den Oberstallmeister; ja sie enthielt sich nicht abermals mit dem Schnupftuche zu winken, als sie ein augenblickliches Stillhalten und Rückblicken mehr vermutete als gewahr ward. (*FA* VIII, 534–35)

> [The beautiful lady directed [...] the telescope a little lower towards a barren, rocky plain over which the hunting party had to pass [...] The clarity and magnifying power of the instrument meant that, with her shining eyes, she could make out the prince and his chief equerry clearly; indeed, she did not keep from waving her handkerchief again as she saw, or thought she saw them pause momentarily and look back.]

The reason for the suppression of the episode in the later version of the *Wanderjahre* has, I think, to do with the nature of *Entsagung*, a theme which is more fully developed in the second version; but it is not so much that, by catching sight of Natalie, Wilhelm has broken the conditions of his journeyman years, according to which he must remain on the move and unattached (which the obvious desire that Wilhelm expresses on finding himself 'ganz in der Nähe des angebeteten Wesens' [quite near that adored being][23] might seem to contradict). Wilhelm is not Faust, and he has not been forbidden, or forbidden himself, to say 'verweile doch! du bist so schön' [stay! you are so beautiful].

Rather, the change has to do with the preoccupation, much more evident in the 1829 version, with human limitations. Just as the letter relating the story of the *Fischerknabe* replaces the episode with the telescope, so Wilhelm's decision, motivated by the memory of the boy's drowning, to become a surgeon in a sense replaces Natalie as the direction for his life. This may seem counter-intuitive: for the profession which he chooses, at that time a relatively lowly one, is in no way commensurate with the 'angebetenes Wesen'. But we have gone beyond the world of the *Lehrjahre*, in which, as Nicholas Boyle shows, Natalie was Wilhelm's ideal.[24] The world of the *Wanderjahre* is more rough-hewn; the ideal, though no less important, has retreated further from view. It is in the spirit of renunciation to accept that direct but unstructured pursuit of the ideal may be less fruitful than the adoption of humbler goals, and conversely that humbler goals may make one more effective in one's slow pursuit of the ideal. That is certainly the sense of the inserted passages in the second instalment of Lenardo's diary, which in turn resonate with the first few maxims in the 'Betrachtungen im Sinne der Wanderer' ['Reflections in the Spirit of the Wanderer']:

> Weil aber niemand Zweck und Ziel seines Daseins kennt, vielmehr das Geheimnis desselben von höchster Hand verborgen wird, so tastet er nur, greift zu, läßt fahren, steht stille, bewegt sich, zaudert und übereilt sich, und auf wie mancherlei Weise denn alle Irrtümer entstehen, die uns verwirren. (*FA* x, 709)

> [But since no one knows the purpose and goal of his existence, the secret thereof being hidden from him, rather, by the divine hand, he can only feel his way, grasp at something, let it go, stand still, move on, hesitate and fall victim to haste, and other such ways in which all those errors arise which confound us.]

> Fahrt fort in unmittelbarer Beachtung der Pflicht des Tages und prüft dabei die Reinheit eures Herzens und die Sicherheit eures Geistes. Wenn ihr sodann in freier Stunde aufatmet und euch zu erheben Raum findet, so gewinnt ihr auch gewiß eine richtige Stellung gegen das Erhabene, dem wir uns auf jede Weise verehrend hinzugeben, jedes Ereignis mit Ehrfurcht zu betrachten und eine höhere Leitung darin zu erkennen haben. (*FA* x, 710)

> [Continue in close contemplation of the day's duty, and, at the same time, examine the purity of your heart and the certainty of your spirit. If you find in a moment of leisure that you can breathe more freely, and have space to raise yourself up, then it is certain you shall find the right attitude towards the sublime, to which we must devote ourselves in admiration at every opportunity. Similarly, we must regard each event with respect and discern therein direction from above.]

We shall see in more detail later how this attitude is borne out in the structure and composition of the novel itself; suffice it to say for now that, in the textual world in which it prevails, there can be no scene in which Wilhelm sees Natalie. As the related themes of renunciation and limitation come more clearly into focus, so the second version of the *Wanderjahre* pulls further away from the *Lehrjahre*. We have already seen that, if the *Wanderjahre* is a sequel, then only in an indirect way: the relationship is one of difference in similarity. This becomes clearer in another, intriguing example of rewriting, to which this pair of episodes — the vision of Natalie, and the story of the *Fischerknabe* which replaces it — is intimately linked.

The final scene of the *Wanderjahre* (1829 version) is reminiscent of a dream which Wilhelm has in Book VII of the *Lehrjahre*; and the pair demonstrates well the dichotomy of similarity and difference that is the relationship between the two novels. Most of the fundamental elements of the two scenes are similar, which shows that this is a conscious reworking, not a coincidence; but their import is significantly different. Both times, Felix is saved from drowning: in the dream, Natalie draws him, apparently by telepathy, to the edge of the pool into which he has fallen, and in the *Wanderjahre*, Wilhelm himself saves his son by the application of his medical knowledge. But in both scenes, death threatens to impinge directly on the world of the living. The pool and the river are suggestive of the waters of Lethe; in the original dream, Wilhelm notices the shades of Mariane and his father, both of whom have departed, as he walks with Natalie, as if in Elysium; and in the closing scene of the *Wanderjahre*, it is implied that he brings Felix back not just from unconsciousness, but from death itself — 'Das Leben kehrte wieder' [life returned] (*FA* x, 744). Moreover, the realm of death is brought closer in each case by the dreaminess of the scene — sleep and death being symbolically close states. Although the closing scene of the *Wanderjahre* takes place in broad daylight, it too has a dream-like quality. The scene materializes as it were from nowhere, and is imbued with that sense of unknown certainty peculiar to the dream world: 'Nun gleitete der Kahn, beschienen von heißer Mittagssonne, den Fluß hinab [...] Das Kornfeld näherte sich dem Strome' [Now the boat, bathed in the hot morning sunlight, drifted downstream [...] The cornfield drew near to the river] (*FA* x, 744). These opening sentences plunge us into the scene without telling us where we are, or which boat, which river, which cornfield this is; but, as in a dream, context seems to matter little. The elliptical style increases the immediacy of the passage: the careful description of the setting in the first paragraph yields suddenly to a flurry of action. And, again as in dreams, each stage flashes up without much attention being paid to the developments which link them — Wilhelm, for example, seems to move with preternatural speed from passive observation to medical intervention. For a short while, it is as though we have passed with Felix to a realm, at once intriguing and slightly sinister, beyond normal consciousness. The deathly aspect of the two scenes confronts the reader with the reality of human loss. In the *Lehrjahre* version, the poignancy of the ghosts from the past retreating ever further out of reach lends a sense of unfinished business to the end of the scene, and indeed Wilhelm awakes 'mit [...] gemischte[r] Empfindung' [with [...] mixed emotions] (*FA* 9, p. 803). At the end of the *Wanderjahre*, too, the joy of repair is clouded by the ongoing possibility of further damage: 'Wirst du doch immer aufs neue hervorgebracht [...] und wirst sogleich wieder beschädigt' [For no sooner are you remade than damaged again] (*FA* x, 745).

The cycle of gain and loss, then, is an unending one. Yet both scenes close with a return to light and to life: in the *Lehrjahre*, Wilhelm wakes from his dream to a room bathed in sunlight, and the *Wanderjahre* ends with the restorative warmth of the sun's rays, and the anticipation of Felix's return to consciousness after a refreshing sleep. Moreover, the two scenes share the striking motif of gemination. In the dream, Natalie unties the scarf with which she had bound Felix's burning brow, and the child appears to divide into two: 'Als sie den Schleier aufhob, sprangen zwei Knaben hervor' [As she lifted the scarf, two boys sprang forth]. (*FA* ix, 802). With the doubling of Felix, new life bursts forth, setting up a further oppositional force to the deathly pull of the ghosts of Mariane and Wilhelm's father. This image is carried over into the description of the reconciliation between father and son as Felix returns to consciousness in the scene from the *Wanderjahre*: 'So standen sie fest umschlungen, wie Kastor und Pollux, Brüder die sich auf dem Wechselwege vom Orkus zum Licht begegnen' [Thus they stood in a tight embrace, like Castor and Pollux, the brothers whose paths cross as they alternate between Orcus and the light] (*FA* x, 745). If only for a fleeting moment, father and son have become peers: and this is the culmination of a theme that has run throughout the *Wanderjahre*, namely the (re-)identification between father and son, even (or perhaps especially) after rivalry.[25] Both scenes move from loss to the possibility, at least, of fulfilment.

Yet, despite all these similarities, the significance of that movement is much weightier in the *Wanderjahre*. In the earlier novel, Natalie restrains Wilhelm from the pursuit of two people whom he has, after all, already lost, and thus pulls him towards life and opportunity. The later novel, however, takes things further, tracing the movement away from loss even through its composition: for the memory of earlier tragedies is transformed symbolically and given redemptive force. This is where the absence of Natalie once again becomes important. In the dream in the *Lehrjahre*, Wilhelm has no hand in his son's rescue, and can only look on in consternation as Natalie draws Felix out of the water. His helplessness in the dream is matched on at least two occasions in his life. For all that he liberates Mignon from the troupe of acrobats with its abusive master, for all that he tries to give her the love and care that she sorely needs, he is, ultimately, unable to save her. Similarly, he is haunted in the *Wanderjahre* by the memory of Adolph, the *Fischerknabe*: his exposition of the story in his letter to Natalie is lengthy, and full of emotion. Yet, in the final scene, Wilhelm is at last able, having renounced dependence on Natalie and found his profession, to take full responsibility for his son's safety, and to save him from Adolph's fate. Wilhelm does here for Felix what he could not do for Mignon: he truly gives him life. In this particular case, rewriting becomes the resolution of former sadness, albeit a partial one (after all, if the way to Orkus is a *Wechselweg*, and Felix is returning from it, then the implications for Wilhelm are sinister); and the pattern of working through dark memories to some sort of reconciliation, however fragile, is one which we have already observed in Goethe's very late poetry.[26]

There is one last example, concerned more directly with the memory of Mignon, which will lead into a fuller discussion of the theme of limitations. The episode set on Lago Maggiore in Book II, chapter 7 is one of the most significant in the novel. The description of the pictures which the artist paints of Mignon is a particularly elaborate instance of the reworking of material from the *Lehrjahre*, and very different in tone from that just discussed. That it surpasses even the other examples of self-consciousness is immediately apparent, for, like 'An Werther' in the *Trilogie der Leidenschaft*, it openly incorporates a sense of the public reception of Goethe's work. Indeed, given its presence in the 1821 edition, it can be seen as initiating in prose this particular type of self-reflexivity characteristic of the very late phase. The artist, we are told, did not know Mignon personally; yet, on meeting Wilhelm, he claims that she is the reason why he too has travelled to the Lago Maggiore region, having been 'leidenschaftlich eingenommen [...] von Mignons Schicksalen, Gestalt und Wesen' [passionately affected [...] by Mignon's fortunes, figure, and being] (*FA* x, 497). What was once the experience of a few individuals has, evidently, become accessible to a much broader public, even within the world of the *Wanderjahre* — either in the form of a myth or, perhaps, of a novel called *Wilhelm Meisters Lehrjahre*.[27] The fictional artist, therefore, apparently shares a reading history, or possible reading history, with the reader of the *Wanderjahre*. The artist's paintings are not given to the reader: we have only their ekphrasis in the passages that we are reading.

The further we read, the stronger the sense of *déjà vu* becomes, for the text is imbued with the language of 'Kennst du das Land' ['Do you know the land']. Or almost: just as, in *Dichtung und Wahrheit IV*, Goethe gives the reader a prose epigone of 'Der Bräutigam' in Book XVII, so here he has transposed another poem into prose, indeed into the prosaic. The references are recognizable, but much of the mystery of the original has been lost, with some details now over-explained and others rendered mundane.[28] The phrase 'der Drachen alte Brut' [the ancient brood of dragons], an example of the spare manner of expression which lends the poem its suggestive power throughout, has been replaced with a fussier equivalent, 'die fabelhaft-furchtbare Drachenbrut' [the fantastical, terrible brood of dragons]. Elsewhere, the original word 'Marmorbilder' [images in marble] is reduced to 'Statuen' [statues], and 'sehen mich an' [look at me] is reversed so that Mignon is now actively 'betrachtend' [observing]; these alterations remove the odd, even eerie empathy of the marble figures with the alienated child whom they eyelessly observe, and render the scene as unremarkable as if she were visiting a museum. The transposition of 'Kennst du das Land' makes a statement about the uniqueness of the poetic utterance. The attempt to explain a poem amounts to the attempt to rationalize a secret — which runs the risk of triviality. Yet this episode within an episode has more to say to us than this: for, although it may appear flat next to the poem 'Kennst du das Land', this is still very fine prose. The surrounding passages bring us closer to its other implications.

Secrets and the limitations of knowledge

The Lago Maggiore episode is the most nuanced treatment in the first edition of a theme which became much more prominent in 1829, namely, what Steve Dowden calls 'human contingency'.[29] This is closely linked to, indeed a form of, self-consciousness: for perceiving the boundaries of one's own knowledge, or even entertaining the notion that there are boundaries, requires a high degree of self-reflection. In a much earlier essay, *Reine Begriffe* (1792), Goethe postulates the need for forms of representation to supplement our limited sensory perceptions, to mediate objects to our minds:

> da die einfachern Kräfte der Natur sich oft unsern Sinnen verbergen, so müssen wir sie freilich durch die Kräfte unseres Geistes zu erreichen suchen und ihre Natur in uns darstellen, da wir sie außer uns nicht erblicken können.[30]

> [since nature's simpler powers often remain hidden from our senses, we must indeed try to reach them through our intellectual powers and to reconstitute their nature within ourselves, since we cannot glimpse them outside ourselves.]

In the Lago Maggiore episode, this mediating function is given to art. Wilhelm, we are told, is not blessed in his appreciation for the natural world, but is helped in this by the artist: 'In gesprächiger Hindeutung auf die wechselnden Herrlichkeiten der Gegend, mehr aber noch durch konzentrierte Nachahmung, wurden ihm die Augen aufgetan' [His eyes were opened through discussion of the changing glories of the region, but even more by means of concentrated imitation] (*FA* x, 499).

The last image is matched elsewhere in the passage by phrases similarly suggestive of revelation: 'ihm sei [...] die Umwelt aufgeschlossen' [the environment was unlocked to his understanding] and 'die Natur [entfaltete] das offenbare Geheimnis ihrer Schönheit' [nature unfolded the open secret of her beauty]. The condition, it is suggested, for this gift of knowledge and understanding is 'Nachahmung' [imitation]: whether this refers to the artist's mimetic renderings of nature, or to Wilhelm's imitations of his imitations, the implication is that the activity of copying, of producing representations of the external world, is an essential stage in reaching some understanding of it. Indeed, representations may be needed in order to understand other representations. The relationship between 'Kennst du das Land' and the equivalent passage in the *Wanderjahre* can also be seen in this context. The prose version is a 'Nachahmung', by means of which we might come to recognize the 'offenbares Geheimnis' of the poem. Sometimes we need prose to help us (literary critics certainly do). Moreover, both the poem and the prose version are ultimately verbal constructs; they aim at once to bring us nearer to an even more recalcitrant secret — Mignon herself — and to perpetuate the mystery that is her life force. Thus works of art are, it is suggested, reflections which help to make one's perceptions more complete, just as, in the narrative of the episode itself, the light shed on land and lake by the rising and setting sun 'sich im Abglanz erst vollkommen verherrlicht' [only reached its full glory in its reflection] (*FA* x, 499).

No sooner is this principle established, however, than it is called into question. For what we are told is not, in fact, that Wilhelm has no understanding for the natural world, but that 'die Natur [hatte] ihm kein malerisches Auge gegeben' [nature had not given him a painter's eye] (*FA* x, 499): that is to say, that he is not talented at this particular way of perceiving and representing it. On closer examination, it becomes clear that, although Wilhelm's experience of the natural world is undoubtedly enhanced by art, what is being described here is less a sudden initiation into nature's innermost secrets than the appropriation of a different perspective: 'nun verschmolz er aber mit seinem neuen Freunde aufs innigste, und lernte, empfänglich wie er war, mit dessen Augen die Welt sehen' [but now he melded with his friend to the highest degree, and learned, open-minded as he was, to see the world with his eyes] (*FA* x, 499). His outlook literally merges with that of the artist, and it becomes clear that the episode is not about nature, or even, first and foremost, about art, but about consciousness. In a chapter as much about mood as it is about nature, Wilhelm is described as spending 'seine Tage und Stunden in durchgreifender Rührung' [his hours and days in the most heightened emotional state] (*FA* x, 497) as a result of the artist's impressions of Mignon. The artist, for his part, works 'mit klugdichtendem Wahrheitssinne' [with a skilful, creative sense of truth] (*FA* x, 498): that is to say, supplementing his *sense* of 'Wahrheit' with his own creativity, not wresting truth from nature and presenting it unchanged. This would be impossible, for, as the *Farbenlehre* reminds us, all the means that we have of accessing the world outside ourselves, including the language which we speak, are mere signposts:

> §751 Man bedenkt niemals genug, daß eine Sprache eigentlich nur symbolisch, nur bildlich sei und die Gegenstände niemals unmittelbar, sondern nur im Widerscheine ausdrücke. Dieses ist besonders der Fall, wenn von Wesen die Rede ist, welche an die Erfahrung nur herantreten und die man mehr Tüchtig-keiten als Gegenstände nennen kann, dergleichen im Reiche der Naturlehre immerfort in Bewegung sind. Sie lassen sich nicht festhalten, und doch soll man von ihnen reden; man sucht daher alle Arten von Formeln auf, um ihnen wenigstens gleichnisweise beizukommen.[31]

> [Sufficient consideration is never given to the fact that language is, in fact, purely symbolic, composed only of images, and can only capture objects in their reflection, never give direct expression to them. This is particularly true of beings which only approach our experience, and which should be called activities rather than objects, such as those in the realm of natural philosophy which are in constant movement. They will not be caught and held, and yet we ought to speak of them; and so we seek all kinds of formulations, in order at least to approach them by means of analogy.]

It follows that misuse of language — or of any form of symbolic representation — can amount to a misuse, or violation, of nature. We cannot approach 'die Gegen-stände' directly, much less grasp them; our only access can be lateral, through the suggestions of likenesses ('gleichnisweise'), through reflections or derivations ('im Widerscheine'). Representations, artistic or otherwise, may narrow the gulf between the isolated subject and the external world of objects, but they always remain rooted in human consciousness: they are not independent ciphers of that external world, which we can only partly know.

However, just as images from storytelling and advertising cloud the judgement of the princess in *Novelle*, so the characters in the Lago Maggiore episode struggle to separate the means from the ends. Art remains the focus of activity throughout, especially for Hilarie and the painter, who seeks to reduce Hilarie's inhibitions in her painting by encouraging her *not* to concern herself too much with the details of the original, but to exercise her own artistic freedom — in other words, to allow the work to flow more from her own subjectivity. Paradoxically, however, the characters' increasing preoccupation with what makes a good painting, with questions of talent and technique, brings with it the illusory sense of becoming more attuned to the mysteries of nature: 'Die herrliche Welt erst Tage lang vor sich zu sehen, und nun die auf einmal verliehene vollkommenere Darstellungsgabe zu empfinden. Welche Wonne in Zügen und Farben dem Unaussprechlichen näher zu treten!' [To see the glorious world for days before him, and now to feel the more consummate gift for representation bestowed upon him all at once. What bliss, to draw nearer to the inexpressible with colours and strokes!] (*FA* x, 509). The phrase 'dem Unaussprechlichen näher zu treten' is matched by the progressive adjective 'vollkommenere', and together these two elements imply that the ability to paint the world well is almost the same as being at one with it. Moreover, the use of the word 'unaussprechlich' is significant: if the wonders of the natural world are 'inexpressible' rather than absolutely unknowable, then the more 'vollkommen' the gift of expression and representation becomes, the closer one will come, apparently, to dispelling the mystery. In the minds of the characters, then, art is gradually becoming indistinguishable from what it seeks to represent.[32]

The extent to which it has begun to govern, rather than simply enhance, their vision and experience of the world becomes clear when the painter sings 'Kennst du das Land'. 'Ihm schwebte Mignons Bild mit dem ersten Zartgesang des holden Kindes vor' [Mignon's image hovered before him with that sweet child's gentle chorus]. The verb 'schwebte' conveys the insubstantial nature of the image, whilst the heaping of 'hold' upon 'zart' makes clear its origins in sentimentality and nostalgia. Yet its hold on him and the other characters is such that it appears as real as if the child herself were present:

> Leidenschaftlich über die Grenze gerissen, mit sehnsüchtigem Griff die wohlklingenden Saiten aufregend, begann er anzustimmen [...] Und als sie nun alle viere im hohen Mondschein sich gegenüber standen, war die allgemeine Rührung nicht mehr zu verhehlen. (*FA* x, 510–11)

> [Driven beyond the pale by passion, and plucking the mellifluous strings with fingers full of longing, he began to sing [...] And now that all four were facing one another in the full light of the moon, their shared emotion could no longer be concealed.]

They become swept along in a stream of literary reminiscences which floods their perceptions of the world. This not only leads them to overstep the mark with some indulgent behaviour; their surroundings also seem the more bald and barren when the heady illusion has passed, and the reality of separation, grimmer than the appealing melancholy which Mignon's song triggers for them, makes itself felt: 'Nun war das Paradies wie durch einen Zauberschlag für die Freunde zur völligen Wüste gewandelt' [Now, as if by a stroke of magic, the friends' paradise was transformed into an utter wasteland] (*FA* x, 511). That the idyll built up over an entire chapter in the minds of its characters can suddenly wither in those same minds into a barren wilderness calls into question man's ability to establish any reliable sense of the nature of things external to himself. The words 'für die Freunde' reinforce this: combined with the element of caprice suggested by 'Zauberschlag', they remind us that both our perceptions and the art which we use to explore and further those impressions are inevitably coloured by our emotions and moods. As Goethe writes in his 1798 essay, 'Das reine Phänomen': 'der Beobachter [sieht] nie das reine Phänomen mit Augen [...], sondern vieles [hängt] von seiner Geistesstimmung, von der Stimmung des Organs im Augenblick, von Licht, Luft, Witterung, Körpern, Behandlung und tausend andern Umständen ab' [the observer never sees the pure phenomenon with his own eyes [...]; a good deal depends, rather, upon his state of mind, upon his ocular state at that particular moment, upon the light, the air, the weather, obstructions, treatment and a thousand other circumstances].[33] There can, therefore, be no total identification between the image and its objective counterpart. The Lago Maggiore episode, and especially its end, dramatizes the erroneous conflation of the two, the consequences of which are 'alle Schmerzen des ersten Grades der Entsagenden' [the full suffering of the first order of renunciants].[34] In a sense, the characters have transgressed a secret with their misunderstanding of the relationship between art and reality — a reality which we cannot know, and a symbol which retains its mystery. Another self-reflexive flourish towards the end of the scene both lightens and darkens the tone: for the tearful embrace of the two couples is a gentle parody of the 'Klopstock!' moment from *Die Leiden des jungen Werthers*, in which the confusion of art and life has more serious consequences.

Latent in the Lago Maggiore episode, therefore, is a concern both with man's imperfect capacity for perception and understanding, and with the fallibility of the aids which we use in an effort to complete our perceptions. The theme of nescience, which this episode plants in the 1821 version, is developed much more fully in 1829. Many of the parts which have been added — the collections of maxims and the two poems, for example, or the greatly expanded material on Makarie — deal intimately with it, with secrets and the unknown. Once again, the prominence of the theme can be attributed to the peculiarities of the very late perspective. Just as a person's perception of the sheer range of things opens up a little more with each advancing stage of life, so the limitations of things also become clearer, and the sense of possibility diminishes even as it increases. An axiom from Makarie's archive encapsulates the idiosyncratic approach which the novel takes to the question of human knowledge: 'Der echte Schüler lernt aus dem Bekannten das Unbekannte entwickeln und nähert sich dem Meister' [The true pupil learns to develop what is unknown from what is known, and thereby draws near to the master] (*FA* x, 746). This can be understood in two ways. The most logical interpretation would be that established knowledge helps the student to edge forward into mastery of the unknown. But the phrase 'das Unbekannte entwickeln' also suggests the unfurling ('entwickeln') of more questions, the perpetuation of mystery as the precondition for any sort of mastery. The best guide to the learner is not, it is implied, an arrogant belief in the ability of the human mind to solve all mysteries, but the coupling of curiosity with doubt. Indeed, the novel demonstrates this through its own structure: in the replacement, as we have seen, of a linear plot with an array of different texts and perspectives, which stand in an enigmatic relation to one another. The challenge of the secret is thus applied in the composition of the text, and the reader is stimulated to reflect and research rather than just follow.[35] Yet that process of research itself generates new enigmas, even as it yields new insights. The secret, then, is both the best stimulus for and the best check on the human desire for knowledge.

The symbol most clearly associated with the theme of the secret is the casket which Felix finds in the Riesenschloss (a cognate, perhaps, of the Stammburg in *Novelle*).[36] Not only does it take most of the novel for the key to be found, but, at the time of its discovery, the casket forms part of a *mise-en-abyme* of secrets: Felix has strayed into a cavern buried within an already labyrinthine building, finds that a crack in the floor opens on to a whole other chamber, and discovers the casket there within a larger chest, which he has to force open. Wilhelm and Felix agree, moreover, to keep the find a secret, even though what they are guarding is an unknown to them too — a secret within a secret. Indeed, the imagery of the whole episode is suggestive of barely fathomed depths. The guide warns Wilhelm and Felix not to stray too far into the Riesenschloss lest they lose their way. It too, as the narrator indicates, has a Chinese-box structure, which recedes potentially *ad infinitum*: 'angeschlossene Säulenwände bildeten Pforten an Pforten, Gänge nach Gängen' [densely spaced colonnades formed portal upon portal, passage after passage] (*FA* x, 301). The general impression, moreover, is one of overwhelming darkness, with sudden waves or chinks of light signalling a find — the 'dämmerhellen Raum' [dimly lit room] on to which the crack in the cavern floor opens, for example, or the glittering of the golden casket which Felix discovers. In a manner reminiscent of the novel's own archival structure,[37] discovery opens on to discovery, and mystery on to mystery. This dialectic of the known and the unknown continues even after the given end of the novel, for the casket remains closed. The jeweller advises Hersilie that 'an solche Geheimnisse sei nicht gut rühren' [it is not right to meddle with such secrets] (*FA* x, 743). For Hans Rudolf Vaget, the jeweller is simply sparing Hersilie from the disappointing discovery that there is nothing in the box.[38] Vaget goes on to suggest that its real significance is not its content, but the meaning which people suppose it has, which they attach to it on the basis of their own desires; and this is certainly a very fruitful notion. But it is, in my view, a mistake to dismiss out of hand the act of not–opening, which has its own symbolism. For if, as Steve Dowden suggests, 'the box serves as a metaphor for the things that lie beyond representation',[39] then the decision to leave it shut implies respect for the things that exceed our understanding. This, indeed, is the sense of the first maxim from Makarie's archive: 'Die Geheimnisse der Lebenspfade darf und kann man nicht offenbaren' [The secrets of life's path cannot and must not be revealed] (*FA* x, 746).

A weight of responsibility evidently attaches to secrets, and Felix soon comes to feel it: 'Ein Geheimnis war ihm aufgeladen, ein Besitz, rechtmäßig oder unrecht-mäßig? sicher oder unsicher?' [He had been burdened with a secret, with property, legitimate or not? safe or not?] (*FA* x, 302). Harbouring a secret raises the question of his right to the possession of an unknown quantity, of the best means of managing it, and its possible effect on him remains uncertain. The psychological pressure exerted by these doubts is expressed in his sudden desire to get away from the place where he found the casket, and the exaggeration of its dimensions in his perception: 'die Säulen kamen ihm schwärzer, die Höhlen tiefer vor' [the pillars seemed darker to him, the hollows deeper] (*FA* x, 302). Significantly, both this and our previous quotation are missing from the 1821 edition. Although, in the earlier version, Felix finds it difficult to be as carefree as before when he has found the casket, that is due more to a sense of excitement, and superiority at knowing something that his playmate does not; and his behaviour elicits this didactic remark from Wilhelm: 'Mein Sohn, wer ein Geheimnis bewahren will, muß nicht merken lassen, daß er eins besitzt' [My son, he who wishes to keep a secret must not let on that he has one] (*FA* x, 45). Although this suggests that the secret is something of value, the concept evidently receives more sophisticated treatment in the 1829 edition. In one of the few examples of the theme that *does* appear in the 1821 edition — namely, Hersilie's letter to Wilhelm, in which she announces her discovery of the key to the casket — she also refers to the ambivalence which surrounds the ownership of this type of knowledge: 'Nun gab es wunderliche Gewissenszweifel, mancherlei Skrupel stiegen bei mir auf. Den Fund zu offenbaren, herzugeben, war mir unmöglich' [Now my conscience began to prick strangely, and all sorts of scruples came to my mind. I could not possibly reveal and hand over what I had found] (*FA* x, 598). There is an additional nuance here, for Hersilie's musings suggest another: does one have the right to own a discovery of note, to conceal it, even if only from one party for the benefit of another? (There is, of course, a certain irony in the situation, for again, secrets mask further secrets: the contents of the casket are still unknown.)

Yet concealment, the preservation of a degree of privacy, can also be a duty, as the jeweller perceives at the end, and as Hersilie remarks in her letter: 'das Kästchen muß zwischen mir und Ihnen erst uneröffnet stehen [...] Ich wollte, es fände sich gar nichts drinnen' [the casket must remain unopened for now by both me and you [...] I could wish that there were nothing inside it] (*FA* x, 599). Accompanying this issue is the question of propriety: 'Mich treibt ein guter oder böser Geist in die Brusttasche zu greifen [...] Bei'm ersten verstohlenen Blick seh' ich, errat' ich, zu Ihrem Kästchen sei es der Schlüssel' [A spirit good or evil drove me to reach in to the breast pocket [...] Stealing a glance I saw, I guessed, that this was the key to your casket] (*FA* x, 597–98). Hersilie's use here of the word 'verstohlen' and the notion of 'ein guter oder böser Geist' suggest that there can be something shameful about human curiosity — or, at least, that it has its dangers. Here, the connotations of the legend of Pandora's box come into full play, and especially when the equivalent symbol of the chest in 'Die neue Melusine' ['The new Melusina'] is taken into account. The human urge to know the mystery contained within a box leads to misfortune in both the legend and, albeit on a less globally devastating scale, in the novella. Makarie, too, knows the effects of curiosity, especially when accompanied by ignorance; she has used disability as a cover for her gift, because 'was sie davon offenbarte wurde nicht anerkannt, oder mißdeutet' [whatever she divulged was not acknowledged, or was misinterpreted] (*FA* x, 735). Secrets can, therefore, also have a protective function. Makarie and others like her need secrets to shield them from the damaging scorn of those whose understanding cannot stretch far enough to accommodate their otherness: 'denn das Unglaubliche verliert seinen Wert wenn man es näher im Einzelnen beschauen will' [for that which is incredible loses its worth if the attempt is made to scrutinize it more closely] (*FA* x, 736). The novel's emphasis on the delicacy of the secret is not a moralistic attempt to stifle human curiosity, but a genuine epistemological position. It has to do with what Clark Muenzer calls 'the deferral of final "meanings"'[40] in the novel.

A word, finally, about the choice of terminology for the casket when Felix first discovers it: *Prachtbüchlein* [splendid *little book*]. Here, the link between the motif of the secret and the theme or device of self-consciousness is at its most evident: in a twist which anticipates Umberto Eco's *The Name of the Rose*, the secret at the heart of the book is itself a book.[41] As we saw at the start, the implication of Goethe's remark to Rochlitz (in which, indeed, he describes the *Wanderjahre* as a 'Büchlein'!) was that the unity of the *Wanderjahre* can only partly be apprehended, and the image of the *Prachtbüchlein* is that notion in performance. For the novel brings a secret, itself a *Büchlein*, out into the open, just as Felix brings the casket to the surface; but the substance of that secret is 'nicht ganz zu fassen', just as the other *Büchlein*, though it is retrieved from a place much deeper and darker than where it ends up, retains much of its mystery. The book knows, and shows, that this is as near as we ever get to the 'offenbares Geheimnis', or to the thing in itself.

Debate and the avoidance of dogmatism

The motif of the secret suggests, then, that only the challenge of competing interpretations and unanswered questions can lead us nearer to true understanding; and this notion is also prominent in the two collections of maxims, 'Betrachtungen im Sinne der Wanderer' and 'Aus Makariens Archiv' ['From Makarie's Archive'], which belong to the 1829 version of the novel. For many years after the reissue of the *Wanderjahre* in 1837, the two collections of maxims were not included. Goethe had said to both Eckermann and Cotta that their function was 'Ausfüllung' [filler material] for the *Ausgabe letzter Hand*, because parts two and three were rather short.[42] Although, as Erich Trunz suggests, Goethe was being disingenuous with that remark,[43] both took him at his word. Cotta's suggestion that some of the aphorisms could be left out prompted Goethe to take a more emphatic position, in a letter to Reichel of 2 May 1829:

> Einzelnen Gebrauch von den Sprüchen aus Makariens Archiv wünsche nicht vor Heraustritt des Werkes. Am Schluß desselben und im Zusammenhang des Ganzen finden sie erst ihre Deutung, einzeln möchte manches anstößig sein.[44]

> [I do not wish for the sayings from Makarie's archive to be deployed individually before the work has been published. They only make sense at the end thereof and in the context of the whole; there is much that might dismay readers if taken separately.]

Yet Eckermann still saw fit to remove them from the 1837 edition, and they were not included again until the *Gedenkausgabe* of 1949 and the *Hamburger Ausgabe* of 1950. The critical consensus now is that they are entirely in the spirit of the rest of the work:

> The aphorisms do not fix meaning but open it up, contributing to the ambiguity of the novel and its ironic texture. They have the function of activating the reader as interpreter and of providing instructions on how to read the world and its representation in the novel.[45]

Both collections move between abstract considerations of the nature of human thought and understanding, and discussions of topics in natural science, aesthetics, and philosophy which had long been important to Goethe. On the one hand, they belong, together with the novellas and inserted letters, to the fictional world of the novel. Even though they are not directly attributed to individuals, they come to us as possible utterances by characters in the novel: Makarie's archive, for example, is alleged in Book I to be excerpts of conversations which Angela has recorded. Yet they also work on a different level from the rest of the piece. They are distilled, focused treatments of some of the many ideas which motivate the *Wanderjahre*, and the relation between the novel's aesthetic and epistemological concerns is in sharper relief here than anywhere else. They are discrete collections of ideas with their own internal relations, and are by nature experimental: some may be expressions of deeply held convictions, but others may be written in play, in jest, or even to be provocative.[46] Part of their attraction is that they can never quite be pinned down. Themes which are familiar from elsewhere in Goethe's *œuvre* — such as the nature of form and development — are given renewed attention, and the laconic form of the reflections leaves plenty of space for potential responses. The maxims have, therefore, a bridging quality, in that they suggest the applicability of the novel and its ideas to the world outside it. They are also a key example of that 'literariness' of life which, as discussed at the start of this chapter, is a major preoccupation in the *Wanderjahre*: for each one is the condensation of experience in words, and thus contributes to the image which the novel develops of a world which cannot be separated from its verbal representation.

The dialectic of limitation and possibility suggested by the motif of the secret is both a thematic concern and a structural feature of the maxims. To take the content first: central to Goethe's maxims is 'die Bemühung, aus diesen menschenkundlichen Einsichten das menschliche Erkenntnisvermögen selbst in seinen Grenzen und Möglichkeiten zu bestimmen' [the endeavour to determine the limitations and potential of the human capacity for understanding, by means of these insights won from the study of humanity].[47] Maxim 3 of the second collection, 'Aus Makariens Archiv', says precisely that: 'Das Wahre ist gottähnlich; es erscheint nicht unmittelbar, wir müssen es aus seinen Manifestationen erraten' [Truth is god-like; it does not appear directly, rather, we must deduce it from its manifestations] (*FA* x, 746). This notion that we can, for the most part, access truth only indirectly, is supported by maxim 93 in the 'Betrachtungen im Sinne der Wanderer', which emphasizes the importance of openness and mobility in thought in order to reduce errors born of dogmatism: 'Nach Analogien denken ist nicht zu schelten; die Analogie hat den Vorteil daß sie nicht abschließt und eigentlich nichts Letztes will'

[It is not an offence to think in terms of analogies; the analogy has the advantage that it does not close off possibilities, and, in fact, that it does not seek finality] (*FA* x, 571). Maxim 144 in the same collection is more acerbic: 'Das Närrischte ist, daß jeder glaubt überliefern zu müssen was man gewußt zu haben glaubt' [Most foolish of all is the belief, held by everyone, that they must pass on what they think they have known] (*FA* x, 579). The framing of the sentence with 'das Närrischte' and 'glaubt' undermines any security that might have rested in 'gewußt', and emphasizes the fragility of what we think we know. Maxims 58 and 59 from 'Aus Makariens Archiv' emphasize a different hindrance to 'das menschliche Erkenntnisvermögen' [the human capacity for understanding], namely, the expressive inadequacy of language: '[der Mensch] denkt und weiß es meistenteils viel besser, als er es sich ausspricht' [for the most part, people think and know a thing much better than they express it to themselves] (*FA* x, 755). Just as the aids which the characters used in the Lago Maggiore episode to supplement their understanding proved to be fallible, so man's most basic tool, language, is also shown to be imperfect, and not to be relied upon too heavily. A last example, one fitting for a novel concerned with specialization and self-limitation to the greater good, is offered by maxim 34 from the 'Betrachtungen', which emphasizes the importance of recognizing one's capabilities and working within them. It reads: 'Der geringste Mensch kann komplett sein, wenn er sich innerhalb der Grenzen seiner Fähigkeiten und Fertigkeiten bewegt' [The least of men can be complete if they operate within the boundaries of their abilities and accomplishments] (*FA* x, 562). Like the motif of the secret, the intention of the maxims is not to discourage research and reflection, but to suggest the care and self-awareness necessary for the responsible acquisition of knowledge. Crucially, reflection itself occasionally becomes the subject of criticism: maxims 2 and 52 from the 'Betrachtungen' assert that it is useless unless combined with practical activity. Thus everything is relativized in the maxims — but in the name of truth, not in denial of it.[48]

The self-consciousness of the maxims lies not only in their intensive engagement with the nature of human thought, but also in the fact that they practise what they preach. Peter Hutchinson observes that: 'In the maxims, we see not only ideas, but, above all, the effort to *structure* the idea. The principle of creating form was one which Goethe elevated above all others'.[49] We have already seen that the aesthetic stance of the novel is conditioned by an awareness of the contingencies of single narratives, and a preference instead for the proliferation of different perspectives; and the maxims are a particularly powerful expression of this. Maxims are by their nature both complete and incomplete. The pithier ones especially appear perfect in their clever verbal patterning, as well as the intellectual punch which they pack. But there is also something inherently fragmentary about them. Their referents may be unknown: who, for example, is the 'ich' that speaks from time to time in the collections? Take, for example, maxim 64 from the *Betrachtungen*: 'Ich schweige zu vielem still, denn ich mag die Menschen nicht irre machen, und bin wohl zufrieden, wenn sie sich freuen da wo ich mich ärgere' [I keep silent on many matters because I do not like to confuse people, and I am quite happy if they find pleasure where I find irritation] (*FA* x, 567). Is this Goethe speaking for himself, implying that he feels increasingly out of tune with the actual public, and chooses more and more to remain silent in their presence, saving his insights for an ideal audience? Or does this voice belong to one of the characters in the novel? After all, Montan had said something similar to Wilhelm in the Pädagogische Provinz:

> das Liebste, und das sind doch unsre Überzeugungen, muß jeder im tiefsten Ernst bei sich selbst bewahren [...] wie er es ausspricht, sogleich ist der Widerspruch rege, und wie er sich in Streit einläßt, kommt er in sich selbst aus dem Gleichgewicht und sein Bestes wird, wo nicht vernichtet, doch gestört. (*FA* x, 535)

> [everyone must keep that which is dearest to them — and that, after all, is our convictions — to himself, in the depth of solemnity [...] as soon as he utters it, contradiction begins to flourish, and if he enters a conflict, he will lose his own equilibrium and the best of him will be, if not destroyed, then still disrupted.]

Yet this remark is not absolutely the same as the maxim. It has a more negative flavour, a stronger element of mistrust of others, apposite to Montan's misanthropic tendencies;[50] by contrast, the maxim suggests a shrug of the shoulders and a quiet smile at how seriously people take themselves and their differences. Finally, whoever the 'ich' in maxim 64 may be, is it the same voice as that in maxim 113? Or maxim 56 in 'Aus Makariens Archiv'?

The maxims also resonate with other works of Goethe's from this very late phase, and his geological writing in particular helps to bring into focus the function of the maxims as a bridge between the world of the novel and the world outside it. Geology is a recurrent theme in the *Wanderjahre*. It dominates the opening chapters, the exploits of Wilhelm and Felix in the mountains and their conversations with Montan; and, through the figures of Makarie and Montan's friend, it forms an important coupling with astronomy. The fragments which form 'Zur Geologie November 1829' promote exactly the kind of thought which we have seen advocated in the two collections; indeed, they themselves have an aphoristic quality:

> Jede Veränderung theoretischer Ansichten über Naturgegenstände muß auf einer höheren philosophischen Ansicht beurteilt werden.
> [...]
> Nun aber wird aller Dogmatismus der Welt am Ende lästig
> [...]
> Und dem allgemeinen natürlichen Gang des menschlichen Geistes gemäß trat die Skepsis ein.
> Die Skepsis fängt mit den Ausnahmen an das Dogma zu befeinden, welches auf einem Gesetzlichen Fuß gefaßt hat.[51]

> [Every alteration in theoretical opinions on natural objects must also be assessed on a higher philosophical level.
> [...]
> Now, all the dogmatism in the world eventually becomes tiresome.
> [...]
> And in accordance with the general, natural course of the human mind, scepticism set in.
> Scepticism uses exceptions to open hostilities with dogma, where dogma takes its stand on regularity.]

Goethe rails against dogmatism and, although he does not fully come down on the side of scepticism (he acknowledges that it lends itself a little too well to 'Überredung', persuasion), the premise for the ensuing investigation of geological formations is flexibility and open-mindedness — for only then can fruitful connections be made: 'Ich ließ die Faktoren isoliert stehen | Aber das Analoge sucht ich auf' ['I allowed the factors to stand in isolation, but I also sought out the analogous part].[52] In addition, 'Geologische Probleme und Versuch ihrer Aufklärung' ['Geological Problems and an Attempt at their Solution'] (1831) begins and ends with frustration at the inadequacy of methods deployed in the field:

> Im ganzen denkt kein Mensch daß wir als sehr beschränkte schwache Personen uns ums Ungeheure beschäftigen ohne zu fragen wie man ihm gewachsen sei? [...] Es sind bloß Worte, schlechte Worte, die weder Begriff noch Bild geben.[53]

> [People forget that when we tackle vast questions, we do so as limited, weak individuals, without asking what qualifies us for this task. [...] We only have words, poor words, which are capable of offering neither a concept nor an image.]

It becomes clear *ex negativo* that here, as in the *Wanderjahre*, the precondition for sound investigation must be self-limitation, awareness of the meanness of the intellectual tools available to us; otherwise, the outcome is simply the propagation of mediocre ideas, which do nothing to help us advance. This rather bad-tempered essay ends with a remarkable echo both of the final two lines of 'Im ernsten Beinhaus', to which we will return in due course, and of maxim 141 from the 'Betrachtungen':

> Wunderliche Art der Erklärungslustigen! Was fest und unerschütterlich ist, soll erst werden und sich bewegen, was ewig fort sich bewegt und verändert soll stationär sein und bleiben, und das alles bloß, damit etwas gesagt werde![54]

> [How strange the methods of those with a particular fondness for explanation! They want that which is firm and unshakeable finally to come into being and to move, and that which truly does move and transform itself without end, they would have brought to a standstill and kept there; and all this, simply in order to have something to say!]

Both here and in the related maxim, doubt itself is turned on its head: for if misplaced, it too can cause human endeavour to stall. The ideas tossed about in 'Betrachtungen im Sinne der Wanderer' and 'Aus Makariens Archiv', then, are rooted both in the novel and in other areas of Goethe's intellectual activity; they connect literary and scientific endeavour, and seek to enhance the contributions that both literature and science have made to the world which they have undertaken to explore.

Yet the maxims may raise more questions in the reader's mind than they answer — perhaps causing confusion, but also stimulating further reflection. As Gerhard Neumann observes: '[Goethe] sucht [...] den Grenzbereich zwischen Sprache und Schweigen für die Erkenntnis nutzbar zu machen, in dem die Gattung des Aphorismus sich ansiedelt' [Goethe seeks [...] to make the border region between language and silence, which the aphorism occupies as a genre, useful for human understanding].[55] This openness is magnified when maxims appear in collections, as they do here. Although each one is a miniature, collectively they offer a formidable array of ideas, and the reader can swiftly feel overwhelmed. This effect is by no means entirely negative. On the contrary, it is connected to some of the postulates which the maxims make for effective intellectual activity. We are advised in maxim 96 of the 'Betrachtungen' to be on our guard against states of thought which feel easy: 'Auch wird [die Mystik] leicht sentimental, so daß wir uns nur was gemütlich ist aneignen' [Mysticism, too, can easily become sentimental, meaning that we only appropriate what is comfortable] (*FA* x, 571). Some discomfort, it is implied, can avert intellectual complacency and narrowness; if the pursuit of truth feels consistently easy, it may not be truth which is being pursued. Certainly, in the collections themselves, nothing is made easy for the reader, although individual examples may exert particular appeal, their brevity, and the fact that they are preceded and succeeded by so many others, prevents any one from dominating. Moreover, if one maxim appears to contradict another, the clash introduces a sense of argument and debate into the collection. 'Jede große Idee,' it is claimed in maxim 102 in the 'Betrachtungen', 'sobald sie in die Erscheinung tritt, wirkt tyrannisch; daher die Vorteile die sie hervorbringt, sich nur allzubald in Nachteile verwandeln' [Every great idea seems tyrannical as soon as it appears; thus the advantages which it produces turn all too soon into disadvantages] (*FA* x, 573). Given that our understanding is always and at best partial, it is important that different perspectives compete in the process of learning if errors are not to become dominant and entrenched.

Through their form and arrangement, then, as well as their content, the maxims are concerned to stimulate critical enquiry — an aim in keeping with the self-consciousness of the novel as a whole:[56] 'Hypothesen sind Wiegenlieder womit der Lehrer seine Schüler einlullt; der denkende treue Beobachter lernt immer mehr seine Beschränkung kennen, er sieht, je weiter sich das Wissen ausbreitet, desto mehr Probleme kommen zum Vorschein' [Hypotheses are lullabies, with which the teacher soothes his pupil; the honest, thinking observer will become ever more familiar with his limitations, he will see that the further knowledge extends, the more problems become apparent] (*FA* x, 579). This comment from the 'Betrachtungen' relates back to Makarie's remarks on discursive learning in Book I, chapter 10. The conversations which provide the material for the maxims in her archive (recorded by Angela), should, she says, 'nichts festsetzen, nichts nach außen wirken, sondern nur uns aufklären wollen, so kann das Gespräch immer vorwärts gehen' [not seek to fix anything or extend any influence, but simply enlighten us, and thus the conversation will always be able to move forward] (*FA* x, 380). The notion of not fixing (or fixating on) anything, together with the image of continuous forward movement, indicates that the type of understanding being promoted is a process of gradual enlightenment, the modification of one's position and insights through the introduction of different perspectives in conversation and debate. Thus the flexibility of thought which the maxims seek to cultivate is also advocated early on by Makarie, and there is further evidence that the maxims and the character Makarie spring from the same intellectual impulse.

Limitation and revelation

We have seen that a strong current of questioning runs through the maxims, and this is equally central to the characterization of Makarie. Clark Muenzer discerns a tension in 'her spiritual discourse, which is neither exclusively serious or [sic] humorous, [and] seems calculated to keep the teleological aspiration in view, while situating it out of reach'.[57] This could be taken further still: for in fact, the Makarie strand of the *Wanderjahre* is serious precisely because it is unserious. The irony in the depiction of the character cannot be overlooked. The approach to her dwelling place which greets Wilhelm and Felix is hyperreal: the gate which apparently opens itself, the indeterminate age of the 'shimmering' building, which manages both to suggest time out of mind and to be in a perfect state of repair. Makarie's first entrance borders on the comic, with the green curtain adding a theatrical flourish, and her conveniently beautiful female companions completing the fantasy. Later on, doubt is introduced: the essay on Makarie in Book III, chapter fifteen is, like so many of the inserted pieces in the *Wanderjahre*, of unstable provenance, 'nicht [...] für ganz authentisch anzusehen' [not to be regarded as wholly authentic], being written 'aus dem Gedächtnis' [from memory] rather than first hand (*FA* x, 733). Its content, moreover, at times becomes quite preposterous: 'aus anderen Angaben läßt sich schließen, daß sie, längst über die Bahn des Mars hinaus, der Bahn des Jupiter sich nähere' [it can be deduced from other accounts that, having long since passed Mars, she is now approaching Jupiter's orbit] (*FA* x, 736). Indeed, this is not just irony, but self-irony: for the novel is laughing at itself here, as we have seen it do at other points. Yet, as we saw earlier, that comic moment in the observatory, when information is first offered, but then withheld, and the novel is mocked for being 'schon mehr als billig didaktisch', is also an example of an extremely subtle dialectic: the moment of supreme authorial control is also the moment when control is loosened, weaknesses acknowledged. This pattern is very telling for Makarie's strand of the novel.

For in the case of Makarie, too, these elements of the ridiculous are not there solely in order to ridicule. Rather, they are linked to the observation in maxim 3 of the second collection that truth cannot be observed or represented directly. Of course Makarie is not to be dismissed out of hand; her understanding of the workings of the cosmos is remarkable, and her insight into the souls of her fellow human beings revelatory: 'es war, als wenn sie die innere Natur eines jeden durch die ihn umgebende individuelle Maske durchschaute' [it was as if she could see through the mask of each individual to the inner nature which it concealed] (*FA* x, 379). But, as we have seen, the inadequacy of representation is emphasized repeatedly in the *Wanderjahre*; and the Lago Maggiore episode highlights the increased fallibility of those representations whose creators believe in them too much. If truth is unrepresentable, then the most honest works are those which, in attempting to handle it, acknowledge their own insufficiency. Thus the air of humour which surrounds Makarie is not intended to extinguish the power which mystery holds, but to keep in focus that the truth which may lie within it will always remain 'out of reach' for all of us, reader and writer: 'Makarie befindet sich zu unserm Sonnensystem in einem Verhältnis, welches man auszusprechen kaum wagen darf' [Makarie's relationship to our solar system is one which we hardly dare to express] (*FA* x, 734). This is something that we shall meet again in relation to the final scene of *Faust II*. Once again, it is evidence of the high degree of self-consciousness at work in these very late texts: the limitations of our understanding are not only the subject of reflection, but are refracted back into the text to become a principle of its own composition.

Everything about the construction of this strand of the novel suggests that we are required to accept it as symbolic. The characterization of Makarie can be related to the excision of Wilhelm's sighting of Natalie. If Wilhelm cannot be shown to see Natalie, then the reader cannot be given a Makarie who is easy to see in the mind's eye, to imagine: 'Dorthin folgt ihr keine Einbildungskraft' [The powers of imagination cannot follow her there] (*FA* x, 737). With her visionary powers, which guide others and reveal them to themselves, she could be called a manifestation of the ideal; at the very least, she possesses ideal perception, by definition a quality beyond the range of ordinary human beings. As Benjamin Sax observes:

> her power of vision is not limited to cosmic movements and events. She has the ability to see the spiritual side of all reality as well. Through this power of vision, she plays an important role in this novel in which there is so much spiritual confusion within and among so many of its characters. Recognizing herself as part of a larger order, Makarie is better prepared to perceive order where others do not. She is able to see the ideal form of individuals [...].[58]

Quite simply, she understands how both the universe and the population of this particular planet work: knowledge which many people would like to have — indeed, some believe that they do — but no one can achieve in its entirety in one lifetime.

Later in the novel, a counterpart to Makarie is introduced in the form of Montan's friend, 'die terrestrische Frau' [the terrestrial woman]. Makarie's insight into the cosmos is paralleled by this woman's instinctive connection with 'alles [...] was man Gestein, Mineral, ja sogar was man überhaupt Element nennen könne' [everything [...] which can be called stone, mineral, indeed, an element] (*FA* x, 728). The material is now placed alongside the spiritual. The anonymous narrator of this part of the novel comments: 'Diese beiden Welten gegeneinander zu bewegen, ihre beiderseitigen Eigenschaften in der vorübergehenden Lebenserscheinung zu manifestieren, das ist die höchste Gestalt wozu sich der Mensch auszubilden hat' [The ability to keep these two worlds moving in equilibrium, to display their reciprocal qualities in life's transient phenomena — that is the supreme form to which people should aspire in their development] (*FA* x, 729). Montan's friend, then, completes the image of perfect human activity and understanding, already so strongly suggested by Makarie; and the words 'wozu sich der Mensch auszubilden hat' make it clear that the function of these figures in the novel is to provide, if not a direct model for development, then encouragement to the ordinary individual to refine his or her blunt perceptions. Without Makarie, the metaphysical substructure of the *Wanderjahre* would be one of overwhelming doubt. As it is, we are given a character, albeit a fantastical one, who upholds the possibility that there might be an ideal towards which to strive; and by underlining its own status as fiction, the novel manages to tell a new kind of truth.[59]

The role of the two poems 'Vermächtnis' ['Legacy'][60] and 'Im ernsten Beinhaus' ['In the solemn vault'][61] is closely related to that of Makarie — that is, promoting the ideal — even if they appear to come at it from different angles. Like the maxims, the poems add yet another, different verbalization of experience to the already diverse textual fabric of the novel; and given that, as we saw in the Lago Maggiore episode, there is something unique about poetry, they are perhaps conceived as the nearest thing in the novel to ideal utterances (though, of course, even they cannot actually represent the ideal). The two poems are related as are the two sides of a coin: they present different aspects of the same material. As befits its title, 'Vermächtnis' draws confidence from history, particularly the history of knowledge; 'Im ernsten Beinhaus', by contrast, is more in tune with the searching, the uncertainty which is the situation of the modern subject. Together, though, they realize that equilibrium between doubt and faith, retreat and assertion, limitation and revelation which, as we have seen, is suggested in different ways throughout the novel. Like the *Prachtbüchlein*, they bring the secret, or secrets, of the novel into the open; but because they are poems, and poems thrive on ambiguity, some of their meaning will always be beyond our reach. Here, then, the text once again displays an almost impossibly sophisticated self-awareness.

Through its Kantianism,[62] 'Vermächtnis' is already intrinsically linked to Makarie. As the editors of the *Frankfurter Ausgabe* note, Wilhelm's reaction, 'ergriffen und erstaunt' [deeply moved and astonished], to the view of the firmament from the observatory to which Makarie's friend the astronomer has brought him resonates with Kant's *Kritik der praktischen Vernunft*:

> Zwei Dinge erfüllen das Gemüt mit immer neuer und zunehmender Bewunderung und Ehrfurcht, je öfter und anhaltender sich das Nachdenken damit beschäftigt: der bestirnte Himmel über mir und das moralische Gesetz in mir.[63]

> [Two things fill a person with admiration and awe, which become ever newer, ever greater the more often and more consistently these things are contemplated: the starry sky above me and the moral law within me.]

The poem and Makarie's strand of the novel share a philosophical ancestor, as it were; and Makarie could be said to represent a conflation of those 'zwei Dinge' — for not only the moral law, but the starry sky itself is within her. Moreover, the poem resonates with several aspects of Makarie's methods and attitudes, as described by Angela. She emphasizes, for example, '[die] Wichtigkeit des augenblicklichen Gesprächs' [the importance of conversation at the time], but attaches equal importance to the preservation and transmission to posterity of 'einzelne gute Gedanken [...] die aus einem geistreichen Gespräch, wie Samenkörner aus einer vielseitigen Pflanze, hervorspringen' [a few good thoughts [...] which spring up from an inspired conversation like seeds from a complex plant] (*FA* x, 387); and this is strikingly similar to strophe five of 'Vermächtnis', with its notion of the present, especially if it is used wisely, as rooted in the past and pregnant with the future: 'Dann ist Vergangenheit beständig, | Das Künftige voraus lebendig, | Der Augenblick ist Ewigkeit' [Then the past endures, the future alive before its time, a single moment is eternity] (ll. 29–31). Equally, the closing lines, 'Denn edlen

Seelen vorzufühlen | Ist wünschenswertester Beruf' [For to anticipate the feelings of noble souls is the most desirable calling] (ll. 41–42),[64] could be read as referring to her dealings with her fellow human beings: perceiving their ideal structures, empathizing with and anticipating ('vorfühlen') their better selves ('edle Seelen'). When it was written in 1829, 'Vermächtnis' was without a home, for the volumes of poetry in the *Ausgabe letzter Hand* had been completed two years before; yet the many resonances with aspects of the *Wanderjahre* indicate that expediency was by no means the sole motivation for its inclusion.

Nonetheless, it appears to sound in a different key from much of the novel, especially in its treatment of truth. Whereas, as we have seen, the *Wanderjahre* is in general extremely cautious in respect of what we know, it is asserted confidently in the second strophe of 'Vermächtnis' that 'Das Wahre war schon längst gefunden' (l. 10) [The truth had long since been known]. There are two ways of approaching this. On the one hand, the continuation of the verse — 'Hat edle Geisterschaft verbunden; | Das alte Wahre fass' es an!' [It has brought together noble minds in communion; grasp it, the old truth!] (ll. 11–12) — suggests that, in this context, 'das Wahre' refers to any type of collective inheritance which has helped mankind to advance. This could be scientific, philosophical, or even technical — think of the generations of weavers whose methods Lenardo admires. Moreover, the poem includes 'das Künftige' in its considerations, and does not, therefore, exclude the possibility that new truths might be discovered. On the other hand, the position of the poem in the novel, and the fact that it never says 'I', always 'you', provide further hints as to how we might read it. 'Vermächtnis' is buried deep within the novel, at the end of the 'Betrachtungen'; thus, although it is an original composition of Goethe's, in the world of the *Wanderjahre* its voice is, like that of the maxims, anonymous. The didactic nature of the poem — it consists, after all, of a set of precepts designed to guide the reader — suggests that whichever voice this is exists on an altogether different level of understanding from the mere mortal, the 'Erdensohn' [son of the earth] (l. 11), whom it addresses. It can therefore speak nonchalantly of 'das Wahre', the principles by which everything functions, whereas the son of the earth, though he may advance his understanding, must ultimately still content himself with trusting that 'Es wird nach seiner Weise schalten' [It will carry on in its own way] (l. 35).[65] The poem is still concerned with limitations;[66] it is just that, for once, this is approached from the standpoint of resounding confidence in 'das Wahre'. In that respect, 'Vermächtnis' performs a similar function in the novel to Makarie (indeed, it is not entirely fanciful to suppose that it might be her voice in the poem). It serves to prevent doubt only from breeding doubt, for it gives encouragement that, though truth, or ideal knowledge, might appear to recede eternally from us, it is nonetheless still there, and worth pursuing.

'Im ernsten Beinhaus' is the obverse of 'Vermächtnis'. The original context of its composition was the identification and removal of Schiller's skull in 1826 from the communal tomb in which his body had been placed over twenty years before; but Goethe deliberately avoids any reference to Schiller in its verses, and, as Albrecht Schöne points out, the 'ernstes Beinhaus' denotes not the tomb from which Schiller was exhumed, but a place half-imagined, half-remembered from earlier times.[67]

Although the poem was written two and a half years earlier, its inclusion in the *Wanderjahre* is not arbitrary; on the contrary, its themes are intimately linked with those of the novel. The placement of 'Im ernsten Beinhaus', like 'Vermächtnis', at the end of a collection of maxims indicates that, within the novel at least, the relationship between the two poems is a semi-symmetrical one. At first sight, they appear wholly in opposition to one another. The first fourteen lines of 'Im ernsten Beinhaus' are full of images of death and distortion ('derbe Knochen' [foul bones], l. 5, 'zerstreut aus Lebensfugen', [scattered, wrenched from their joints] l. 9), and are drained of colour; this is in stark contrast to 'Vermächtnis', which has the sun as its dominant image. Although the mood of those lines is not one of horror, exactly, or desperation, there is a strong sense of depression and emptiness: 'niemand kann die dürre Schale lieben | Welch herrlich edlen Kern sie auch bewahrte' [no one can feel affection for the desiccated shell, however magnificent the kernel it once housed] (ll. 13–14). Again, this differs greatly from the sense of accomplishment and optimism which runs through 'Vermächtnis'. The serenity which that poem exudes is reinforced by its structure: the neat, regular strophic pattern, the aphoristic quality of each verse. 'Im ernsten Beinhaus', on the other hand, has the air of a monologue, reflective and personal, exploratory rather than conclusive.

Yet the development of the poem is such that it becomes 'not a *memento mori*, but rather a celebration of life'.[68] Indeed, as it draws to a close, the poet turns away from the house of decay, and towards the sun which has shone throughout 'Vermächtnis': 'Dich höchsten Schatz aus Moder fromm entwendend | Und in die freie Luft, zu freiem Sinnen, | Zum Sonnenlicht andächtig hin mich wendend' [Retrieving you, greatest treasure, with grave solemnity from the mildew, I turn to the fresh air, to free contemplation, to the sunlight] (ll. 28–30). 'Im ernsten Beinhaus' moves, in fact, from doubt — 'Ihr Müden lagt also vergebens nieder' (l. 10) — through recognition and revelation — 'Doch mir Adepten war die Schrift geschrieben, | Die heil'gen Sinn nicht jedem offenbarte' [Yet the writing was clear to me, the adept, though it does not reveal its sacred meaning to everyone] (ll. 15–16) — to celebration: 'Was kann der Mensch im Leben mehr gewinnen | Als daß sich Gott-Natur ihm offenbare?' [What higher reward can there be for man in life than that God-Nature be revealed to him?] (ll. 31–32). Although the tone remains different throughout, 'Im ernsten Beinhaus' begins, after the turn in lines 15–16, indicated by the word 'doch', to move towards the affirmation of life which 'Vermächtnis' represents. The opening lines, with their emphasis on death and decay, had seemed to defy the assertion that 'Kein Wesen kann zu nichts zerfallen, | Das Ew'ge regt sich fort in allem' [No being can crumble to nothing, for the eternal being lives on and moves in all things]; but line 21, 'Als ob ein Lebensquell dem Tod entspränge' [As if a fountain of life had sprung up from death], suggests a revival of faith in 'das Ew'ge', even if the subjunctive of 'als ob [...] entspränge' indicates continued caution. The reasons for this belief are the same in both poems: the sheer plurality and diversity of life's forms ('Das flutend strömt gesteigerte Gestalten' [From its floods surge more consummate forms, 'Beinhaus', l. 25; 'Durch Auen reichbegabter Welt' [The world richly endowed with meadows], 'Vermächtnis', l. 25), and the wondrous laws which govern them ('Die gottgedachte Spur, die sich erhalten!' [The divinely conceived trace which has been preserved], 'Beinhaus', l. 23; 'Denn Gesetze | Bewahren die lebend'gen Schätze | Aus welchen sich das All geschmückt' [For laws preserve the living treasures with which the cosmos is adorned], 'Vermächtnis', ll. 5–7 — note the emphasis in both on preservation, *bewahren/erhalten*).

Thus, for all their superficial differences, 'Vermächtnis' and 'Im ernsten Beinhaus' are both celebrations of life. Yet, while 'Vermächtnis' suggests the voice (whose we cannot know) of one who is *au fait* with the laws which preserve 'die lebend'gen Schätze', who has seen them in their purest form and thus can hand out advice to the less experienced addressee of the poem, 'Im ernsten Beinhaus' traces a development in the life of the lyric 'I' towards the *possibility* of that kind of confident knowledge of the workings of the universe. The line 'Zum Sonnenlicht andächtig hin mich wendend' is crucial here, for it expresses the kind of intellectual attitude which we have seen at work throughout the *Wanderjahre*: the notion, namely, of edging forward, of gradual enlightenment ('Zum Sonnenlicht [...] mich wendend'), always tempered by the unknowability of the absolute ('andächtig'). The poem does mark the attainment of a new level of understanding: 'Als ich in Mitten solcher starren Menge | Unschätzbar herrlich ein Gebild gewahrte' [When, amid that rigid mass, I discerned a form inestimable, magnificent] (ll. 17–18). This is more than simply recognizing which skull might have belonged to Schiller. The *anagnōrisis* with the skull is, rather, an image of the moment of insight, the recognition of an aspect of the workings of Gott-Natur which the speaker is not entirely willing (or able) to share with us. Indeed, we are not told *what* he has discovered, simply *that* he has discovered. For Karl Vietör, 'wenn nun in den letzten Versen das Geheimnis selbst, dies höchste, unschätzbare, ausgesprochen wird, geschieht es ganz knapp nur und in einer so allgemeinen Formulierung, daß man von Hinweis eher als von Lösung sprechen darf' [now if, in these last verses, the secret itself is proclaimed, that highest, priceless secret, it only happens briefly and in so general a formulation that it would be more appropriate to speak of a clue than a solution].[69] Even this, I think, is an understatement: for the return to life and the celebration of form with which the second part of the poem is taken up is not the same as uncovering 'das Geheimnis selbst', the messages from the oracle of which the poet writes in line 26. Just as the Kästchen at the heart of the novel remains closed, so the secret revealed to the poet is not represented here; rather, the poem remains a 'Hinweis' throughout.

Moreover, that insight (whatever it is), although achieved partly by the poet's own skill, is ultimately the product of revelation, 'Die heil'gen Sinn nicht jedem offenbarte' (l. 16). Despite the use of the word *Adept*, which traditionally meant one initiated into the secrets of alchemy, and came in Goethe's vocabulary to mean one who could discern the secrets of nature,[70] the active verbs in this part of the poem ('geschrieben', 'offenbarte') are assigned not to the adept, but to *Gott-Natur* — out of the control, that is, of *der Mensch*. The notion of revelation appears again later on: 'Was kann der Mensch im Leben mehr gewinnen | Als daß sich Gott-Natur ihm offenbare?' (ll. 31–32). *Gott-Natur*, or truth, or the absolute, may reveal itself to a person, especially if he or she has prepared the mind in the right way, and is competent in interpreting nature's 'Schrift'; but self-limitation is also an essential part of the process, and is itself a form of recognition. For revelation, wisdom cannot be forced through arrogance — it can only be a gift: 'Geheim Gefäß! Orakelsprüche *spendend*, | Wie bin ich wert dich in der Hand zu halten?' [Secretive vessel, which generously *pours forth* the counsel of oracles, how can I be worthy to hold you in my hands?] (ll. 26–27, my emphasis). Here, too, the theme of the secret appears; indeed, this is the second mention of it in the poem, for, in line 21, the delight of form is its mystery, the fact that part of it will always elude perception or analysis: 'Wie mich geheimnisvoll die Form entzückte' [How its form delighted me with its mystery]. Thus, in its position at the end of Book III, 'Im ernsten Beinhaus' becomes as it were an afterword to the novel, refocusing themes which have been suggested and explored in myriad ways throughout. But even this is not the final word, for the words 'Ist fortzusetzen'[71] at the end suggest that discovery, the subject of the poem and of the novel, is an eternal process, just as the ever-changing nature of the forms of life is their permanence: 'Wie sie das Feste läßt zu Geist verrinnen, | Wie sie das Geisterzeugte fest bewahre' [As it allows what is firm to trickle away into spirit, and as it preserves, firmly, what spirit has engendered] (ll. 33–34).

Notes to Chapter 3

1. Jane Brown argues that even discrepancies in style which are due to the transition between the two versions, and which appear not to have been smoothed out, should be understood as intentional:

     Differences in technique between chapter three [of Book II], which was written in the summer of 1807, and the following two chapters (summer 1823) might seem at first due simply to this time lag. Yet it is absurd not to accept these differences as deliberate; Goethe clearly could have recast the first part in the style of the second, as he did the introduction, had he so chosen. (Jane K. Brown, *Goethe's Cyclical Narratives: 'Die Unterhaltungen deutscher Ausgewanderten' and 'Wilhelm Meisters Wanderjahre'* (Chapel Hill: University of North Carolina Press, 1975), p. 60)

   Different stages of Goethe's output are preserved in the novel, like the strata of a rock, and *Novelle* likewise was conceived considerably earlier. The inclusion of earlier ideas in new material is, as we have seen, an essential aspect of very late style.
2. *FA* VIII, 536. Further references to this volume will be given after quotations in the text.
3. Nicholas Boyle, 'Goethe, *Novelle*', in *Landmarks in German Short Prose*, ed. by Peter Hutchinson (Berne: Peter Lang, 2003), pp. 11–27 (p. 21).
4. This is the term which Goethe uses of the paragraph beginning 'Der Fürst, dem seine militärischen Erfahrungen auch hier zu statten kamen' (*FA* VIII, 549) in his final plan for the story (given in the commentary, *FA* VIII, 1057–60).
5. David E. Wellbery, 'Afterword', in *The Sorrows of Young Werther; Elective Affinities; Novella / Johann Wolfgang von Goethe*, trans. by Judith Ryan and Victor Lange, ed. by David E. Wellbery (New York: Suhrkamp, 1988), pp. 283–96 (p. 296).
6. See Boyle, 'Goethe, *Novelle*', p. 19.
7. See *FA* VIII (commentary), 1084.
8. *FA* VII.1, 456.
9. Boyle, 'Goethe, *Novelle*', p. 25.
10. Steve Dowden, 'Irony and Ethical Autonomy in *Wilhelm Meisters Wanderjahre*', *DVjs*, 68 (1994), 134–54 (p. 135).
11. *FA* X, 862–63. Further references to this volume are given after quotations in the text.
12. For a fuller treatment of the place of the *Wanderjahre* within 'the tradition of the self-reflexive text' see Wright, *Novel Poetics*, pp. 1–68.

13. I concur fully with Heinz Schlaffer's distinction (in relation to *Faust*) between the modernity which Goethe experienced, and 'our' modernity, and with his concern to avoid the assumption that 'es reiche Goethes Moderne noch ungebrochen in die Gegenwart' (*Faust Zweiter Teil: Die Allegorie des 19. Jahrhunderts* (Stuttgart: Metzler, 1981), p. 7).

14. 'Indem die *Wanderjahre* sich als Produkt vieler Erzählinstanzen und Textsorten [...] darstellen, verdeutlichen sie, daß mimetische Weltreferenz und dichterische Integrationsfähigkeit in der Moderne problematisch geworden sind. An ihre Stelle treten perspektivisch gebundene Zeichenordnungen, über die nicht mehr ein souveräner Erzähler verfügt; vielmehr bemüht sich ein Redaktor ohne rechten Erfolg, das heterogene Material zu einer geschlossenen Romanwelt zu homogenisieren.' (Günter Saße, *Auswanderung in die Moderne: Tradition und Innovation in Goethes Roman 'Wilhelm Meisters Wanderjahre'* (Berlin: De Gruyter, 2010), p. 20)

15. Hans Reiss, 'Wilhelm Meisters Wanderjahre: Der Weg von der ersten zur zweiten Fassung', *DVjs*, 39 (1965), 34–57 (p. 37).

16. For the same reason, less will be said in this chapter about the various *Novellen*, for, with the exception of 'Nicht zu weit' and the later passages of 'Der Mann von funfzig Jahren', they all belong to much earlier stages of composition, some (including 'Die gefährliche Wette', even though it was not included in the 1821 edition) dating back as far as 1807.

17. Jane Austen, *Mansfield Park*, ed. by Claudia L. Johnson (New York and London: Norton, 1998), p. 312.

18. See also Joan Wright, who draws attention to the novel's internal mirroring:

> The sections of the novel which tell the story of Lenardo and Susanne — that is, the two parts of 'Lenardos Tagebuch', 'Das nußbraune Mädchen' and the exchange of letters between Makarie and her nieces and nephew — represent a complex and wide-ranging mise en abyme for the whole book. [...] Lenardo's wanderings through the Swiss mountains reduplicate, on a smaller scale, Wilhelm's wanderings through the whole landscape of the text' (*Novel Poetics*, pp. 159–60)

19. Ehrhard Bahr, 'Wilhelm Meisters Wanderjahre oder die Entsagenden (1821/1829)', in *Interpretationen: Goethes Erzählwerk*, ed. by Paul Michel Lützeler and James E. McLeod (Stuttgart: Reclam, 1985), pp. 363–95 (on Goethe and Joyce, pp. 367–74).

20. *FA* x, 709–10.

21. See Ehrhard Bahr, *The Novel as Archive: The Genesis, Reception, and Criticism of Goethe's 'Wilhelm Meisters Wanderjahre'* (Columbia, SC: Camden House, 1998).

22. Benjamin C. Sax, *Images of Identity: Goethe and the Problem of Self-Conception in the Nineteenth Century* (New York: Peter Lang, 1987), p. 118.

23. *FA* x, 163.

24. 'Natalia belongs, as far as Wilhelm is concerned, to the ideal world [...] The essence of her character is a moral principle, something which speaks to us from beyond the empirical altogether' (Boyle, *Goethe: The Poet and The Age*, II, 380)

25. This theme is again one which comes to greater prominence in the 1829 version, and I treat it more fully in '"Wenn ich Leben soll, so sei es mit dir!" The Relationship of Father and Son in Goethe's *Wilhelm Meisters Wanderjahre*', GLL, 64 (2011), 489–500.

26. Although the *Fischerknabe* story is based on an experience about which Goethe wrote to Sophie von La Roche as early as 1774 (see *FA* x, 1141–42), the biographical dimension is of much less import than the pattern itself, the act of delving deep into and reworking old material, and the resolution which that can bring — which, as we saw in the chapter on poetry, is the achievement of very-lateness. It matters little in this case *whose* past is being transformed — Goethe's, Wilhelm's, or even that of the text; what matters is the *possibility* of such a transformation as recorded in this scene.

27. See Brown, *Goethe's Cyclical Narratives*, p. 63.

28. See Hannelore Schlaffer: '[Goethe beschreibt] einen Kunstbetrieb, dessen schneller Tausch auf rasches Erfassen der Oberfläche, auf leichte Begreifbarkeit zielt' (*Wilhelm Meister: Das Ende der Kunst und die Wiederkehr des Mythos* (Stuttgart: Metzler, 1989), p. 23).

29. See note 10.

30. *FA* XXIII.2, 69.

31. *FA* XXIII.I, 244.

32. I cannot agree with Günter Saße's claim that the pictures of Mignon serve the function of giving 'Sehnsucht' (embodied by Mignon and aroused in Wilhelm by her) aesthetic form, and thereby containing it so that those who once felt it might go forth and lead more useful lives:

> durch die ästhetische Gestaltung verliert [die Sehnsucht] ihr Gefahrenpotential und wird genießbar. [...] die Gemälde erregen zwar die Sehnsucht, aber nur, um sie in kathartischer Dialektik sogleich wieder stillzustellen [...] damit [die Rezipienten] sich umso ungestörter ihren praktischen Pflichten zuwenden können. (*Auswanderung in die Moderne*, pp. 104–05)

First, this almost reads like a continuation of the ingrained (but, to my mind, quite objectionable) strain of argument in critical writing on the *Lehrjahre*, according to which Mignon must be 'overcome' in order for Wilhelm to complete his development. (See, for example, Helmut Ammerlahn, who argues that the self-appointed task of the novel is 'zu zeigen, wie Wilhelm Mignon zu überwinden vermag, wie der Sturm und Drangmensch sich durchdringt zum bewußten, tätigen und freien Menschentum': 'Wilhelm Meisters Mignon — ein offenbares Rätsel: Name, Gestalt, Symbol, Wesen und Werden', *DVjs*, 42 (1968), 89–116 (p. 112).) Second, though, it does not recognize the slipperiness of representation, its potential to confuse as well as enhance human perception: a theme which is as prominent in the Lago Maggiore episode as it is in *Novelle*.

33. *MA* VI.2, 820. The essay postulates that knowledge of 'das reine Phänomen' would have to be the result of all possible 'Erfahrungen und Versuche'; even then, the pure phenomenon (what Goethe later calls the *Urphänomen*) remains an 'Erscheinung', and therefore distinct from the thing in itself.

34. *FA* X, 511.

35. The active role of the reader in the *Wanderjahre* is, of course, a very common theme in the secondary literature, which is why I do not develop it any further. Benjamin Bennett pays it particularly sustained attention in *Beyond Theory: Eighteenth-Century German Literature and the Poetics of Irony* (Ithaca: Cornell University Press, 1993). It is also a major concern of Joan Wright's study *The Novel Poetics of Goethe's Wilhelm Meisters Wanderjahre*.

36. Here I part company with the editors of the FA, who write that:

> Während das Kästchen [...] in der ersten Fassung noch das Motiv des 'Geheimnisses' vertritt, wie es traditionellerweise zu einem Schauer- oder Abenteuerroman gehört, bezieht die zweite Fassung das geheimnisvolle Kästchen dann auf das Rätsel der Beziehung zwischen Mann und Frau, die Montan schon in der ersten Fassung nur wie nebenbei ausspricht: daß nämlich der Schlüssel zu diesem Kästchen 'kompliziert' sein werde. (pp. 976–77)

The relationship between Felix and Hersilie certainly does become more prominent in the second version, and with it the motif of the casket — the erotic symbolism of the lock and key is clear. Nonetheless, its significance stretches beyond that; as I show in this section, the secret plays far more subtle a role than simply the motor of an adventure novel, and in fact becomes more defined, not less, in the version of 1829.

37. The structural feature of inserted texts creates the sense of delving deeper into a theme without necessarily being sure of what one will find — much the same effect as opening an archive or other closed source of information.

38. Hans Rudolf Vaget, 'Johann Wolfgang Goethe: Wilhelm Meisters Wanderjahre', in *Romane und Erzählungen zwischen Romantik und Realismus: Neue Interpretationen*, ed. by Paul Michael Lützeler (Stuttgart: Reclam, 1983), pp. 136–64 (p. 153).

39. Dowden, 'Irony and Ethical Autonomy', p. 153.

40. Clark E. Muenzer, *Figures of Identity: Goethe's Novels and the Enigmatic Self* (University Park: Pennsylvania State University Press, 1984), p. 104.

41. Joan Wright also notes the parallel with Eco: see *Novel Poetics*, pp. 263–64.

42. See Erich Trunz in the notes to the *HA* VIII, 637.

43. 'Es ist nun Goethes Art, da, wo er begründen muß, zuerst äußere Gründe zu nennen und die inneren für sich zu behalten' (ibid.).

44. *WA* IV.45, p. 261.
45. Bahr, *The Novel as Archive*, p. 48. R. T. Llewellyn is not entirely wide of the mark with his assertion that: 'The aphorisms are clearly relevant [...] But the "all is relevant" approach of the editors who have insisted on re-introducing them together with the poems whilst claiming a unified formal organization for the novel seems excessive' (Llewellyn, 'Parallel Attitudes to Form', pp. 413–14). It would certainly be possible to exaggerate the nature of the formal unity of the *Wanderjahre* in an effort to prove that Goethe remained in control of his material to the end. But the aphorisms and the interpolated poems are more than simply 'relevant': they proceed from the same spirit of enquiry, experiment, and self-limitation as the rest of the novel.
46. This is certainly a technique used elsewhere in the novel: not all utterances are necessarily to be taken seriously, or as representative of Goethe's own convictions. Wilhelm's assertion in Book I, chapter 10 (pp. 384–85), for example, that glasses worn to correct short-sight are only an illusory aid, and that people ought to remain within their natural limitations, is impractical, and from the perspective of anyone who is short-sighted, plainly ridiculous! (Indeed, although we cannot know exactly how this was meant, and Goethe occasionally expressed ambivalence about glasses and people who wear them, the *FA* cites his conversation with Eckermann of 5 April 1830 as evidence that Wilhelm's notion that 'die Gewohnheit Annäherungsbrillen zu tragen an dem Dünkel unserer jungen Leute hauptsächlich Schuld hat' was *not* a view which he supported.) The impossibility of knowing what is to be taken seriously and what is not is part both of the narrative strategy of the novel — its irony, and the active role demanded of the reader — and, of course, of its realism. For no one, not even Goethe, can know what is right all the time.
47. Gerhard Neumann, *Ideenparadiese: Untersuchungen zur Aphoristik von Lichtenberg, Novalis, Friedrich Schlegel und Goethe* (Munich: Fink, 1976), p. 644.
48. Steve Dowden argues that: 'There is no ideal totality that determines the order of things [in the *Wanderjahre*] [...] Perfection, total harmony, and wholeness are ideals that Wilhelm Meister (and all the rest of us) must learn to do without' ('Irony and Ethical Autonomy', pp. 137–38). Here Dowden veers very close to the assertion that there is no truth, which is not, I think, in the spirit of the novel. It is clear from the maxims that 'das Wahre' *is* a preoccupation in the *Wanderjahre*; the point of the maxims and the motif of the secret is that perfection, totality, etc. *do* exist, or could, but will almost never be grasped by man's limited understanding, and therefore must remain guiding ideals.
49. Peter Hutchinson, 'Introduction', in *Maxims and Reflections by Johann Wolfgang von Goethe*, trans. by Elisabeth Stopp, ed. with introduction and notes by Peter Hutchinson (London: Penguin, 1998), pp. ix–xvi (p. xiii).
50. In his incarnation as Jarno in the *Lehrjahre*, he was cuttingly dismissive of Mignon; and, during his conversation with Wilhelm at the beginning of the *Wanderjahre*, he comments: 'Die Menschen wollt' ich meiden', to which Wilhelm replies, *lächelnd*: 'Es steht doch nicht so ganz schlimm mit ihnen' (*FA* x, 291).
51. *FA* xxv, 642.
52. Ibid., p. 643.
53. *FA* xxv, 653.
54. Ibid., p. 656. Maxim 141 reads as follows: 'Unser Fehler besteht darin, daß wir am Gewissen zweifeln und das Ungewisse fixieren möchten' (*FA* x, 579).
55. Neumann, *Ideenparadiese*, p. 631.
56. See, for example, Joan Wright, who argues that: 'Metafictional literature aims at a fusion of the creative with the critical, an amalgam of theory and praxis, so that it both thematizes and incorporates within its structure its own critical system' (*Novel Poetics*, p. 3).
57. Muenzer, *Figures of Identity*, pp. 120–21.
58. Sax, *Images of Identity*, p. 128.
59. This endeavour runs throughout Goethe's very late works. With reference to *Novelle*, Nicholas Boyle writes:

> What differentiates Goethe from later German writers, particularly of the twentieth century, is not that he is unaware of, or indifferent to, the perplexities and incompleteness of life and the human quest for reality [...] he does not compromise that disillusioned understanding of our lot, but he manages, like Shakespeare, to

incorporate it in a literary work which, largely through its refusal to conform to the requirements of any particular genre, also includes intimations of wholeness, and assurances, however fleeting, of consolation. (Boyle, 'Goethe, *Novelle*', p. 27)

60. *FA* x, 585–86.
61. Ibid., p. 774.
62. For a detailed treatment of this dimension of 'Vermächtnis', see Nicholas Boyle, 'Kantian and Other Elements in Goethe's "Vermächtniß"', *MLR*, 73 (1978), 532–49.
63. *FA* x, 1077.
64. Here I use different line numbers from the *FA*, which counts, somewhat confusingly, from one again after the page-turn.
65. See n. 64.
66. Nicholas Boyle observes that:

> [t]he individual must begin his pilgrimage by recognising, in both the natural and in the human world, realities which surpass and are independent of his own individual faculties, and towards which his proper attitude is one of attachment, thankfulness, and reverence: only after that can he establish order within the microcosm that is himself. ('Kantian and Other Elements in Goethe's "Vermächtniß"', pp. 544–45)

67. Albrecht Schöne, *Schillers Schädel* (Munich: Beck, 2002), pp. 56–57. Schöne writes extensively on the poem's relation to Goethe's scientific study, especially his long-standing interest in osteology. His analysis is so thorough that I shall focus on other aspects here; but the evidence which Schöne offers makes it plain that 'Im ernsten Beinhaus' is as deeply resonant with the rest of Goethe's life's work, and therefore yet another instance of poetic *Steigerung*, as any of the other very late poems.
68. Swales and Swales, *Reading Goethe*, p. 55.
69. Karl Vietör, 'Goethes Gedicht auf Schiller's Schädel', *PMLA*, 59 (1944), 142–83 (p. 153).
70. See Schöne, *Schillers Schädel*, pp. 61–62.
71. The editors of the *FA* argue that the words must refer only to the poem (p. 1272); but since the themes of 'Im ernsten Beinhaus' are clearly, if subtly, intertwined with those of the rest of the *Wanderjahre*, I think it by no means impossible that they refer both to the poem and to the novel. Moreover, as in every canto in *The Divine Comedy*, the last line of the poem repeats the rhyme of the middle line of the tercet, creating an abab effect in the last four lines, which diverts the potentially infinite flow of the *terza rima*, and thus allows the poem to end. Indeed, the poem ends emphatically, in terms of both form and content. But the concluding two lines suggest a potentially infinite process, and the novel as a whole is deliberately constructed so that, in a reminder of Goethe's words to Rochlitz, 'es eine Art von Unendlichkeit erhält, die sich in verständige und vernünftige Worte nicht durchaus fassen läßt'. The words 'Ist fortzusetzen' are, I think, to be read more in the spirit of the 'Unendlichkeit' that the novel both tries to capture and seeks to stimulate, than as referring to any concrete additions that Goethe may or may not have had in mind, either for the poem or for the novel as a whole.

CHAPTER 4

Faust

Faust. Zweiter Teil shares, even outdoes, the literariness of *Wilhelm Meisters Wander-jahre*, and bears all the hallmarks of very late style which we have identified so far. It is densely allusive, acknowledging the legacy of past poetic works through references to them, and spinning its own distinctive poetry out of their influence.[1] As Martin Swales observes, 'the theatrical statement is as knowing, as quotational, as the multiple textuality which it explores'.[2] That knowingness is linked, as it is in the *Wanderjahre*, to the theme of limitations: in the poetry[3] of *Faust*, a high degree of self-awareness is always coupled with an implicit acknowledgement of its own inadequacy, as a product of the human mind. *Faust* is the most thoroughly, but also the most urgently, self-conscious of all Goethe's works. For out of the highly reflective poetic framework steps a central character who blunders because he reflects only sporadically, and acts still less often on the understanding which he gains from reflection.[4] *Faust*, and especially Part II, brings the moral importance of self-questioning into sharper relief than any other work by Goethe.

The premises of the argument which is to follow differ, respectfully but profoundly, from those adopted by Benjamin Bennett in *Goethe's Theory of Poetry: 'Faust' and the Regeneration of Language*, the fullest study to date of self-consciousness in *Faust*. For him, self-consciousness is a problem, and it is Faust's problem:

> The beginning of *Faust* [...] strongly emphasizes the idea of the tragedy of self-consciousness, tragedy rooted in an internal division of the self. Our self-consciousness, by separating us from ourselves, denies us satisfaction even from what we actually possess [...].[5]

As I shall argue, Faust's tragedy is indeed rooted in the sense, explored in the scene 'Nacht' ['Night'], of division from nature and from his own spirit, and of longing for a superior state of being; but although, as Fichte recognized first, self-reflection presupposes a split between an experiencing self and a conscious self, I disagree with the suggestion that it is this ability of man's to reflect which brings about his isolation from nature and from his own spirit. This is a contemporary Romantic dogma, shared by Rousseau and Schiller, that Goethe rejects. The situation arises, rather, from the inherent limitations of human understanding; as Goethe observes in his little essay 'Bedenken und Ergebung' ['Doubt and Surrender'] (1820): 'Der Verstand kann nicht vereinigt denken, was die Sinnlichkeit ihm gesondert überlieferte' [the intellect cannot unify in thought things which the senses delivered to it in parts].[6] For Goethe, reflection may in fact stretch those limitations, if it cannot conquer them completely: he concludes his piece 'Erfahrung und Wissenschaft' ['Experience and Science'] (1798) with the observation that, although perception of 'das reine Phänomen' [the pure phenomenon] would be 'das Resultat aller Erfahrungen und Versuche' [the result of all our experiences and experiments], and, as such, impossible, the human mind is capable of modest progress in that direction: 'es sind am Ende doch nur, wie mich dünkt, die praktischen und sich selbst rektifizierenden Operationen des gemeinen Menschenverstandes, der sich in einer höheren Sphäre zu üben wagt' [in the end, these are, it seems to me, simply the practical operations of the meagre human intellect, bent on self-correction, as it ventures to try itself in a higher sphere].[7] Moreover, Faust's problem, especially in the later stages of Part II, is more likely to be a *lack* of reflectiveness, owing not least to the terms of the wager, than an excess of it; as Michael Jaeger observes: 'Der Zwang des Subjekts zieht die Distanzen ein und vernichtet das Objekt und mit ihm zugleich die Möglichkeit der Selbsterkenntnis' [the pressure of the subject draws in all distances and destroys the object, and with it also any opportunity for self-understanding].[8] My own analysis rests, then, on the contention that the character Faust is *not* the agent of self-consciousness in the work, and, moreover, that self-consciousness in Goethe's work holds the status less of a problem than of an opportunity.

   The actual agent of self-consciousness is the poetry of *Faust*. Again, this marks a significant divergence from Bennett's position. He identifies what he calls 'levels of consciousness' in the work, and argues that the movement between them must take the form of 'a rhythm of articulation and submergence':[9] 'for the normal direction of reflective consciousness is upward [...] But if the process of consciousness were irreversible, its content would become insupportable — not in mass so much as in complexity [...] Therefore there must also be in our experience an opposing or simplifying movement, a movement downwards.'[10]

   Poetry, he contends in a comment spurred by Chiron's words 'G'nug, den Poeten bindet keine Zeit' [In short, the poet is not bound by time] (l. 7433), is one such movement:

> Poetry conquers time by plunging it as into a whirlpool (7483), toward its unmoved center (7481), toward intensity of submergence and containment, on a *lower* level of consciousness, approaching the narrow limits of the 'instant' (9418) that is also eternity.[11]

The difficulty here is that this is precisely not the pattern of the poetry of *Faust*, or of the very late Goethe in general. As we have seen, one of the chief characteristics of Goethe's very late style is not lowering, but heightening: the reflective incorporation of the patterns of the past to yield a fuller, more self-conscious poetic present. The poetry of *Faust* is the culmination of this tendency; and the movement of its own climax, the scene 'Bergschluchten', is unambiguously an ascent. The career of Faust himself, however, is not. Contrary to the claims advanced in perfectibilist readings of the work, Faust's story is not one of progress; at most, he can be said to experience occasional flashes of insight which are never sustained. Bennett's sophisticated notion of 'the rhythm of articulation and submergence' could, therefore, be attributed instead to the constant sense of rupture between the reflective play and its comparatively unreflective central character. It is that disjunction which will be the focus of what follows. I shall trace the career of the character Faust, highlighting the consequences of his underdeveloped or underused capacity for reflection, and I shall contrast it with the superior level of reflection represented by the literary self-consciousness of the text.

The search for the ideal

The story of *Faust*, from start to finish, is that of a search for the ideal — and, of course, of the often misguided paths which that search takes. The ideal, or the intuition of one, stimulates the human mind and spirit to progress; but it also gives rise to a feeling of absence, for it is necessarily difficult of access. Early in Part I, in 'Nacht', Faust, the frustrated scholar, longs to understand 'was die Welt | Im Innersten zusammenhält' [what binds the world together in its innermost] (382–83): that is, to apprehend what Goethe referred to elsewhere, notably in the *Maximen und Reflexionen*, as the *Idee*: 'das was immer zur Erscheinung kommt und daher als Gesetz aller Erscheinungen uns entgegen tritt' [that which is always appearing to us, and which we thus encounter as the law of all appearances].[12] The *Idee*, as the law which governs and gives rise to the appearances by which we know the world, is indeed that which 'holds the world together' at the deepest level, *im Innersten*. However, although the *Idee* is constantly appearing to us, we are, for the most part, unable to perceive it in appearances: 'Die Idee ist ewig und einzig [...] Alles was wir gewahr werden und wovon wir reden können, sind nur Manifestationen der Idee' [The Idea is eternal and unique [...] All things which we perceive and of which we can speak, are but manifestations of the Idea].[13] Only an extraordinary level of perception and understanding is equal to the task of perceiving the single, eternal principle which underlies the multiplicity of shifting manifestations. This is where the ideal becomes relevant. Of the *Urphänomen* [archetypal phenomenon], a close relative of the *Idee*, Goethe wrote:

> Urphänomen
>   ideal, als das letzte Erkennbare
>   real als erkannt
>   symbolisch weil es alle Fälle begreift:
>   identisch mit allen Fällen.[14]

> [Archetypal phenomenon: ideal in the sense of the last discernible things, real in that it can be discerned, symbolic because it encompasses every instance: identical to every instance.]

The ideal, then, is not some distant, unreal quality; it is precisely the real, the most real. As Karl Ameriks writes, it 'can be taken to be simply the purposive structure or [...] optimal form of our world of ordinary objects'.[15] Yet, as Faust senses, recognizing that purposive structure requires a level of understanding beyond the capabilities of most humans. Knowledge of the ideal, then, is also a state of ideal understanding — and Faust desires both: 'Daß *ich erkenne* was die Welt | Im Innersten zusammenhält' [that *I may recognize* what binds the world together in its innermost] (my emphasis). This line resonates, through the verb 'erkennen', with the maxim on the *Urphänomen*. The search for the ideal merges with the desire for self-knowledge as the striving mind seeks to recognize and overcome its own deficiencies, and to reach a state where everything, including itself, is transparent to it.

The scene 'Nacht' sets the conditions for the entire play, turning as it does on Faust's thwarted desire to apprehend a presence superior to human understanding. It forms part of the earliest stratum of the work, namely the *Urfaust* of 1774, but it is not anachronistic to deploy in the analysis of this early scene terminology (such as *Idee*) which became important to Goethe some years later. In many ways, 'Nacht' anticipates the major philosophical debates of the late eighteenth and early nineteenth centuries; indeed, it influenced them, for it was published in 1790 in the *Fragment*, and was read by, among others, Hegel and Schelling. In retrospect, therefore, the scene forms part of a reciprocal exchange between Goethe and other thinkers. The desire expressed by Faust to overcome the dichotomy between subject and object, between mind and nature, was also a chief concern of the German idealists; and, in turn, notions such as the *Idee* developed in Goethe's mind at least partly under the influence of the philosophical climate in the decades immediately before and after 1800. Moreover, *Faust* underwent so many revisions that it is legitimate to read the earliest strata *both* as residual elements of a much earlier period of creativity, *and* as overlaid with meaning which might not have been fully or consciously intended when they were first written, but which emerged as a result of later developments. Once *Urfaust* entered Part I (completed in 1806), it became something different (though, of course, it can and should be taken seriously on its own terms also); and the 1808 stratum in turn became part of a greater whole with the completion of Part II in 1832. In Part II, Goethe takes up again the themes launched in Part I, and especially in 'Nacht', and treats them in the light of the preoccupations of the very late phase.

'Nacht' establishes a tension between striving and dissatisfaction which informs the rest of the work. The unending activity of nature is the suggestion most tangible to the mind of that superior presence which it dimly suspects; and Faust's various attempts to approach nature, to 'grasp' it, form the substance of the scene. He desires both total, unreflective immersion in its beauty, as exemplified by the moonlight — 'Von allem Wissensqualm entladen | In deinem Tau gesund mich baden!' [freed from the thick smoke of knowledge | to cleanse myself in your dew] (396–97) — *and* full understanding of its works: 'Daß ich erkenne was die Welt | Im Innersten zusammenhält' (382–83). In the context of the scene, this latter wish is not, or not only, the urge of an obsessive scientist to penetrate and possess the world's every secret — the impulse which, for example, drives Wagner's activity in Part II: 'Was man an der Natur geheimnisvolles pries, | Das wagen wir verständig zu probieren, | Und was sie sonst organisieren ließ, | Das lassen wir kristallisieren' [We honoured these mysteries as the preserve of nature, and now we dare to test our understanding against them; and what nature once organized, we now crystallize]. (6857–60) Rather, it is first and foremost Faust's desire to know what binds his innermost self. We saw in Chapter 1 that, for Goethe, knowledge of the external world (including nature) and self-knowledge are inextricably linked: and it follows that any limitations of the one will also apply to the other.[16] This is the state of ignorance about the relationship between the self and nature that Faust is trying to overcome in this scene. He tries repeatedly to establish his own position in relation to nature: 'Ihr schwebt, ihr Geister, neben mir' [You spirits hovering near me] (428), 'Ich schau' in diesen reinen Zügen | Die wirkende Natur vor meiner Seele liegen' [In these pure lines I see the workings of nature before my soul] (440–41), 'Wo fass' ich dich, unendliche Natur?' [Where shall I grasp you, infinite nature?] (455). Yet his longing to exist in complete identity with nature must, he knows, remain unfulfilled: the subjunctive in 'Ach! Könnt' ich doch auf Berges-Höh'n, | In deinem lieben Lichte gehn' [Ah! Could I but walk the mountain tops by your sweet light] (392–93) limits the expression to a wish rather than an expectation of fulfilment. His situation corresponds to the one rather bleakly described in the *Maximen und Reflexionen*:

> Alle Verhältnisse der Dinge wahr
> Irrtum allein in dem Menschen
> An ihm nichts wahr als daß er irrt
> Sein Verhältnis zu sich zu andern zu den Dingen nicht finden kann.[17]

[All relations between things are true, error is in man alone; nothing about him is true except that he errs, and cannot make out his relation to himself, to others, to things.]

Faust's world, that of lonely scholarship, has broken off from the world of nature and has become arid, and he with it, and his recognition of this lies behind his bitter words: 'Das ist deine Welt! das heißt eine Welt!' [That is your world! You call that a world?] (409). This sense of being at once part of nature and fatally adrift from it is intimately linked with his sense of being alienated from himself:

> Und fragst du noch, warum dein Herz
> Sich bang' in deinem Busen klemmt?
> Warum ein unerklärter Schmerz
> Dir alle Lebensregung hemmt? (410–13)

[And do you still ask why your heart remains cramped and anxious in your breast? Why a mysterious pain hampers your every living movement?]

> Dein Sinn ist zu, dein Herz ist tot! (444)

[Your senses are closed, your heart is dead!]

The sense of loss which pervades the scene is the result of Faust's separation, perceived or real, from both the natural world and from the forces within him which give life to his own self. Faust's attempts to return to nature, of which he knows he must be part, even if he cannot fathom how, are thus also attempts at self-knowledge; or, as Jane K. Brown has it, 'Faust faces a double dilemma — to know the unknowable self and to know unknowable nature'.[18]

Faust vacillates between hubris and humility in his search for understanding. This is especially evident in his exchange with the Erdgeist. Faust's sense of awe, of being belittled, at the appearance of the spirit is so great that he must look away: 'Weh! Ich ertrag' dich nicht!' [Ah! I cannot bear to look upon you!] (485). This is a mutation of a motif from the Old Testament, in which the appearance of God is deemed too much for the human mind and its eye to bear:

Und der Engel des Herrn erschien ihm in einer feurigen Flammen aus dem Busch [...] Und Mose verhüllte sein Angesicht, denn er furchte sich Gott anzuschauen. (2. Mose, 3: 2, 6)

[And the angel of the Lord appeared unto him in a flame of fire out of the midst of a bush [...] And Moses hid his face; for he was afraid to look upon God.]

Und sprach weiter: Mein Angesicht kannst du nicht sehen: Denn kein Mensch wird leben, der mich siehet. (2. Mose, 33: 20)[19]

[And he said, Thou canst not see my face: for there shall no man see me, and live.]

The Erdgeist is not God, not the absolute, but still manifestly a being which, when it appears, challenges the very basis of Faust's existence; it is monstrous because it is an *Erscheinung* the like of which the human mind is not equipped to perceive with understanding. Yet a few lines later, Faust is able to say: 'Geschäftiger Geist, wie nah fühl' ich mich dir!' [Busy spirit, how close to you I feel!] (511). It is, namely, his persistent hope that a way back and into nature will be found, be it through magic or by some other means; and, moreover, that the separation between his mind and the objective world will end in the revelation that the 'weaving' of 'alles sich zum Ganzen' [everything to form the whole] (447) is the work of an all-encompassing intelligence — and one which happens to be coextensive with the mind of a human subject like himself. That is the sense of his protest, 'Ich Ebenbild der Gottheit!' [I, made in God's image!] (516). Faust is, in fact, profoundly unsure of who, or even what he is: 'Bin ich ein Gott?' [am I a God?] (439), he speculated only a few lines earlier. Yet he clings to the hope, planted in his mind no doubt by the claim in Genesis that God made man in his own image, that he is somehow a manifestation of a greater being: and not, in his vocabulary, just an image, a *Bild* or an *Abbild*, but an *Ebenbild*, an equal. He yearns for confirmation that his stake in the world is as great at least as that of the Erdgeist, and that the highest truth accessible to the human mind is not simply the recognition 'daß wir nichts wissen können!' [that we can know nothing] (364). But the Erdgeist taunts him with what he already suspects, namely that his intelligent activity has resulted only in the creation of an inner world which bears little or no relation to external reality: 'Wo ist die Brust? die eine Welt in sich erschuf?' [Where is that heart now which created an entire world within itself?] (491). The final blow dealt by the spirit, 'Du gleichst dem Geist den du begreifst, | Nicht mir!' [You are equal to the spirit which you can comprehend, not to me!] (512–13), both reinforces the vexed question of Faust's identity, recalcitrant even to his own understanding ('Nicht dir? | Wem denn?' [Not you? Then who?], 514–15), and belittles the only power which might enable him to solve it, namely his intellect, the capacity of *Begreifen*.

Thus the conditions for the play are set: what unfolds will be various phases of Faust's reaction against the limitations which the Erdgeist forces him to confront. This begins with his cynical bet with Mephistopheles, of which a significant side-effect is access to manifold, indeed potentially infinite, experience: 'Und was der ganzen Menschheit zugeteilt ist | Will ich in meinem innern Selbst genießen' [And I wish to experience the pleasure of man's whole lot within my inner self]

(1771–72) — an ambition which lends some justification to the charge of fanatical subjectivism which Michael Jaeger levels at Faust.[20] The unfortunate paradox of the wager, which Faust does not seem to recognize, is that, even as it appears to promise him the absolute and the infinite, it makes transience compulsory, and loss inevitable. For Faust has wagered against the value of permanence: 'Werd' ich zum Augenblicke sagen: | Verweile doch! du bist so schön! | Dann magst du mich in Fesseln schlagen, | Dann will ich gern zu Grunde gehn!' [And if ever I should say of a single moment: Stay! you are so beautiful! | Then you may clap me in chains | Then I shall willingly go to my destruction!] (1699–1702). Hence he must go from loss to loss, as much as from gain to gain, if he is to win. The final phase of the saga is Faust's project of land-reclamation, which is symbolic of his desire finally to subjugate nature's forces to his own will: 'Zu überschaun mit einem Blick | Des Menschengeistes Meisterstück' (11247–48) [To survey with a single glance the masterpiece of the human spirit] — almost, it is tempting to suppose, as if to spite the Erdgeist, to prove that the 'Menschengeist' *is* equal to it in its scope after all. Angus Nicholls writes of Goethe's adoption in the 1790s, under the influence of Kant and in a reaction against the unlimited subjectivity represented by Werther, of an attitude which he characterizes as *Weltfrömmigkeit*;[21] and he suggests that, for Goethe,

> when the subject perceives itself as a finite being situated within the expanse of the entire world [...] its subjective desires, longings, projects and theories must adopt a sense of humility and self-limitation that is appropriate to its place within this wider order.[22]

Faust's career could be described as the failure to adopt that sense of self-limitation, as the '[repudiation of] all human concern and commitment'.[23] The wager marks his initial refusal to do so; and it yokes him to his hubris so that, even in the rare moments when he does show a flash of real understanding, he is unable to act upon it.

An exception to this trajectory is the opening scene of Part II, 'Anmutige Gegend' ['Pleasant landscape']. The scene is parallel to 'Nacht' in more than just its setting at night, and its position in Part II;[24] but in accordance with the pattern, by now familiar, of poetic *Steigerung*, it varies, in some cases even reverses, the themes and motifs which it picks up from the earlier scene. The longing voiced in Faust's address to the moon (392–97) appears to have been answered. Ariel and his elves harness night's gentler forces to bring him back to health, to 'bathe' him as he had wished that other night, albeit in a different dew: 'Dann badet ihn in Tau aus Lethes Flut' [Then bathe him in dew from Lethe's torrents] (4629). Faust himself recognizes that nature has come to his aid when he awakes:

> Du Erde warst auch diese Nacht beständig
> Und atmest neu erquickt zu meinen Füßen,
> Beginnest schon mit Lust mich zu umgeben,
> Du regst und rührst ein kräftiges Beschließen,
> Zum höchsten Dasein immerfort zu streben. — (4681–85)

> [Earth, this night too you have endured, and you breathe refreshed at my feet, already you envelop me with new joys, you stir in me the powerful resolution ceaselessly to strive for the supreme existence. —]

Yet the dash indicates a pause: a hesitation, even if only a reflective one, as to the accessibility of this 'höchstes Dasein'. The ambition to 'strive' is less arrogantly formulated than before,[25] and the remainder of Faust's speech is given over to this element of uncertainty. The lines immediately following are a paean to the manifold energy of nature, the beauty of the paradise which, as Faust looks round, develops 'um mich her die Runde' [all around me] (4694); but, in spite of his sense of being surrounded by its healing, inspiring activity, Faust's words come increasingly to express, once again, a sense of apartness from it. His experience of this detachment is both less bitter and less hubristic than in 'Nacht'. Faust's comment, as he gazes up at the rising sun, that '[d]er Berge Gipfelriesen' [the mountains' giant peaks] receive its rays before his own kind (4696–98), amounts to an admission of the lowliness of his place in the mighty hierarchy of the cosmos. Faust has, it seems, learned that the capacity of his own mind is less than absolute: that his creativity and understanding can never be equal in extent to that 'höchstes Dasein' suggested by both the work of nature and the resplendence of the sun on high. He now realizes that he cannot coexist (as he had hoped in 'Nacht') in full communion with the surrounding world, and from there with that which is absolute or transcendent, because he will always be pulled up short by his inadequacy. He turns away and shields his eyes from the sun (4702–03) as he had to once before from the glare of a different light; but here he does voluntarily what the Erdgeist forced him to do. The affirmative line 'So bleibe denn die Sonne mir im Rücken!' [Then let the sun shine on behind me!] (4715) makes this turning away into a positive action, a renunciation of his own delusions of grandeur.

At the same time, he recognizes that another figuration of light is more commensurate with his own understanding: 'Am farbigen Abglanz haben wir das Leben' [It is in the reflected colours that our life consists] (4727). Iris is the messenger of the gods in Greek mythology;[26] and just as the arc of the rainbow which hovers over the waterfall in 'Anmutige Gegend' suggests the formation of a bridge over the ravine, so human understanding requires a mediating force to gesture across and beyond the gulf of ignorance which separates it from the absolute. In his 1825 essay 'Versuch einer Witterungslehre' [Attempt at a Theory of the Weather], Goethe dwells more explicitly on what that force might be:

> Das Wahre, mit dem Göttlichen identisch, läßt sich niemals von uns direct erkennen, wir schauen es nur im Abglanz, im Beispiel, Symbol, in einzelnen und verwandten Erscheinungen; wir werden es gewahr als unbegreifliches Leben und können dem Wunsch nicht entsagen, es dennoch zu begreifen.[27]
>
> [Truth, which is identical to the divine, can never be perceived by us directly, we may only see it in reflections, in examples, in symbols, in individual and related appearances; we see it first as an incomprehensible living force, and yet we cannot renounce the desire to comprehend it.]

The vocabulary of these lines resonates strongly with Faust's closing couplet in 'Anmutige Gegend': '[Dem Regenbogen] sinne nach und du begreifst genauer: | Am farbigen Abglanz haben wir das Leben' (4726–27). Faust's desire to understand is no less ardent than it was in 'Nacht'. However, the word 'begreifen', which became so significant in its use by the Erdgeist, has taken on a new aspect: for it now suggests a process of edging patiently, with the limited resources which we have, towards an understanding which is less incomplete. It is revealing — and perhaps, in a Goethean way, a little ironic[28] — that Faust's greatest insight, the moment in his earthly life when he is closest to ideal understanding (though he still has not reached it), is when he is able to look his deficiencies squarely in the face. At any rate, the moment is as transient as the rainbow itself: for Faust soon forgets this understanding as he becomes caught up in the action of Part II.

The search for the past

The search for ideal knowledge, or knowledge of the ideal, fuses in Part II with the preoccupation with memory (both personal and cultural) characteristic of Goethe's very late phase. In the first three acts, the search for the 'das letzte Erkennbare' is modulated into the effort to recover the past — that is to say, into the search for a *lost* ideal, symbolized (in the eyes, at least, of those invested in the search) by the world of classical antiquity. This, too, is in part an attempt at self-knowledge: for the past, and, more specifically, the past as it appears to man in memory, determines and structures his sense of self in the present — be that in the life of the individual, or in the development of an entire civilization or culture. Yet, as we saw in Goethe's autobiographical works, and as will become clear in *Faust*, the past cannot be reached directly: what once was cannot suddenly be willed, unchanged, back into the present, just as 'das letzte Erkennbare' cannot be perceived unmediated. Whereas Faust's own attempts to recover the ideal veer in Part II between a naive belief in the accessibility of the past and a hubristic aversion to remembering, the poetry of *Faust* displays a more constant commitment to memory, and a superior awareness of the forces — such as art, such as myth — which both enable us to maintain a connection with the past, and transform it so that it reaches us in a form different from its original reality.[29]

The point of transition from the search for the *Idee* to the search for an ideal past (now lost) is 'Finstere Galerie'. The Kaiser has given Faust the task of producing the perfection of humankind:

> Der Kaiser will, es muß sogleich geschehn,
> Will Helena und Paris vor sich sehn;
> Das Musterbild der Männer, so der Frauen,
> In deutlichen Gestalten will er schauen. (6183–86)

[The Emperor wishes — it must be done directly — wishes to see Helena and Paris, the paragon of man and womankind clearly formed before him.]

The wording here is important: for what the emperor explicitly demands is the real, or at least realistic, embodiment ('in deutlichen Gestalten') of the ideal ('das Musterbild'), rather than some fabulous hocus-pocus imitation; he articulates his desire in terms of history and mythology. He demands to see Helena, the woman whose beauty is the stuff of legends. Regardless of whether she 'really' existed, she has entered history by means of her story and its influence. The longing for perfection thus merges with the longing for the return of what has been, or is said to have been.[30] The link between the two versions of the search is also made clear in the solution which Mephistopheles proposes to the impossible task of reviving the past, namely the visit to 'die Mütter' [the mothers]. He describes them, albeit with his tongue in his cheek, as a 'höheres Geheimnis' [higher secret] (6212). Faust's search in 'Nacht' is couched in the same terms: 'Drum hab' ich mich der Magie ergeben, | Ob mir, durch Geistes Kraft und Mund, | Nicht manch Geheimnis würde kund' [That is why I gave myself over to magic, that, through the power and intercession of the spirit world, I might perhaps discover many a secret] (377–79); 'Und dies geheimnisvolle Buch, | Von Nostradamus eigner Hand, | Ist dir es nicht Geleit genug?' [And this book of secrets, by Nostradamus's own hand, is it not guide enough for you?] (419–21). As we saw in the *Wanderjahre*, the notion of the secret is closely related to that of the ideal (and Mephisto's ironic tone throughout the scene does nothing to change this): both are essential, but essentially hidden 'im tiefsten, allertiefsten Grund' [in the deepest depths] (6284). This first attempt to bring Helena back to life does not involve time-travel, but travel *beyond* time, and beyond space: 'Entfliehe dem Entstandnen, | In der Gebilde losgebundne Räume' [Flee from all that has been created, into the unbound realm of patterns] (6276–77). The 'Bilder aller Kreatur' [images of all the animal world] (6289) which surround 'die Mütter', the 'Schemen' [silhouettes] (6290) which they see are the essential, eternal forms — 'des ewigen Sinnes ewige Unterhaltung' [the eternal play of the eternal mind] (6287) — which both precede and outlast the manifold variations which appear in historical time: 'Gestaltung, Umgestaltung' [Formation, transformation] (6286). The Helena whom Faust, as a result of his visit to that realm, is able to conjure in 'Rittersaal' [Hall of the Knights] is not yet a historical figure, as she is in Act III, but the pure idea. Faust's attempt to embrace her is the equivalent of looking directly at the sun, or of imagining himself to be the equal of the Erdgeist. The explosion which knocks him unconscious is a renewed reminder of his limitations, and of the need for a mediating force in the search for the ideal.

Act I also inaugurates an important pattern in Part II: Faust's tendency, namely to confuse spectacle or artifice with reality, even when the show is of his own making. The involvement of 'die Mütter' means that there is more to this interlude than the sophisticated masks and conjuring tricks of the Mummenschanz [masque],[31] as, indeed, first the Herald and then the Astrologer suggest, with an element of enjoyment of their own portentous tones: 'Mein alt Geschäft, das Schauspiel anzukünden, | Verkümmert mir der Geister heimlich Walten' [My old task of announcing the spectacle is now confounded by the secret workings of spirits] (6377–78). But although the power conferred on Faust by 'die Mütter' exceeds his understanding, he has sufficient insight to use it in his orchestration of the shadow play for the court. Indeed, the clever juxtaposition of 'Geister' and 'Meister' by the Astrologer (6443) is a reminder that these shadows, these ideas are not moving freely at this point, but are being manipulated before our eyes. It is, as Mephistopheles observes, sheer folly for Faust, like Pygmalion before him, to become infatuated with a being whom he has invoked, if not actually created: 'So faßt euch doch, und fallt nicht aus der Rolle!' [Just pull yourself together, and keep to your role!] (6501), 'Machst du's doch selbst, das Fratzengeisterspiel' [It's your own work, this ghastly spirit play] (6547). Faust is at this point hardly any more discerning than the populace in 'Weitläufiger Saal' ['Spacious Hall'], who are so caught up in the masque that the illusion is only dispelled when the trinkets at which they grasp become insects, and the contents of the treasure chest become molten and spurt into their faces. The irony, of course, is that Faust himself, in his guise as Plutus, was responsible for this second transformation, using the Herald's staff to transform the treasure, and thus that he 'has also not absorbed the lesson he himself gave'.[32] This inability to learn, too, becomes an established pattern in Part II.

Illusion is one of the guiding themes of Act I, including the scenes preceding 'Rittersaal'. Not only is it played out on stage, in the form of the disguises adopted by the players in the *Mummenschanz*, but it is also an inherent preoccupation of the type of theatre which this act emulates, namely, as Jane Brown writes, 'world theatre':

> The essential difference between world theater and Aristotelian drama is that the first is not mimetic. The action is [...] rather a game or play that observes certain given conventions, as the very word *play* suggests. The frequency of the play-within-the-play motif in Shakespeare, Calderón, and *Faust* reflects the extreme self-consciousness of such texts with regard to this trait.[33]

Once again, Act I has a pronounced quality of literariness: Brown shows, for example, that Goethe both revives and radically modernizes the Jonsonian court masque in the Mummenschanz.[34] Moreover, in spite of its large scale and grand design, Act I does not make excessive claims for its powers of representation. The crucial moment, Faust's visit to 'die Mütter', is not shown. This is not to say that (within the magical world of the play) it does not happen,[35] but simply that it is recognized as an event and a realm which lies beyond anything that art, that theatre and poetry can represent. This poetic self-limitation can also be detected in the framing of the episode. The elements of parody and humour — such as the excessive theatricality of Faust's exit ('FAUST *stampft und versinkt*' [Faust stamps and sinks into the stage]), or Mephisto's ironic tone throughout — do not detract from the essential seriousness of the episode (although it need not be read with excessive seriousness for this to be appreciated). Rather, as with Makarie in the *Wanderjahre*, the humour is an acknowledgement of the insufficiency of our attempts to grasp the Absolute, or even to write about it. Thus the resolute awareness in the play of the pervasiveness of illusion and of the limitations of art clearly surpass Faust's own capabilities in this act. Act I operates at the very high level of self-consciousness which we shall come to expect in *Faust II*, and is the first major example of the disjunction between the play and its central character.

The first scene of Act II announces the theme of the return of, or to, the past. It is a move into the past: but this is a past that is marked by decay. Faust's study, to which we have returned, is even gloomier and more run down than it was at the beginning of Part I. Though it appears 'unverändert' [unchanged] in the main, Mephistopheles notes that:

> Die bunten Scheiben sind, so dünkt mich, trüber,
> Die Spinneweben haben sich vermehrt;
> Die Dinte starrt, vergilbt ist das Papier [...] (6572–74)

[The stained glass seems to have dulled, the spiders' webs have multiplied; the ink has congealed, the paper is yellowed.]

This state of things is, of course, a source of great satisfaction for him: he rejoices in the swarm of insects which burst out of Faust's coat and which live off death, as do the crickets which inhabit the 'Hohlaug' jener Totenköpfe' [eye sockets of those skulls] where they lead their 'Moderleben' [life of decay] (6613–15). Yet this decaying and indeed hated past can hardly be the lost ideal which is sought: the 'hochgewölbtes enges, gotisches Zimmer' [high-vaulted, narrow gothic room] was, after all, a prison for Faust in his unhappiness in Part I. Faust is searching not just for any past, but for one projected as a better place. The words of Homunkulus make clear that this is to be the role of the 'Klassische Walpurgisnacht' ['Classical Walpurgis Night']:

> Jetzt eben, wie ich schnell bedacht,
> Ist klassische Walpurgisnacht:
> Das Beste was begegnen könnte
> Bringt ihn zu seinem Elemente. (6942–43)

[It occurs to be that now, this very minute, is the Classical Walpurgis Night: what could be better, he will be in his element.]

More can be read into that last line: the German construction (literally 'will bring him to his element') suggests not only that he will feel at home, but also that he will meet his 'Element', both his own true self and the ideal beauty of which or of whom he dreams. Moreover, the disparaging remark which Homunkulus makes to Mephisto, 'Im Düstern bist du nur zu Hause' [You are only at home in darkness] (6927), suggests that a move south-eastwards (6951) to a lighter, brighter place, to the southern Mediterranean of the ancient world, is required to restore clarity of vision to those from the North, caught up in the 'Wust von Rittertum und Pfäfferei' [jumble of knights and clerics] (6925). Thus the search for the ideal begins to work on two levels: Faust's personal longing overlaps with a broader cultural quest for an improvement to the present situation, carried out in the spirit of late eighteenth-century philhellenism.[36] Yet Homunkulus adds a qualifier: 'Romantische Gespenster kennt ihr nur allein, | Ein echt Gespenst auch klassisch hat's zu sein' [You only know romantic ghosts; for a ghost to be genuine it must also be classical] (6946–47). The mischievous double use of 'Gespenst' introduces an element of doubt into the undertaking: the question, namely, whether the supposed revival of the past can be much more than a ghostly image.

Certainly, Faust travels in the 'Klassische Walpurgisnacht' in the belief that it *is* possible. He greets each mythological figure whom he encounters with breathless delight: 'Wie wunderbar! das Anschaun tut mir Gnüge, | Im Widerwärtigen große tüchtige Züge' [How wonderful! A satisfying sight and their features, though repulsive, are grand] (7181–82) — although he appears oblivious to the irony that, at the high point of his search for the embodiment of the ideal, he encounters so many strange bodies. Moreover, the vision of Leda and her companions bathing, stimulated by the suggestive language and sight of the nymphs, leaves Faust profoundly moved. The strange sensation of bliss which he describes is aroused not only by the sensuous beauty of the maidens, but by the return in his mind of a similar moment from his own, personal history:

> So wunderbar bin ich durchdrungen.
> Sind's Träume? Sind's Erinnerungen?
> Schon einmal warst du so beglückt. (7274–76)

[How strangely, how intensely I am moved. Are these dreams? Are they memories? You knew such bliss once before.]

This 'schon einmal' is both his recent dream in 'Laboratorium', which dwelt on a similar scene, and a more distant, but more real, experience, namely the love which he shared with Margarete. It is the apparent resurrection of a perfect moment, now past, which overwhelms Faust here; and his pursuit of Helena is motivated by a similar desire for revival: 'Und sollt *ich* nicht, sehnsüchtigster Gewalt, | Ins Leben ziehn die einzigste Gestalt?' [And should *I* not, by the power of all my yearning, bring to life that most unique form?] (7438–39). He seeks the past exactly as it was. Towards the opening of the scene, Faust lists what he recognizes from accounts he has read as if he were a tourist of the ancient world, with that world genuinely restored before his eyes: 'Vor solchen hat einst Ödipus gestanden' [Oedipus once stood before similar beings] (7185), etc. He continues his historical tourism with Chiron, who half complies, and Faust tries to move in conversation through a catalogue of past heroes until he reaches Helena, '[die] schönste [...] Frau' [the most beautiful woman] (7398), 'mein einziges Begehren' [the sole object of my desire] (7412). The terms in which he speaks of her make clear her status as his ideal: 'die einzigste Gestalt, | Das ewige Wesen' [the most unique form, the eternal being] (7439–40), that is, the ultimate form, eternal in its validity, realized once, now lost. In spite of Chiron's scepticism (7446–47), Faust once again insists on trying to grasp the absolute, or, in Manto's words, 'Unmögliches' [the impossible] (7488). Convinced that, having moved back into the ancient world, and forward from the time of the pre-Olympian creatures with which the 'Klassische Walpurgisnacht' opens, he has at last reached Helena's own era, Faust descends out of time, into the deathly realm of Persephone, in order finally to bring her back to life.

Yet it is made clear from the start of the 'Klassische Walpurgisnacht' that the realm that we have entered is something other than the classical past of which it seems to remind us. The characters are strikingly aware of their legendary status: that is, of what has been said and written about them since the time when they originally 'lived'. Erichtho refers bitterly to her characterization by Lucan in the *Pharsalia*:

> Nicht so abscheulich wie die leidigen Dichter mich
> Im Übermaß verlästern [...] Endigen sie doch nie,
> In Lob und Tadel [...] (7007–09)

[I am not so abominable as those tiresome poets, with their exaggerated, slanderous portraits, would have me be [...] They never know when to stop, be it in praise or censure.]

The Sphinxes likewise demonstrate a preternatural awareness of developments after their own time, for they are able to tell Faust, who is looking for Helena: 'Wir reichen nicht hinauf zu ihren Tagen, | Die letztesten hat Herkules erschlagen' [We did not last until her day, for Hercules slew the last of us] (7197–98). Indeed, for all that the scene is entitled '*Klassische* Walpurgisnacht', the figures which inhabit it are not particularly 'classical': as Albrecht Schöne notes, their world is not that of Olympian gods and Homeric heroes, who are not represented in this scene.[37] It is, rather, an imaginative distortion of the classical world, just as the 'Walpurgisnacht' in Part I is a distortion of a modern, Germanic reality. The figures in the 'Klassische Walpurgisnacht' are the dream-figures of the ancient world as imagined by a modern mind (that is to say, by Goethe). Indeed, Heinz Schlaffer goes so far as to contend that: 'Die Antike in *Faust II* ist ein vergegenständlichter Bewußtseinsinhalt der Moderne' [The ancient world in *Faust II* is the objectified content of the modern consciousness].[38] It is significant also that Homunkulus pits 'klassisch' against 'romantisch' in lines 6946–47, for this itself is an act of literary historicization. It signals that the major literary and philosophical developments in Weimar and Jena around the turn of the nineteenth century, to which Homunkulus's words are a subtle allusion, have themselves become history for the very late Goethe: for the literary-historical terms 'klassisch' and 'romantisch' which he puts into Homunkulus's mouth, and which have become commonplaces for us, were applied retrospectively, rather than by the actual exponents of those movements.[39] Just as the figures in the scene are able to recognize the place of their existence on the temporal continuum, so their poet acknowledges the passing of stages of his personal development into history. The decision to populate the 'Klassische Walpurgisnacht' with unclassical figures is perhaps an implicit interrogation of the accuracy or usefulness of the word 'klassisch'. It has become synonymous with antiquity, with the world of the Greeks; but although this appears a very solid concept it has, in fact, always been rather nebulous, as Charles Grair indicates:

> For writers at the close of the eighteenth century, 'antiquity' did not signify a coherent historical or philosophical system; it was rather [...] an absent ideal that reflected the dreams and ambitions of artists and their frustrations with their own imperfect age.[40]

The 'classical' world, then, is one that has been imagined and reimagined more times than we tend to realize; and the apparently incongruous choice of figures here perhaps reflects the element of arbitrariness that obtains in how we recreate the past, and in the names which we give to our versions.

The setting of the 'Klassische Walpurgisnacht' is thus not the ancient past as it once happened, but that past as it has been worked up by historians and by poets ever since — often using characters who were always only imagined. This process is at its most complex in the marine pageant with which the act closes. The glory of creation is celebrated in the idiom of Greek mythology. Galatea, the figure at the pinnacle of the festivities, emerges from Cyprus (8359), and her procession is 'Angelernt vor alten Zeiten' [Learnt in times of old] (8354). In a sense, she acts as Homunkulus's ideal in his search for form: she is the *telos* of his journey to the source of life, from the starting point of the sterile German laboratory. Yet, in artistic terms, the scene is anything but a straightforward return to the ancient world. Even the reference to Cyprus is trans-historical, for it is followed by allusions to the various powers who ruled the island during and after antiquity: the lines 'Wir leise Geschäftigen scheuen |

Weder Adler noch geflügelten Leuen, | Weder Kreuz noch Mond' [We, who go quietly about our business, fear neither the eagle nor the winged lion, neither the cross nor the crescent] (8370–72) refer to the symbols of Rome, Venice, the Crusaders and the Ottoman Empire respectively. Jane Brown traces the bewildering variety of sources upon which Goethe drew in the composition of this scene: from Ovid's *Metamorphoses* and the *Histories* of Herodotus, to the paintings of Raphael and Botticelli for his own version of Galatea; and she shows that, throughout the act, 'the implicit history of ancient sculpture is mediated by Renaissance images with which Goethe had had much more direct experience'.[41] The past which we witness in the 'Klassische Walpurgisnacht' is thus not the pure past which Faust, perhaps, believes he has entered; rather, it is the accretion, layer upon layer, of literary and artistic developments through the centuries. Brown concludes that 'the act [is not simply] framed by Renaissance gestures but [...] the 'recovery of antiquity' in the act is at every moment self-consciously modern'.[42] What is recovered, then, is a past mediated through, and shaped by, memory, both personal and cultural, and by other developments leading up to the present.

The self-consciousness of the scene is clinched by the poetic irony which runs through it: the gentle self-parody which indicates to the audience that this crucial episode is both serious and playful, an intellectual game as well as an earnest exploration of the past and our relation to it. Erichtho's lamentation of her mis-representation at the hands of 'die leidigen Dichter' (7007), for example, is an ironic, or self-ironic, meditation on the role of poets in the telling of history and the making of culture, one which casts them as meddling and inaccurate (although scholars, 'Philologen', receive similarly short shrift from Chiron in lines 7427–28). We have already seen something similar in the Mummenschanz in Act I: in the lines of the 'Satiriker' — 'Wißt ihr was mich Poeten | Erst recht erfreuen sollte? | Dürft ich singen und reden | Was niemand hören wollte' [Do you know what would truly make me happy as a poet? If I could only sing and say what no one wants to hear] (5295–98) — or in the remarkable stage direction, immediately following the satirist's words: 'Die Nacht- und Grabdichter lassen sich entschuldigen, weil sie soeben im interessantesten Gespräch mit einem frisch erstandenen Vampiren begriffen seien' [The night and graveyard poets make their apologies, for they are in the middle of an interesting conversation with a freshly resurrected vampire]. Although this second example is a gibe specifically directed at 'die neuste Art der Autoren, welche sich mit dem Abscheulichen abgeben' [the most recent breed of writer, with their fascination for the abominable],[43] both Act I and Act II are the work of a poet not above smiling at his own profession. Moreover, the 'Greisen'/'Greifen' pun in lines 7092–94, and the ensuing game of etymology, is a moment of reflection on two fundamentals of poetry: the sound and sense relations between words which give life to it, and the bibliographical forms in which it is recorded. The amusing confusion between 'Greisen' [old man] and 'Greifen' [gryphon], which derives from the similarity of the letters 's' and 'f' in *Fraktur* (as well as from Mephistopheles's compulsion to mock), pulls the audience briefly out of the rarefied mythological and phantasmagorical atmosphere, and into the most basic, material reality of texts. Moments such as these, together with the complex historical consciousness of the episode, ensure that it functions at a level of awareness, of 'knowingness', beyond anything that Faust demonstrates. This is most clearly expressed in the exchange with Chiron: in response to his words 'G'nug, den Poeten bindet keine Zeit' [In short, the poet is not bound by time] (7433), Faust responds: 'So sei auch sie [Helena] durch keine Zeit gebunden!' [Then let Helena, too, be not bound by time!] (7434). Once again, Faust muddles poetic with empirical reality. The point which Chiron was making, and which is made repeatedly through the form of the scene, is that poetry may conjure up a legendary figure, may fashion her over and over: 'Ganz eigen ist's mit mythologischer Frau; | Der Dichter bringt sie, wie er's braucht zur Schau' [It is quite different with the mythical woman; the poet depicts her as he requires] (7428–29). But this is not the same as plucking her unchanged from the realms of the past, even of death, which is what Faust takes Chiron to mean. The consequences of this misapprehension are explored in Act III, when it becomes clear that the embodied ideal beauty contained in the realm of Persephone (to which Faust descends in the 'Klassische Walpurgisnacht', as he descended to 'die Mütter' for the pure idea) cannot become historical reality for a second time.

The loss and return of the past

In Act III, the multiple difficulties attendant upon the attempt to recover the past come fully to the fore. There is Helena's longing, and the denial of that longing, to return to her own past; and the whole act depicts a failed attempt to pluck life from the dead, to achieve a revival which is more than ghostly.[44] When we meet Helena, she is profoundly aware that her person has already become the stuff of legends. Her first words, 'Bewundert viel und viel gescholten Helena' [Helena, much admired and much cursed] (8488), resonate with those of Erichtho, and especially with the Gryphon's line: 'Zwar oft gescholten, mehr jedoch gelobt' [Oft cursed, it is true, but praised more often still] (7101). Her use of the third person in respect of herself signals her awareness that, owing to the work of *fama*, of admiration and envy, of gossip and storytelling, her name is heavy with history. As the scene progresses, it transpires that this fictional 'superidentity' has almost come to overshadow the 'real' person who she so desperately tries to be. The first words of the chorus reflect this: 'Denn das größte Glück ist dir einzig beschert, | Der Schönheit *Ruhm* der vor allen sich hebt' [For you alone have been granted the greatest happiness of all, the *fame* of beauty, which rises above all else] (8518–19; my emphasis). The implication here is that the reputation of her beauty, the stories which are told about it, have become more significant than the quality itself — a development which is not quite so great a 'Glück' as the chorus supposes. Later, it becomes clear that Helena has undergone so many different representations that she herself no longer knows who she is, or where she has come from:

> Ist's wohl Gedächtnis? war es Wahn, der mich ergreift?
> War ich das alles? Bin ich's? Werd ich's künftig sein,
> Das Traum- und Schreckbild jener Städteverwüstenden? (8838–40)

[Can it be memory? is it madness that seizes me? Was I all those things? Am I now? In times to come, shall I still be dream and nightmare to those city-destroyers?]

Her confusion here is a variant of the problem of self-knowledge which with Faust grappled in 'Nacht'. She, too, struggles to locate or maintain a stable personal identity: for history has made of 'Helena' a character-construct related to, but distinct from, her 'true' self. Phorkyas picks up the word 'Bild' from Helena's own usage to torment her with the sense that any uniqueness or idiosyncrasy is now denied her: 'Doch sagt man, du erschienst ein doppelhaft Gebild, | In Ilios gesehen und in Ägypten auch' [Yet they say that your image appeared twice, seen in Ilios and in Egypt too] (8872–73). The notion 'ein doppelhaft Gebild' is itself a reference to one of the literary versions of her story, namely Euripides' *Helena*.[45] This detail only serves to reinforce what Phorkyas implies here, namely that Helena's existence is no longer one of flesh and blood, but that of an imagined reality in the minds of many. She has been reduced to a mere image or illusion, and one which can easily be multiplied. As Helena's last words before her swoon make plain — 'Ich schwinde hin und werde selbst mir ein Idol' [I fade away, and become an idol even to myself] (8881) — the accumulation of so many fictions leads ultimately to the effacement of any 'true' identity. Jane Brown is correct in her assertion that Helena recovers her strength by deciding to embrace artificiality:

> Helen [...] first gives up her consciousness of herself (she faints); but when she awakens it is to become conscious of herself not as a sentient but as an artificial being. Rousseau's Galatea steps down from her pedestal; Goethe's Helen does the reverse when she becomes herself a statue (*Idol*, l. 8881).[46]

Yet it will become increasingly clear throughout the act that artificiality cannot compensate indefinitely for a lost connection to the world, and to oneself.

Closely linked to this entanglement in narratives is the disorientation which results from trying to recapture a lost essence. The desire to escape from a recent past by moving into a deeper past governs Helena's first two speeches. Standing before her home in Sparta, she cries: 'Laßt mich hinein! und alles bleibe hinter mir, | Was mich umstürmte bis hierher, verhängnisvoll' [Let me in! And may all the fateful turmoil that has hitherto surrounded me be left behind] (8508–09). Both speeches are replete with the language of return and repetition: *Rückkehr, wieder, wiederkehrend*. This combines with the recurring references to family and childhood — *Vater, schwesterlich*, even *vaterländisch* — to fuel the expectation, both within Helena and for us, that this will be a return to origins, an opportunity to recapture a lost essence. Yet she falters as she mounts the stairs of the house so 'lang entbehrt, und viel ersehnt, und fast verscherzt' [long absent, much missed, and almost forfeited for ever] (8606); it is as though, in the moment when that sense of loss is met by the potential for recovery, the result is in fact the realization for Helena of the *distance* that has opened up between her past, embodied in the family house, and her present state. The words of the chorus, though positive in tone, reflect this disparity between past and present: the house hovers between two epochs in their description, 'das alte das neugeschmückte' [the old, newly adorned]; and the anticipation is that Helena will here reflect upon, *gedenken*, rather than relive her youth. The sense of difference in similarity which the chorus articulates in sympathy with Helena becomes a violent rupture with the introduction of Mephistopheles-Phorkyas, the sinister figure who bars Helena's way to 'dem Schoße des Herdes'

(8674), the hearth and heart of her home, the symbolic point of origin. Phorkyas has been described as 'the agent of historical change';[47] but her first appearance in this act serves also to remind us of the heaving, disturbing mass of time which settles itself between those lost origins which we long to recover, and the place to which history has brought us. A spirit of ugliness, she is the direct antithesis of Helena: and her physical appearance reminds us that passing time disfigures as well as nourishes. The 'hohle[r], blutig-trübe[r] Blick' [hollow gaze, clouded with blood] (8689) into which Helena runs as she tries to flee confronts her once again with the yawning gap (hohl) left within her by what she has lost, and by the terrible cloudiness (trüb) of the retrospective, remembering Blick which tries to recover it. Through the personal crisis which this episode unleashes for Helena, we witness the dizzying nature of dislocation from one's origins, which throws into question not just where one has come from, but where one is going to: Phorkyas also bars Helena's way out as she tries to flee the house. Thus the scene resonates with the insights offered by Goethe's autobiographical writings into the difficulty of uncovering the past, and in particular with that closing sentence of Dichtung und Wahrheit IV: 'Erinnert er sich doch kaum, woher er kam' [For he can scarce remember whence he came].[48]

These details, which expose the difficulty of recovering the past, are crucial for our understanding of the rest of the act. Continuing the trend established in Act II, the search for personal origins is replicated on the cultural level. Just as Helena seeks a return to a more innocent period of her life, so the quest of the second scene is to bring a deep, remote past — the Classical era, the cradle of Western civilization — into the present via a more recent, recognizably Germanic, past. The journey of collective memory moves further and further into the realms of fiction. Accepting that she cannot go back, Helena makes radical steps forward, familiarizing herself with the trappings of the medieval world, and mastering a 'newer' prosody. Whereas 'Vor dem Palaste des Menelas' [Before Menelaus's Palace] is written in unrhymed iambic trimeters, the principal metre of Greek tragedy, Helena begins in 'Innerer Burghof' [Inner Courtyard] to speak in blank verse, associated both with Shakespeare and with Goethe's own 'classical' plays, before learning finally, with Faust's help, to rhyme. Faust for his part prepares to meet Helena by moving backwards in time once again, now fashioning himself into a medieval knight, and celebrating the perfection of his lady in the manner of the courtly lyric: 'Erst knieend laß die treue Widmung dir | Gefallen, hohe Frau' [On bent knee I beg that you accept my faithful dedication, most gracious lady] (9359–60). For a time, the union appears to be a success. The chorus dwells in the second scene on the rapidly developing proximity of the two:

> Nah und näher sitzen sie schon
> Aneinander gelehnet,
> Schulter an Schulter, Knie an Knie,
> Hand in Hand wiegen sie sich [...] (9401–04)

[Nearer and nearer already they sit, leaning against one another, shoulder to shoulder, knee to knee, hand in hand they cradle one another]

This physical intimacy is entirely new, and marks a development since Faust's disastrous attempt to embrace the shadow-Helena in 'Rittersaal'. Each seems to bring to the other something that was missing. Absence cedes to presence: 'Ich fühle mich so fern und doch so nah, | Und sage nur zu gern: da bin ich! da!' [I feel so far away and yet so near, and all too willingly I say: here I am! Here!] (9411–12). And that which is foreign becomes familiar: 'In dich verwebt, dem Unbekannten treu' [Bound up in you, faithful to a stranger] (9416). But the ensuing episode with Euphorion makes it clear that, despite the flashes of inspiration that it can bring, the attempted rapprochement between disparate times is an inherently unstable process.

On the one hand, Euphorion embodies the bond between Faust and Helena, and seems to hold within himself the power to compensate for the sense of loss from which Helena in particular suffered before. She speaks of 'Das schön errungene | Mein, Dein und Sein' [That beautiful accomplishment, mine, yours, and his] (9733–34). Instead of being threatened with extinction as it had been previously, her sense of self, of 'mein', seems now to be given substance by the union which created Euphorion and which he perpetuates — a pattern which is reinforced here by the internal rhymes of the second line. But, despite the validation which he seems to afford his parents, and the swooning by the chorus over his beauty and energy ('All' unsre Herzen sind | All dir geneigt' [All our hearts are devoted to you], 9765–66), Euphorion is inherently insubstantial. His development, from conception to death, is telescoped into a few bursts of adolescent passion and activity. He is precociously formed when he is born, literally springing into life — 'da springt ein Knabe von der Frauen Schoß zum Manne' [a boy leaps from a woman's lap to his father] (9599) — and seeking greater independence with each single leap:

> Springt er auf den festen Boden, doch der Boden gegenwirkend
> Schnellt ihn zu der luft'gen Höhe, und im zweiten dritten Sprunge
> Rührt er an das Hochgewölb. (9604–06)

[He jumps on firm ground, yet the ground itself exerts contrary force and propels him into the airy heights, and as he leaps a second time, a third, he touches the vault on high]

He dies without reaching full maturity, as his distressed parents lament: 'Kaum ins Leben eingerufen, | Heitrem Tag gegeben kaum' [Scarce brought into the world, scarce held out to the bright day] (9877–78). The manic energy which is his life, but is also the death of him, is a sign of imbalance.[49] It is a reminder that he is the product of a process which is essentially anachronistic. For in the fictional play of his parents, two very disparate eras have been yoked together in a way which, though it has some creative potential, does not have enough substance to last. In his essay 'Klassiker und Romantiker in Italien, sich heftig bekämpfend' [Classics and Romantics in Italy, arguing fiercely] (1817), Goethe warns that an exclusive focus on the past will inhibit life in the present: 'wer bloß mit dem Vergangenen sich beschäftigt kommt zuletzt in Gefahr das Entschlafene, für uns mumienhafte, vertrocknet an sein Herz zu schließen' [those who only concern themselves with the past will eventually run the risk of clasping to his breast what has long since gone to sleep, something withered and mummy-like].[50] Although, by Act III, Faust has recognized the need for some guise which mediates between modernity and antiquity if he is to reach his Helena, the pseudo-medieval persona which he adopts is regressive. He dons a mask of selected features from a previous era, rather than undergoing a genuine, progressive transformation, and this deficiency is reflected in Euphorion's fate:

> in the 'Helena' as a whole it appears that a return to the past — a wedding of the modern-romantic to the ancient-classical — can only be impermanent and that the fruit of such a union can only be the imbalance, the instability, symbolized by Euphorion.[51]

The fraught opening of Act III was thus the presentiment, Euphorion's death the proof, of the difficulties, even dangers attendant upon any artificial recovery of the past.

Yet the ultimate failure of these various attempts at revival is by no means an endorsement of the cynical premise of the wager, namely that nothing is worth preserving, that each experience should be thrown off and the arrival of the next hastened. On the contrary, the work is driven by a passionate belief in the value of what is past, and of keeping it somehow alive in memory (though as an active presence, not a museum piece). There are suggestions in Act III that the past *can* genuinely be fused with the present, even if only for a moment. In 'Innerer Burghof', Faust and Helena are transported, with the aid of poetry, beyond normal time and space into an ideal realm: 'Es ist ein Traum, verschwunden Tag und Ort' [It is a dream, place and time have disappeared] (9414); and for a few lines, a real synergy of past and present, Classical and Germanic is achieved. The theme of rhyme, which Helena has learnt, suggests that a successful balance between disparate qualities has, temporarily, been reached: for rhyme depends for its existence on the interplay between similarity and difference. Moreover, both Faust and Helena are overwhelmed by a new sense of presence. Helena, who in the previous scene was tormented by the infinite regress into which her own identity was threatening to disappear, can now exclaim 'da bin ich! da!' (9412). With the words 'Dasein ist Pflicht und wärs ein Augenblick' [Being is our duty, even if it were only to last a moment] (9418), Faust, for his part, goes entirely against the grain of his own wager. There he had asserted that *Dasein*, existence *per se* as opposed to restless, ambitious activity, has no value: 'Werd' ich zum Augenblicke sagen: | Verweile doch! du bist so schön! | Dann magst du mich in Fesseln schlagen' [And if ever I should say of a single moment: Stay! you are so beautiful! | Then you may clap me in chains | Then I shall willingly go to my destruction!] (1699–1701).

That the moment in 'Innerer Burghof' is one of genuine synthesis, rather than a mere flight of fancy, is confirmed on the structural level. There, too, the past enters the present: for the poetic transport of Faust and Helena is a heightened version of the most sincere moment in Part I, namely the kiss in 'Ein Gartenhäuschen' ['A Summerhouse']. The stage directions for Margarete, *ihn fassend und den Kuß zurückgebend* [clasping him and returning the kiss], indicate that this is likewise a singular instance of reciprocity and balance, and one which will not be repeated on stage. The next time the word 'fassen' appears, it is in the context of absence and longing: 'Ach dürft' ich fassen | Und halten ihn!' [If I could only grasp him and hold him tight!] (3408–09), and the next time we see them kiss, it is frenzied and forced: 'Küsse mich! | Sonst küss' ich dich!' *Sie umfaßt ihn* [Kiss me! Or I shall kiss you! *She clasps and embraces him*] (4491–92). Moreover, this most serious moment in respect of Faust's character — the moment in which he can see beyond the wager — is also a high point of literary self-reflexivity: the discussion of rhyme is a metapoetic moment *par excellence*. Faust and Helena are aware of the fragility of what they have found: the words 'Und sage nur zu gern' (9412) and 'und wärs ein Augenblick' (9418) convey their presentiment that it will not last. And indeed, both the moment in the summerhouse and that in 'Innerer Burghof' are interrupted by Mephistopheles (the second time in the guise of Phorkyas). It is arguably that awareness, as opposed to the hubris which soon returns to Faust, which makes this moment distinct, and full of a potential which we have rarely seen in Faust's dealings in Part II. Act III may not appear to take a different course after this: Helena continues to rhyme, and her intimacy with Faust increases rather than diminishes. But the harmony has been disrupted with the entrance of Phorkyas; what follows is increasingly artificial and insubstantial, until it eventually collapses altogether.

Indeed, Phorkyas induces Faust, with almost predictable punctuality, to forget the consummate 'Augenblick' and to desire something grander, something more his own. Towards the end of the virtuosic speech through which Faust conjures up the *locus amoenus* to which the characters repair from the 'Innerer Burghof', he renounces memory in favour of (he thinks) a new ideal: 'So ist es mir, so ist es dir gelungen, | Vergangenheit sei hinter uns getan' [And it is my achievement and yours, let the past be put behind us] (9562–63). The hubris of this is made all the greater by the fact that, as Katharina Mommsen observes, the removal of Helena from Sparta to Arcadia is a transgression of the conditions set by Persephone.[52] Faust, it seems, has become convinced that he can cheat death, and can create, out of his own resources, a permanent and real dwelling for himself and his ideal: 'Noch zirkt, in ewiger Jugendkraft | Für uns, zu wonnevollem Bleiben, | Arkadien in Sparta's Nachbarschaft' [A place beckons, one of eternal youth, where we might endure in bliss — Arcadia, Sparta's neighbour] (9567–69). Yet Arcadia is little more than an imagined space: 'Was Faust mit Helena erlebt, ist phantasmagorische, nicht natürliche Wirklichkeit' [what Faust experiences with Helena is a phantasmagorical reality, not a natural one].[53] Time has long since ceased to be important — at the very latest since Helena and the chorus entered time's mists at the end of the first scene of this act — and now the domain is wholly that of the metaphorical. Euphorion, born of parents who are themselves players in an increasingly thick fantasy, is a fiction within a fiction — or as Eudo Mason has it in respect of the relationship of Faust and Helena, 'a dream within a dream'.[54] For all the semblance of control which the speech at the end of 'Innerer Burghof' lends Faust, the situation is, in fact, already spiralling out of control. He may have orchestrated the situation, but, as in Act I, he is drawn in to such an extent that he fails to keep sight of the problem which is plain for all to see. Whereas, in Act I, he mistook spectacle for reality, now he has mistaken death, or at best ghostliness, for life.[55]

The genuine recovery of an ideal, lost past can, therefore, only be momentary — if it happens at all. Yet the very difficulty of the undertaking renders it more important, not less: the ideal would not be ideal if it were easy of access. And, as we saw in the *Wanderjahre*, that access cannot be forced: it can only be given. After the poignancy and disappointment of the end of Act III, Act IV opens with one of the rare moments of reflective insight on Faust's part, and one which affirms the importance of memory. In a symbolic reading of the changing movements of the clouds, which represent Helena and Margarete, Faust watches the splendid focus of his recent past, 'ein göttergleiches Frauenbild' [the divine image of a woman] (10049), yield to a 'jugenderstes, längstentbehrtes höchstes Gut' [long-lost, greatest treasure of my earliest youth] (10059). Though this 'holde Form', the cirrus, which wafts round Faust in the second part of his monologue in 'Hochgebirg' ['High Mountains'], is from a more distant past than the other female form, she is — to judge even by the number of lines devoted to her — a stronger presence for Faust than her recently departed regal avatar. In the Helena cloud, the cumulus, Faust contemplates historic grandeur: 'Und spiegelt blendend flüchtger Tage großen Sinn' [And reflects the great meaning of fleeting days, dazzling me] (10054). The use of the word 'blendend' recalls the words of Phorkyas in 'Vor dem Palaste' ('Tritt hervor aus flüchtigen Wolken hohe Sonne dieses Tags, | Die verschleiert schon entzückte, blendend nun im Glanze herrscht' [The high sun of this day emerges from fleeting clouds, and though delightful when she was veiled, now, resplendent in her glory, she is dazzling], 8909–10), and links with the motif of turning away, blinded, to suggest a certain inaccessibility about this cloud; and indeed, Faust stands and observes it from a distance, 'Wie majestätisch lieblich mir's im Auge schwankt' [How majestic, how lovely it is as it hovers in my sight] (10051). The 'zarter lichter Nebelstreif' [gentle, light wisp of mist] (10055), by contrast, moves more intimately around him, caressing 'Brust und Stirn' [his breast and forehead] (10056), and causes treasured memories to burst forth from deep within him ('Des tiefsten Herzens frühste Schätze quollen auf' [the oldest treasures rise up from the bottom of my heart], 10060). In Part II, we rarely see Faust so moved as he is in the few lines dedicated to the cirrus. Again, this return of the past is repeated on the structural level: for the reminiscence of the early love which suddenly overwhelms Faust resonates with the opening poem of the play, 'Zueignung' ['Dedication'], itself a reflection on the mysterious interplay of past and present:

> Ihr bringt mit euch die Bilder froher Tage,
> Und manche liebe Schatten steigen auf;
> Gleich einer alten halbverklungnen Sage,
> Kommt erste Lieb' und Freundschaft mit herauf [...] (9–12)

> [You bring with you the images of happy days, and many dear shadows stir and rise; like an old legend, which has half died away, our first loves and friendships rise up too.]

This, then, is a moment full of memory: and early, formative experiences, however modest they appear, become vividly present. Here, fleetingly as in 'Innerer Burghof', Faust and *Faust* are almost at one, for the self-consciousness of *Er-innerung* — self-knowledge as knowledge of the past, 'das Beste meines Innern' [the best of my innermost soul] (10066) — brings the central character into step with the poetic mode of the play.

In his poem 'Howards Ehrengedächtnis' ['In Honour of Howard'] (1817), Goethe associates the cirrus with transcendence:[56] 'Doch immer höher steigt der edle Drang! | Erlösung ist ein himmlisch leichter Zwang' [Yet the noble impulse heads higher and higher! And with a heavenly, light compulsion comes redemption] (strophe headed *Zirrus*, lines 23–24). In 'Hochgebirg' likewise, the cirrus moves onwards, moves upwards, and, in an anticipation of the final scene of the play, takes part of Faust, 'das Beste meines Innern' (10066), with her. It becomes clear at this moment that Faust needs his past, and in particular this aspect of his past, to reach the ideal, whether it be beauty, now become spiritual, 'Seelenschönheit', or true self-knowledge, the fruition of 'das Beste meines Innern'. The love of Margarete was the most perfect experience he has known, as he attests with the words 'überglänzte jeden Schatz' [would outshine every treasure] (10063). Victor Lange claims: 'In diesem erinnernden Blick auf Vergehendes und Vergangenes sind die Voraussetzungen für die neuen letzten Lebensstufen gestaltet, der heroische Wille zur Tat und der Glaube an jenes "Beste meines Innern"' [This retrospective survey of things passing and things past forms the conditions for the next steps in this last part of Faust's life, the heroic will to act and the belief in 'the best of my innermost soul'].[57] Yet the cirrus draws the best of his self away, 'mit sich *fort*' (10066, my emphasis), and the Faust who remains is worse off. Faust's 'erinnernder Blick' *could* be the precondition for better things; but Lange does not recognize that, like the poetic transport in 'Innerer Burghof', this moment of reminiscence and insight cannot last, nor is he alive to the critical and tragic elements of Acts IV and V.

The events which follow do *not* unfold in memory of Margarete: quite the contrary.[58] She has gone once more, and it is that obliteration of a better influence which causes things to take the terrible turn that they do, particularly in Act V. Eudo Mason writes that:

> Mephisto now rejoins Faust, who sets out on further adventures. Helena is completely banished from his mind, as Gretchen had been. He never recalls her, expresses no regret for her loss, and seems to have learnt nothing of what might have been learnt from his encounter with her.[59]

This is not quite true: Faust *has* learned something. The lines 'Den schnellempfundnen, ersten, kaum verstandnen Blick, | Der, festgehalten, überglänzte jeden Schatz' [That first, fleetingly felt gaze, scarcely understood, which, had it been held, would have outshone every treasure] (10062–63) show that he has come to appreciate the value of permanence: the loving gaze of which he speaks becomes resplendent when it has crystallized from a fleeting thrill ('schnellempfunden') into a quality which endures and, presumably, is reciprocal. Moreover, he recognizes that this is an experience which slipped through his grasp: for 'überglänzte' is in the subjunctive, and is conditional upon 'festgehalten'. The problem is that 'festhalten' [to hold on to, hold tight] is something which he was and is still unable to do — or, rather, which he is contracted by the terms of the wager not to do. Faust's fundamental error is that he has committed himself to forgetting, and so must rush from one situation to the next without allowing the insights gained from experience time to work.[60] The monologue in 'Hochgebirg', like the flash of recognition at the waterfall in 'Anmutige Gegend', is a rare reflective pause; but the wisdom and, crucially, the self-understanding which Faust shows does not, in either case, carry over into what follows. What Faust senses in the final line of his monologue, as he watches the Gretchen cloud float away, and just before Mephistopheles steps back into the foreground, is that he is soon to forget her again.

The rejection of the past and delusions of a future

Through Acts IV and V, Faust's attention shifts from the past to the future, and the search for the ideal is more or less displaced by a desire for domination. Faust's description in 'Hochgebirg' of his plans 'Das herrische Meer vom Ufer auszu-schließen, | Der feuchten Breite Grenzen zu verengen | Und, weit hinein, sie in sich selbst zu drängen' [To expel the imperious sea from the shore, to narrow the borders of that great wet plain, and to drive it far into itself] (10029–31) differs significantly in tone from the opening of the scene. That moment, 'staunend' [full of wonder] (10045), 'entzückend' [delightful] (10058), has yielded to a bitter competitiveness, especially against the forces of nature, as if Faust were once again rising to the taunts of the Erdgeist: 'Da wagt mein Geist sich selbst zu überfliegen, | Hier möcht' ich kämpfen, dies möcht ich besiegen' [My daring spirit outdoes itself, here I wish to fight, this I wish to conquer] (10220–21). By Act V, his plans have taken a markedly subjectivist turn, expressed here in the proliferation of first-person pronouns and possessive pronouns:

> Die wenig Bäume, nicht mein eigen,
> Verderben mir den Welt-Besitz.
> Dort wollt ich, weit umher zu schauen,
> Von Ast zu Ast Gerüste bauen,
> Dem Blick eröffnen weite Bahn,
> Zu sehn was alles ich getan [...] (11241–46)

[The few trees which are not mine spoil the world, which is my possession. I wanted to build platforms from branch to branch, to survey the land for miles around, to broaden the view, to look upon all that I have done.]

This is arguably nothing more than a politicized version of the desire he expressed in 'Studierzimmer II': 'Und was der ganzen Menschheit zugeteilt ist | Will ich in meinem innern Selbst genießen' [And I wish to experience the pleasure of man's whole lot within my inner self] (1771–72). The boundaries of his own self have come (in his mind) to overlap with the boundaries of the territory over which he presides — and his ambition in both cases is for there to be no boundaries at all. The moment of insight in 'Anmutige Gegend', 'Am farbigen Abglanz haben wir das Leben' (4727), has long since been forgotten. The coastal lands which Faust exploits in Act V are a reward from the Emperor for his 'service'; but the record of Act IV provides a base as solid as quicksand for Faust's ambitions. The victory over the Anti-Emperor is brought about by multiple deceptions — deceptions by Faust, but, as Ulrich Gaier observes, also *of* Faust.[61] Faust is as entangled as ever in Mephisto's dangerous game, and his visions of future mastery are predicated on dependence — a condition which, for Gaier, is peculiarly characteristic of the age of technological advancement.[62]

In Act V, grandiose plans for the future are coupled with a rejection of the past. Philemon and Baucis are not only very elderly — 'Alt schon jener Tage' [Old even in those days] (11054) — but they are also figures residual from another era. They bear the names given by Ovid, at a point when the play has moved through the Napoleonic wars[63] (Act IV) into an image of industrial and technological modernization; and the frantic rate of that development jars with, indeed ultimately stamps out, the 'vita beata' which they represent.[64] The terms in which Faust describes his frustration with Philemon and Baucis are revealing: 'Vor Augen ist mein Reich unendlich, | Im Rücken neckt mich der Verdruß, | Erinnert mich durch neidische Laute: | Mein Hochbesitz er ist nicht rein' [My kingdom stretches infinite before my eyes, an irritation behind me nags away — those jealous sounds remind me that my great estate is not pure] (11153–56). The past ('im Rücken'), which they and their modest dwelling represent, interferes with his grandiose visions of the future ('vor Augen'). Moreover, that word 'erinnert' (11155) carries more weight than a simple reminder to Faust that his territory is not wholly in his possession: it is also the past *per se*, all that is 'behind him', of which he does not wish, or cannot bear, to be reminded. His exclamation 'Verdammtes Läuten!' [damned ringing] (11151) also makes this clear. Bells have always been evocative for him, and the irritation evident in 'verdammt' is arguably a sign of some suppressed emotional conflict; but whereas, in 'Nacht', he submitted to the call of the Easter bells and the heavenly choruses ('Erinnerung hält mich nun, mit kindlichem Gefühle, | Vom letzten, ernsten Schritt zurück' [Now memory, with childish feeling, restrains me from taking the last, grave step], 781–82), now he attempts to harden his heart against the past and memory. Although he deludes himself, as their home is engulfed by flames, that there will be a place for Philemon and Baucis in his new development — 'Da seh ich auch die neue Wohnung, | Die jenes alte Paar umschließt, | Das, im Gefühl großmütiger Schonung, | Der späten Tage froh genießt' [I can see the new dwelling, too, which will house that old pair, and, knowing that they have been generously spared, they shall spend their last days in good cheer] (11346–49) — his words beforehand make plain that, in his mind, nothing less than the eradication of this pair, and the past which they represent, will remove the obstacle which they pose to his future: 'Die Alten droben sollten weichen, | Die Linden wünscht ich mir zum Sitz, | Die wenig Bäume, nicht mein eigen, | Verderben mir den Welt-Besitz' [The old folk over there must move, I want the linden trees for my estate, etc.] (11239–42). Even if he does not envision their removal in the form orchestrated by Mephistopheles, he cannot tolerate their presence. Act V need not necessarily be understood as a critique of modernization, of technological advancement *per se*; rather, it seeks to expose the consequences of rushing headlong into a future projected as more advanced, and of trampling on the past, and all that is valuable about it, in the process.

Michael Jaeger's claim that Faust never feels any shame or remorse[65] is perhaps a little overstated. Faust is not entirely unrepentant: almost as soon as he has cursed Philemon and Baucis and 'Das verfluchte *hier*!' [this accursed word 'here'!] (11233), he pauses and says: 'Und wie ichs sage schäm' ich mich' [And no sooner have I said it than I feel ashamed] (11238). Similarly, the words 'mich, im Innern, | Verdrießt die ungeduldge Tat' [this over-hasty action sickens me to the stomach] (11341–42), suggest that Faust's actions, or Mephistopheles's interpretations of his wishes, go against his better instincts — and that he knows it. But Jaeger is right that Faust tends to flee from 'die moralischen Bedenken der Selbstreflexion' [the moral doubts stimulated by self-reflection].[66] Just as, in 'Wald und Höhle' in Part I, he rails against Mephistopheles's crude, cruel insinuations about Gretchen, but still allows himself to be complicit in her ruin ('Mag ihr Geschick auf mich zusammenstürzen | Und sie mit mir zu Grunde gehn' [May her fate crash down on me, and may she go to ruin with me], 3364–65), so here, neither his anticipation of disaster nor his remorse in its early stages is strong enough for him to change his course. Moreover, he comes close in 'Mitternacht' to expressing regret at the path which he has chosen: 'Könnt ich Magie von meinem Pfad entfernen | Die Zaubersprüche ganz und gar verlernen' [If I could but rid my path of magic, could purge the magic spells from my memory] (11404–05), 'Das war ich sonst, eh ich's im Düstern suchte, | Mit Frevelwort mich und die Welt verfluchte' [Such was I once, before I turned to search in darkness, and cursed myself and the world with heinous words] (11408–09). Yet, as with every other moment of insight on Faust's part, in 'Anmutige Gegend', in 'Hochgebirg', this one passes and is unsupported by change; he returns at the end of the scene to his destructive project, and the 'inner light' (11500) which he fancies that he perceives is another of his delusions. He is severely, almost wilfully, blinkered in Act V even before he is blinded by Sorge [Care]: he tries to wriggle out of acknowledging his own guilt in the Philemon and Baucis affair, just as he did in respect of Gretchen in 'Trüber Tag. Feld' ['Gloomy day. Field']; and he persists in seeing new beginnings in the destruction which Lynkeus describes in lines 11304–37 — which is the more vivid because it is fed directly into our imaginations, rather than being shown to us on stage — just as he later mistakes the sound of his own grave being dug for work on his kingdom (lines 11539–43).

Thus, although Faust is not wholly unreflective in Act V, indeed throughout Part II, he is incapable of sustaining those brief moments of understanding; and the overall result is that he learns very little. Moreover, subjectivism of the kind which he displays at the beginning of Act V is almost the opposite of self-awareness: for it is a refusal to recognize the limits of one's own self, and as such is a profoundly *unselfconscious* mode of being. It is in this respect that Faust, the character, and *Faust*, the play, diverge. For if Faust's career is marked for the most part by a lack of real awareness, by forgetfulness, resulting in a trajectory that is repeatedly two steps forward, one step back, the play itself is constantly developing, rooted in a past which is progressively heightened and transformed. Günther Mieth senses this kind of development in Part II:

> [Fausts letzter] Monolog [ist] durch das poetische Prinzip sich wechselseitig steigernder Spiegelungen strukturiert [...] Im Prozeß dieser Steigerung werden bei Faust bisher latente Qualitäten frei. Als *vollkommen* in seiner Art muß er *über seine Art hinausgehen*. Im Grunde transzendiert Faust seine geschichtliche Realität in Form einer *poetischen* Antizipation.[67]

> [Faust's final monologue is structured according to the poetic principle of reflections, which are engaged in a process of reciprocal heightening [...] This sets free qualities which have hitherto been latent in Faust. Because he has reached *perfection* in himself, he must *transcend himself*. In essence, Faust transcends his historical reality in the form of a *poetic* anticipation.]

Where Mieth is mistaken, I think, is in attributing this to Faust himself. Even if, as John Williams argues (following Eudo Mason's lead), the subjectivism of Faust's speeches early in Act V yields here to a desire to work more to the common good[68] — 'Eröffn' ich Räume vielen Millionen' [I shall open up space for many millions] (11563), 'Auf freiem Grund mit freiem Volke stehn' [Shall stand on free land with a free people] (11580) — the moment is too brief for it to be proof that he is now, in Mieth's terms, 'vollkommen', or in a position to anticipate being such.[69] Indeed, this is arguably another delusion, an ambition in the same unsupported vein as his belief in 'die neue Wohnung, | Die jenes alte Paar umschließt' [I can see the new dwelling, too, which will house that old pair] (11346–47). Moreover, personal interest has by no means disappeared from his plans, and he remains as reluctant as ever to accept his limitations: 'Es kann die Spur von meinen Erdetagen | Nicht in Äonen untergehn' [The trace of my earthly days cannot disappear into aeons] (11583–84). Even if Faust's final monologue does represent some minor development (and I am far from convinced that it does), this does not take place on the scale which Mieth and others suggest. The situation on the poetic level, however, is quite different.

Self-conscious poetry

We have seen throughout that the poetry of *Faust* runs counter to the blunderings of the character Faust.[70] Where he forgets, the work remembers; where, as in Act II, he is determined to uncover the past directly, the work offers a form of imitation which allows for variation. The work is replete with references to the artistic and literary past, which have 'the function of opening up the long perspective of the Western cultural inheritance':[71] that is to say, of the heritage from which the play draws inspiration and on which it builds. Harold Jantz makes even more of the presence of echoes and parallels with other works, arguing that: 'the implications of the poetic technique of symbolic extension are that the poet is active, deliberate, sovereign in his use of the past for the purpose of understanding the vistas and the relationships'.[72] Moreover, Part II resonates hundreds of times over, and deliberately, with Part I. Stuart Atkins uncovers any number of subtle parallels. He shows, for example, that Chiron is the 'converse of [...] the supernatural black horse'[73] which Faust once rode to reach the imprisoned Margarete, and that 'the absurdity of [Euphorion's] childhood without infancy' is a 'pathetic reminder that [Faust] never saw a child by Margarete'.[74] He also makes the interesting suggestion, by way of a parallel with Klärchen's appearance in the guise of Freiheit to the sleeping Egmont, that the vision of Helena in Part II, Act I may be 'imagined as Margarete in the classical dress so often worn by women in *tableaux vivants*'.[75] Reflections and echoes are an important manifestation of the self-consciousness of the work. As Charlie Louth observes: 'Self-questioning is already implicit in forms which imitate a mirror-like reflection: the reflection in the form points to a reflection on the form and thus to a self-reflection within the poem'.[76]

In the later acts of Part II, the level of allusiveness inevitably dips a little as we enter a phase concerned less with the past than with contemporary events (or with very recent history), and less overtly with poetry and myth than with war and technological advancement; but this is still self-conscious writing. Since the 'Prolog im Himmel', Mephistopheles has served as a 'witnessing figure [...] who moves between picture and frame',[77] and this role is made more explicit than ever in Act IV. Twice he addresses the audience directly (both lines 10210–11 and lines 10327–30 are marked *ad spectatores* in the stage directions) — three times if we take 'den Wissenden', in the stage directions preceding lines 10554–64, to mean, or at least to include, the audience. This direct address is equivalent to the interruptions by the narrator in the *Wanderjahre*, discussed in the previous chapter, and places him at an even further remove from the dramatic 'reality' than he is when he makes remarks under his breath which Faust does not hear (as in Part I, line 3325, 'Gelt! daß ich dich fange!' [I care not! I shall have you yet], marked *für sich* [*to himself*]), or when he is left alone to a soliloquy (as in Act I, 'Kaiserliche Pfalz', lines 5061–64): now he steps out of the picture *in medias res* rather than in the fading moment of a scene. By Act IV, then, Mephisto's movement between picture and frame serves *both* to provide an ironic commentary on Faust's progress,[78] *and* to remind the audience that they are party to a work that has been constructed, to action that can be paused at any time, rather than to unmediated reality (or, alternatively, to remind the reader that there is an audience). Once again, this is evidence of a poetry that can distance itself from itself.

Moreover, in addition to reflections of Part I, there are now also reflections of earlier scenes in Part II. Act IV, for example, shares a number of motifs with Act II. The conversation between Faust and Mephistopheles in 'Hochgebirg' about likely models for the development of the earth — a series of volcanic explosions versus gradual formation and reformation — recalls the debate between Thales and Anaxagoras in the 'Klassische Walpurgisnacht'. A number of fantastical characters are also reintroduced, including the Undinen, who are related in kind both to 'die Mütter' and to the daughters of Nereus, and the gryphon. This time, though, the gryphon — seen vying with an eagle in the sky — indicates a sea-change in Faust's attitude. His naive confusion of myth and reality yields to a delusion altogether more dangerous, that of power: 'Gib acht: gar günstig scheint es mir. | Greif ist ein fabelhaftes Tier; | Wie kann er sich so weit vergessen, | Mit echtem Adler sich zu messen?' [Pay attention: the omen seems favourable. The gryphon is a legendary creature; how can he so forget himself as to think himself equal to the eagle?] (10626–29). In Act V, 'Mangel', 'Not', 'Schuld', and 'Sorge' recall the allegorical figures ('die Grazien', 'die Parzen', 'die Furien', 'Furcht', 'Hoffnung' and 'Klugheit') in the Mummenschanz. The speech of 'Sorge' (the only one of the four who is given more than a line or two) is similar in cadence — half riddle, half timeless truth — to those of the figures in Act I; only this time, her words are not uttered in jest. The gravity of her presence is increased by the echo of Faust's own soliloquy in 'Nacht' in her words: 'Unruhig wiegt sie sich und störet Lust und Ruh; | Sie deckt sich stets mit neuen Masken zu' [She hovers restlessly, destroying rest and appetite; she always shrouds herself with different masks] (Faust, 646–47), 'In verwandelter Gestalt | Üb' ich grimmige Gewalt' [Transformed yet again I wield my terrible powers] (Sorge, 11426–27). The presence of which he tried to rid himself that night long ago returns in this, the last night of his life, in a more defined shape than ever.[79] The process of repeated reflection throughout Acts IV and V culminates, as we shall see, in 'Bergschluchten', the final scene.

As usual in Goethe's very late work, neither the allusions to Part I nor those to other literary and cultural sources are simple verbatim repetitions. Goethe's treatment of his numerous 'source' texts is always decidedly idiosyncratic: for example, with the novel inclusion in the *Urfaust* of Margarete's tragedy, his play is, from the earliest stages of its composition, as much of a departure from the traditional Faust legend as a confirmation of it. Moreover, as the examples from Stuart Atkins's commentary make plain, the events and motifs lifted from Part I undergo significant changes before they enter Part II. Implicit in Harold Jantz's term 'symbolic *extension*' (my emphasis), is the notion of growth and transformation: and Part II is yet another example of poetic *Steigerung*. The most striking example of this is the line of development that connects the two leading female figures: for Helena could be described as a *gesteigerte Margarete*. They are introduced together in Part I, Helena appearing immediately before Margarete's first entry; but Mephisto's sneering insinuation that the witch's potion is both an aphrodisiac and a hallucinogen — 'Du siehst, mit diesem Trank im Leibe, | Bald Helenen in jedem Weibe' [With that drink inside you, you will soon see Helen in every wench] (2603–04) — is hardly firm evidence that the two characters are related. It is, rather, their role in Faust's life which links them. Both provide Faust with a glimpse of the ideal: the moment in the summer house and its cognate in 'Innerer Burghof' represent 'Dasein' at its zenith, the possibility of which Faust had wagered against. Margarete does this by her love, Helena by the momentary restoration, in and through her presence, of a lost past. The two women are, of course, as different as they are similar. In social and aesthetic terms, Helena is quite literally a heightened version: the pretty but obscure young girl has been transformed into a queen and demigoddess, whose beauty is legend. Moreover, Helena is differentiated from Margarete by a degree of self-awareness. Helena is, as we have seen, acutely conscious of her own history, of the way in which others have described and perceived her. She also 'self-consciously learns to speak in the new manner'[80], that is, she appropriates with skill the stylized metre and rhyme-scheme of an epoch very distant from her own. Margarete, by contrast, is relatively unselfconscious, which is reflected in her speech: it is powerful because it is unadorned, and directly from the heart. Indeed, Faust admires this in her: 'Ach, daß die Einfalt, daß die Unschuld nie | Sich selbst und ihren heil'gen Wert erkennt!' [Ah, simplicity and innocence never knows itself, or its sacred worth!] (3102–03). She too has a story when Faust meets her, which she tells in 'Garten'; but although it is even more moving than that of Helena, it is of course much more concrete and narrower in scope. Part II is even more steeped in history than Part I, and the contrast between Helena and Margarete is typical of that development.

Yet the point of the process of *Steigerung* is not that the later avatar is wholly superior to the earlier one: the transformation is not complete with the donning of a 'mask of unsurpassable splendour', which for Stuart Atkins makes Margarete into Helena.[81] In 'Hochgebirg', the delicate cirrus rises above the cumulus: at that point, in other words, Margarete surpasses Helena. This suggests that *Steigerung* is a circular, or helical, development as much as a linear one, and that the deeper past, however much it is refined and embellished by what comes after it, never ceases to be important and to exert its influence. In 'Bergschluchten' ['Mountain Gorges'], Helena's majesty and Margarete's innate purity are finally brought together in the image of the Mater Gloriosa, and she transcends them both. The penitent woman 'sonst Gretchen genannt' [once called Gretchen] is, as Jane Brown observes, one of the 'more mediate manifestations' into which the Mater Gloriosa is 'repeatedly reflected and fragmented'.[82] The hideous distortion of motherhood which Faust's betrayal and Margarete's infanticide brings about in Part I is reversed as the immaculate figure, the transcendent mother in the Christian faith, calls to Margarete, 'Komm!' [Come!] (12094). Despite belonging to a very different tradition, Helena is also a relative of this figure. Doctor Marianus's paean to her, 'Lasse mich, im blauen, | Ausgespannten Himmelszelt | Dein Geheimnis schauen' [Let me look upon your mystery in the vast azure firmament] (11998–12000) recalls the adoration of Lynkeus, the *Turmwärter*, for Helena in Act III, which likewise dwells on the exceptionality of the adored, even in the infinite expanse of the universe: 'Statt der Erd- und Himmelsweite, | Sie die Einzige zu spähn' [To look not upon the vast expanses of heaven and earth, but upon her unique form] (9228–29). Moreover, Doctor Marianus describes her as 'Göttern ebenbürtig' [equal to the gods] — that is to say, as Albrecht Schöne observes, 'mit den gleichen Worten, die zuvor der antiken Helena galten' [with the same words which once were used in respect of Helena].[83] The Mater Gloriosa is not a conventional Catholic Madonna, as the culminating word in the phrase 'Jungfrau, Mutter, Königin, | *Göttin*' [Virgin, Mother, Queen, *Goddess*] (12102–03, my emphasis) makes plain. Rather, in her, the two figures most important to Faust are remembered and transformed. The connections between Margarete and Helena form the spine of the work, the most tangible points of intersection between Parts One and Two; and through those connections, the past is both upheld and transcended.

Goethe recognized that this was a more realistic way of preserving or reviving the past than is the attempt to reconstruct it exactly as it was. This principle has its roots in his much earlier writing on morphology, in which he argues that form is mobile, a continuous development:

> Betrachten wir aber alle Gestalten, besonders die organischen, so finden wir, daß nirgends ein Bestehendes, nirgends ein Ruhendes, ein Abgeschlossenes vorkommt, sondern daß vielmehr alles in einer steten Bewegung schwanke. Daher unsere Sprache das Wort Bildung sowohl von dem Hervorgebrachten, als von dem Hervorgebrachtwerdenden gehörig genug zu brauchen pflegt.[84]

> [But if we consider all forms, especially organic ones, then nowhere do we find evidence of endurance, of rest, of closure, rather, we find that everything oscillates in constant movement. That is why, in our language, we tend quite appropriately to use the word *Bildung* [formation, development] in respect both of things that have been created and of things that are being created.]

If nothing is 'abgeschlossen', then neither can the past have an ultimate, 'fixed' form simply by virtue of being the past: it too must be caught up in this 'stete[r] Bewegung'. The preoccupation with the past to the complete exclusion of the present inhibits that life-giving movement, resulting, as Goethe asserts in 'Klassiker und Romantiker', in something dry and 'mummy-like'. This is what Mephistopheles does, with almost perverse intent, when he equips his army in Act IV: 'Sonst waren's Ritter, König, Kaiser, | Jetzt sind es nichts als leere Schneckenhäuser. | Gar manch Gespenst hat sich darein geputzt, | Das Mittelalter lebhaft aufgestutzt. | Welch Teufelchen auch drinne steckt, | Für diesmal macht es doch Effekt.' [Once, they were knights, kings, emperors, now they are mere empty snail shells. Now scores of ghosts have dressed up in them, bringing the Middle Ages to life again. Who knows what little devils may be in there, but it makes a good show.] (10559–64). Ideally, a mode of remembering (both personal and cultural) should be found which allows the past to live on in the present, but not quite in its original form: rather, influenced in its turn by the very developments which it helped to bring about. In the specific literary-critical context of that essay, he argues that commitment to the present by no means precludes the acknowledgement and creative use of the wisdom of the past — quite the contrary:

> jeder, der von Jugend an seine Bildung den Griechen und Römern verdankt, [wird] nie ein gewisses antikes Herkommen verleugnen, vielmehr jederzeit dankbar anerkennen [...] was er abgeschiedenen Lehrern schuldig ist, wenn er auch sein ausgebildetes Talent der lebendigen Gegenwart unaufhaltsam widmet und, ohne es zu wissen, modern endigt wenn er antik angefangen hat.[85]

> [Anyone who owes his education to the Greeks and the Romans will never deny the influence of the ancients; on the contrary, he will acknowledge in tireless gratitude his debt to his departed teachers, even if, inevitably, he devotes the talent which he has honed to the living present and, without knowing it, finishes in a modern style what he had begun in the ancient mode.]

This is exactly what Goethe has done in *Faust*: older motifs from antiquity and the Christian tradition, together with newer ones from the Western cultural heritage, have been remoulded to produce a thoroughly modern piece of poetry; and a work begun in Goethe's early youth has been progressively revised and expanded, stratum laid upon stratum, to form his last and most complex contribution.[86]

'Bergschluchten'

'Bergschluchten' is arguably the most self-conscious scene of all in *Faust*. Like the rest of the play, in particular the 'Klassische Walpurgisnacht', it draws on a multiplicity of sources, combining them this time to produce a syncretic mix of the sacred and the secular. The density of reminiscences, or rather revisions, of images or excerpts from earlier moments in the play, is also greater here than in any other scene.[87] Thus the allusive tendency characteristic of the play as a whole is itself heightened here, and the text is swelled more than ever by (poetic) memory, ancient and recent. The redemption which the scene describes is possible not because of anything Faust has done, but because of what the text itself does (and, of course, because of the love of Gretchen). As in *Novelle*, the text produces its own harmony.

The clearest example in 'Bergschluchten' of a parallel with another part of the play is the address to the Mater Gloriosa by the woman who was once called Margarete: 'Neige neige, Du Ohnegleiche, | Du Strahlenreiche, | Dein Antlitz gnädig meinem Glück' [O matchless, resplendent lady, incline thy merciful gaze to my great joy] (12069–72). This is, of course, a transfiguration of Gretchen's desolate plea in the scene 'Zwinger' in Part I. We saw in relation to the closing scene of the *Wanderjahre* that rewriting can have a certain redemptive force; and here, too, a pain-filled memory is transformed into an expression of joy at the return of 'der früh Geliebte' [my first beloved] (12073) whom she once lost. She is described, moreover, as 'sich anschmiegend': nestling, presumably, against Faust's soul, just as the wisp of cloud hovered tenderly around Faust's 'Brust und Stirn' in 'Hochgebirg'. Elsewhere in the scene, Doctor Marianus's words 'Werde jeder bessre Sinn | Dir zum Dienst erbötig; | Jungfrau, Mutter, Königin, | Göttin bleibe gnädig' [May each worthy spirit be always ready to serve thee; Virgin, Mother, Queen, Goddess, look graciously upon us] (12100–03) are an almost exact echo of the sirens in the 'Klassische Walpurgisnacht': 'Dir zu jedem Dienst erbötig, | Schöne Luna, sei uns gnädig!' [Ever ready to serve thee, beauteous moon, look graciously upon us] (8042–43). 'Bergschluchten' also bears many similarities with the opening scene of Part II. Despite its Christian coloration, the 'Geisterchor' [chorus of spirits] is not so very far removed from the 'Geister Kreis' [ring of spirits] of 'Anmutige Gegend'. The spirits are given in the stage directions as 'schwebend bewegt', moving tenderly around the unconscious Faust, just as the life-giving 'Blüten Frühlings-Regen | Über alle schwebend sinkt' [the showers of spring and blossoms which hover, which fall all around] (4613–14); and Ariel juxtaposes their movements with the task of cleansing which he has given them, and links their gentle hovering to the release of the patient from past horror: 'Die ihr dies Haupt umschwebt im luftgen Kreise | [...] Besänftiget des Herzens grimmen Strauß' [You who hover in a ring of air around this head [...] soothe this heart's grim struggle] (4621–23). In 'Bergschluchten', the connection between hovering and healing is even more pervasive. Although it begins in the curious 'Heranschwanken' of the forest and the levitation of Pater Ecstaticus, the movement quickly becomes global, equally applicable to angels and penitent women: the place of each member in the hierarchy is mobile, and the whole company is joyfully borne aloft. The condition for this movement is purification: Faust, for example, is redeemed by the influence of those purer than he, and the 'selige Knaben' express the hope that he, too, will become an example.

There is, however, a crucial disparity between these two scenes: whereas 'Bergschluchten' is full of memory, 'Anmutige Gegend' invokes the opposite — 'badet ihn in Tau aus Lethes Flut' [Then bathe him in dew from Lethe's torrents] (4629). The difference has to do with the situation depicted in each: for 'Anmutige Gegend' takes place in a wholly natural realm, 'Bergschluchten' in a transcendentally human one. Nature, as depicted in the 'Klassische Walpurgisnacht', with the annual return of Galatea and the celebration of Pharsalus, operates cyclically: repetition is simply part of its process. It has no need of memory, a reflexive and quintessentially human function. Although the natural and the human coexist peacefully at last, they are still distinct entities in 'Bergschluchten', with nature working independently of humanity: 'Sind Liebesboten, sie verkünden | Was ewig schaffend uns umwallt' [They are love's emissaries, who tell of that infinite creative power which surrounds us] (11882–83). As the scene moves up from the deep and middle regions into the 'höhere Atmosphäre' [higher atmosphere], the natural world shifts out of focus, and the world of human spirituality becomes central. Whereas, in 'Anmutige Gegend', purification was a gift from nature, which used its own forces, mysterious to us, to wash Faust clean, now humanity itself can fulfil that role, drawing on memory and community to expiate wrongdoings. Of course, there is another force at work in 'Bergschluchten', which *is* at one with nature, namely 'Gottes Gegenwart' [the presence of God] (11921), 'Ewigen Liebens Offenbarung | Die zur Seligkeit entfaltet' [the revelation of eternal love, which unfurls to supreme bliss] (11924–25). This force of eternal love (equivalent to the 'Gott-Natur' of 'Im ernsten Beinhaus') is the ultimate condition of the transcendence of the human spirits in this scene; yet collectively, they are able at last to raise themselves to the point where they are more permanently receptive to its gifts.

Whereas the rest of Part II was marked by a disjunction between the poetry of the play and the actions of its central character, now there is a near-total integration of form and content. *Steigerung* on the poetic level is intimately linked to the scene's 'action', if it can be called that. Albrecht Schöne argues that one of the controlling concepts of the scene is *apokatastasis pantōn*, especially as advocated by Origen: that is to say, the redemptive resurrection of all, not a final separation into the damned and the saved, but 'eine liebende, versöhnende Rückführung zu Gott, die alles erfaßt, was einmal von ihm ausgegangen war' [the loving, conciliatory return to God of everything which he once sent into the world].[88] In Goethe's (secular) adaptation of the doctrine, the notion of restitution is understood to include change. Indeed, as Schöne observes:

> der polyphone Ausgang des Spiels beschränkt sich nicht auf eine variierende Wiederholung und summierende 'Engführung' von Vergangenem: in einer mächtigen umartenden Steigerung hebt er das alles über sich selbst hinaus.[89]

> [the polyphonic end of the play is not limited to variations on a theme, to a 'stretto' which summarizes what has passed: rather, he has all the material transcend itself in a powerful, transformative process of heightening.]

The passing moment of insight and ascension in 'Hochgebirg' now becomes sustained: for the movement previously confined to the cirrus, 'Wie Seelenschönheit *steigert* sich die holde Form' [Like the beauty of souls, the lovely form rises] (10064, my emphasis), now involves Faust and the whole company. The scene describes a continuous upward motion, rising as it does from the depths of the mountain ravines to the heights of the sky. The company is held in hovering suspension, each member now lower, now higher than his or her fellows: Faust's *Unsterbliches* [immortal part], for example, is progressively stripped of its unworthy elements until he begins to overtake his mentors ('Er überwächst uns schon' [Already he outgrows us], 12076, 'Er wird uns lehren' [He will teach us], 12083). It is the reciprocal influence upon and care of each other that enables the figures collectively to move upwards. The supreme example of this in the scene is the relationship between Faust and Margarete. The Mater Gloriosa says to her:

> Komm! Hebe dich zu höhern Sphären,
> Wenn er dich ahnet folgt er nach. (12094–95)

[Come! Lift yourself up to higher spheres; when he senses you, he will follow.]

Margarete's abiding love is the force which bears Faust aloft, as she in turn is drawn towards the Mater Gloriosa. Thus, as Faust himself anticipated in 'Hochgebirg', the best of the past is the condition for healing and transcendence in this scene. The past which has formed the present must be upheld; but the present must also be transformed. In Doctor Marianus's final speech, the remoulding or refinement of the inner essence, the *Art*, of a thing is explicitly linked with the higher existence for which all the figures yearn:

> Blicket auf zum Retterblick
> Alle reuig zarten,
> Euch zu seligem Geschick
> Dankend umzuarten. (12096–99)

> [Turn your eyes upwards to the saviour's gaze, all you gentle, penitent souls,
> and transform yourselves in thanks and readiness for a blessed existence]

Umartung is another word for metamorphosis, which has been prominent in the scene since the image of the chrysalis used by the *selige Knaben*: 'Freudig empfangen wir | Diesen im Puppenstand' [Joyfully we welcome him in his chrysalis] (11981–82). Metamorphosis, transformation, is thus the condition for approaching the ideal, represented here by the Mater Gloriosa, the 'höchste Herrscherin' [Queen and ruler] (11997), the 'Unberührbare' [inviolate] (12020). This is, of course, also a piece of self-reference on Goethe's part: for it is yet another elaboration, this time in poetic form, of the morphological principles central to his own thought.

The theme of the transformation of life at the end of life is mirrored on the formal level by the transformation of the play's language at the end of the piece; and just as *Umartung* enables the company to rise above themselves, so the process of repeated reflection and heightening enables language and thought to move beyond itself, towards what it can barely imagine. That is the gesture on which the scene ends: 'zieht uns hinan' [draws us on]. But that ending is a continued movement, not an arrival. We do not see the culmination of the process of *Umartung*. Faust is still 'blinded by the new day' (12093); and, although the Mater Gloriosa calls Margarete — and, by proxy, Faust — to her, we do not see them reach her. She is, as Jane Brown observes, 'an eternally receding ideal'.[90] Doctor Marianus exhorts the company to lift its gaze not 'zum Retter' but 'zum Retter*blick*' (my emphasis), which suggests that, once again, the ideal cannot be viewed directly — though the linking of 'blicket auf' and 'Retterblick' nonetheless suggests reciprocity, the possibility of engagement, even if it cannot be total. Moreover, even though the Chorus Mysticus says the word 'hier' — 'Hier wird's Ereignis', 'Hier ist es getan' — we are given no indication whatsoever where 'hier' is (although those lines are a resounding reversal of Faust's 'Das verfluchte *hier*!' earlier in Act V).

The point of the scene is categorically not, as Peter-André Alt argues, that: 'der Schluß des *Faust* [reflektiert] die Möglichkeit der poetischen Sprache, das Inkommensurable zu erfassen und zu vergegenwärtigen' [the close of *Faust* reflects the ability of poetic language to grasp the incommensurable and to make it manifest].[91] Rather, the scene itself remains a *Gleichnis*, a reflection. Albrecht Schöne argues that its Catholic imagery is not to be taken at face value, that it prepares the mind, rather, to look beyond the earthly.[92] Although it may appear extravagant in its design, 'Bergschluchten' is in fact marked by caution in respect of what it can represent. In this respect, it is a relative of the Makarie strand of the *Wanderjahre*. If the scene seems far-fetched, or even parodic, it is not because Goethe has succumbed completely to doubt and scepticism, and has decided to make a mockery of his own play;[93] rather, the element of humour in its composition, and the smile which it might prompt in the reader, is part of the self-questioning of a text which upholds a commitment to the existence of the ideal, but does not presume to represent it. The sense of the line 'Das Unzulängliche, | Hier wird's Ereignis' [What was unreachable is here made manifest] is partly, as Erich Trunz writes, that: 'Was auf Erden *unzulänglich*, unvollkommen ist, wird dort vollkommen' [What is *inadequate*, imperfect on earth, there becomes perfect].[94] But this is also a moment of self-irony, an acknowledgement that the words becoming 'Ereignis' as we read or watch the play are, for all their virtuosity, still inherently insufficient. The hubris of Faust, who, in his earthly life, tries against his better judgement to force access to the ideal, is not reproduced in the poetry of the play; and those words from *Novelle*, 'Ist es möglich zu denken' [If it is possible to imagine], would serve well as the motto for this scene.

Yet Alt is not wrong to claim a special role for poetry on the basis of the scene. For 'Bergschluchten' is an extended gesture towards *das Unbeschreibliche*, even if 'the indescribable' is not actually represented *per se*: the figures on stage are all on the ascent towards it, and the language of the scene is poised between revelation and reticence, between intuition of the truth and an admission of ignorance. In Act III, poetry was ultimately not enough; and 'Bergschluchten' remains reserved about the potential of human discourse in its various forms — 'nur ein Gleichnis' [but a likeness]. But the scene dares nonetheless to offer a vision, albeit an abstract, even private one, of the conditions required in order to draw closer to the ideal: understanding ('Doch dieser hat gelernt | Er wird uns lehren', 12082–83), love ('Wenn er dich ahnet folgt er nach', 12094–95), transformation ('Euch zu seligem Geschick | Dankend umzuarten', 12098–99). The scene's poetry thus seeks to fulfil the function postulated for the *Abglanz* in 'Anmutige Gegend' and 'Versuch einer Witterungslehre': namely, to point beyond human ignorance, to mediate between 'das Wahre' and the limitations of our minds, and thus to enable the ascent towards the ideal understanding which, in his earthly life, Faust has always sought but never found. This is where the integration of form and content in 'Bergschluchten' becomes so important. For if the process of *Umartung* brings Faust and the company closer to the ideal, or the ineffable, then the many layers of reflection and heightening which have gone into the composition of the scene seek to prepare the mind to look beyond the earthly, to a plane of meaning and love of which it still cannot conceive. Although Faust's attempts at knowledge stall catastrophically during his earthly life, in 'Bergschluchten' he is involved in an upward, and unending, spiral of understanding, in which he both teaches ('Er wird uns lehren') and is taught ('Vergönne mir ihn zu belehren' [I beg the indulgence of teaching him], 12092); and the play likewise traces, through its poetry, a pattern of ever-increasing self-awareness, which culminates in this scene. The type of knowledge which Faust, now *unsterblich*, is supposed to have reached in this realm, remains unknowable to readers and spectators; but its earthly equivalent, the play's poetry suggests, is self-knowledge, which, in its most genuine form, continuously challenges and renews itself.

Notes to Chapter 4

1. This is a preoccupation for many critics, but Horst Rüdiger's article 'Weltliteratur in Goethes "Helena"', *JDS*, 8 (1964), 172–98, remains one of the most sophisticated treatments of the topic.
2. Martin Swales, 'Goethe's *Faust*: Theatre, Meta-Theatre, Tragedy', in *Goethe's Faust: Theatre of Modernity*, ed. by Schulte and others, pp. 197–208 (p. 202).
3. *Faust* is a poetic drama, and I shall refer to it both as poetry and as a play over the course of the chapter.
4. Here I agree with Michael Jaeger, who writes: 'Abgeschnitten von der kritischen Selbstreflexion, bleibt Faust die Wurzel des Übels im eigenen Bewußtsein immer verborgen' (*Fausts Kolonie: Goethes kritische Phänomenologie der Moderne* (Würzburg: Königshausen und Neumann, 2004), p. 430).
5. Bennett, *Goethe's Theory of Poetry*, p. 24.
6. *HA* XIII, 32.
7. Ibid., p. 25.
8. Jaeger, *Fausts Kolonie*, p. 405.
9. Bennett, *Goethe's Theory of Poetry*, p. 123.
10. Ibid., p. 120.
11. Ibid., p. 121.
12. *MA* XVII, 909.
13. Ibid., p. 783.
14. Ibid., 946.
15. Karl Ameriks, 'Introduction', in *The Cambridge Companion to German Idealism*, ed. by Karl Ameriks (Cambridge: Cambridge University Press, 2000), p. 8.
16. See Frederick Beiser:

    Because the identity of the self depends on its place within nature, it ceases to be self-sufficient and perfectly transparent to itself. The identity of the self depends on the whole of nature, which it can know but imperfectly. Deep within myself there lie the mysterious energies and powers of nature itself, which I cannot entirely know or control. (*German Idealism: The Struggle against Subjectivism, 1781–1801* (Cambridge, MA: Harvard University Press, 2002), p. 358)

17. *MA* XVII, 947.
18. Jane K. Brown, 'Theatricality and Experiment: Identity in *Faust*', in *Goethe's Faust: Theatre of Modernity*, ed. by Schulte and others, pp. 235–52 (p. 235).
19. References taken from *Biblia, das ist: Die ganze Heilige Schrift Alten und Neuen Testaments, durch Doctor Martin Luther in das Deutsche Übersetzt* [...] (Schaffhausen: Johann Conrad Müller, 1770).
20. Jaeger, *Fausts Kolonie*, p. 405.
21. The term comes from the Abbé's letter to Wilhelm in Book II, chapter 7 of the *Wanderjahre*.
22. Nicholls, *Goethe's Concept of the Daemonic*, p. 201.
23. Fred Hagen and Ursula Mahlendorf, 'Commitment, Concern and Memory in Goethe's *Faust*', *The Journal of Aesthetics and Art Criticism*, 21 (1963), 473–84 (p. 476).
24. If, that is, we regard 'Zueignung', 'Vorspiel auf dem Theater', and 'Prolog im Himmel' as belonging to a 'frame' external (though, of course, deeply connected) to the plot, and 'Nacht' therefore as the opening of the action proper of Part I. The decision to place the title page, which reads 'Der Tragödie Erster Teil', *between* the 'Prolog im Himmel' and 'Nacht' in the *Ausgabe letzter Hand* suggests that this is indeed what Goethe had in mind.
25. There has, of course, been some debate as to whether the line should be 'immerfort zu streben' or 'immer fortzustreben'. See Albrecht Schöne in his commentary to the FA, VII.2, 409. My own view is that both versions accord in their semantics with the spirit of what is being said.
26. See Philip Fisher, *Wonder, the Rainbow, and the Aesthetics of Rare Experience* (Cambridge, MA: Harvard University Press, 1998), p. 12.

27. *MA* xiii.2, 275.

28. Ehrhard Bahr distinguishes between a rhetorical 'ironie qui sait' and a metaphysical 'ironie qui cherche', arguing that the latter is more typical of Goethe. In his work, it is the function of irony 'immer wieder herauszustellen, daß die Dinge nicht eindeutig festzulegen sind, sondern immer problematisch bleiben müssen, wenn man ihnen gerecht werden will'. Irony 'reißt den Menschen fort vom Hängen am Relativ-Wahren, an der begrenzten Einzelmeinung und Einzelerscheinung und hält ihn im Zustand der Schwebe offen und bereit für das Schauen des Absolut-Wahren' (Ehrhard Bahr, *Die Ironie im Spätwerk Goethes* (Berlin: Schmidt, 1972), pp. 18 and 20).

29. I cannot accept Wilhelm Emrich's interpretation of 'Anmutige Gegend' and the pattern which it suggests for the rest of the play: 'Tat ist nichts anderes als produktiv schaffender, vergessender, traumhafter Eintritt in immer neue Bereiche unter Abbruch aller lastenden Erinnerung. Die Spontaneität und Unvermitteltheit der Tat macht einen Verjüngungsakt und ein gnadenreiches Vergessen geradezu zur unabdingbaren Voraussetzung' (Wilhelm Emrich, *Die Symbolik von Faust II: Sinn und Vorformen* (Frankfurt am Main: Athenäum, 1964; 1st edn 1943), p. 108). This may be the kind of escapism which Faust himself espouses, but Goethe's poetry shows us, I think, something quite different.

30. See Emil Staiger: 'Goethe wagt sich damit an ein Problem, das ihn schon lange quält, das aber noch nie so unmittelbar, ausdrücklich und zentral zum Thema seines Schaffens geworden ist: Bewahrung des vergangenen, Wiederbelebung des abgeschiedenen Daseins' (*Goethe: 1814–1832* (Zurich: Atlantis, 1959), p. 296).

31. It is not, I think, helpful to become stuck on the question of whether 'die Mütter' are 'real' or 'fictional'. In one sense, of course, they are complete fantasy; but so is much of what happens in the play (it is, after all, a play), and, indeed, in other works — are we so concerned to know whether Shakespeare's Ariel is 'real', or whether Prospero *really* conjured up his tempest? It is arguably a simple dramatic necessity that, within the total fiction of the whole, 'die Mütter' represent something more than fiction: otherwise the *Schattenspiel* would be superfluous, a recapitulation of the problems exposed by the *Mummenschanz*. Moreover, Faust's first descent is followed in Act II by another, to Persephone: and the consequences of that descent, however myth-bound Hades is, have to be accepted for Act III to be understood.

32. Jane K. Brown, *Goethe's* Faust: *The German Tragedy* (Ithaca: Cornell University Press, 1986), p. 163.

33. Ibid., p. 20.

34. Ibid., pp. 156–61.

35. The realm of 'die Mütter' is, I think, more than simply 'a brilliant improvisation' on the part of Mephistopheles, as Stuart Atkins suggests in *Goethe's 'Faust': A Literary Analysis* (Cambridge, MA: Harvard University Press, 1958), pp. 134–35.

36. See for example Philip J. Kain, who writes of the

> attempt (and also the ultimate failure) on the part of certain German thinkers to construct a particular humanistic ideal for social and political institutions. This ideal was patterned after the cultural conditions of ancient Greece and was based on modern aesthetic concepts. It was designed to overcome alienation and estrangement in the modern world [...] For these thinkers, ancient Greece represented a lost ideal, a high point of the human condition.

Philip J. Kain, *Schiller, Hegel and Marx: State, Society, and the Aesthetic Ideal of Ancient Greece* (Kingston and Montreal: McGill-Queens University Press, 1982), pp. 6–7.

37. Albrecht Schöne, *FA* vii.2, 521.

38. Heinz Schlaffer, *Faust Zweiter Teil: Die Allegorie des 19. Jahrhunderts* (Stuttgart: Metzler, 1981), p. 109.

39. See Dieter Borchmeyer: 'It has [...] been convincingly demonstrated that the early Romantic authors did not use the words "romantisch, Romantik, Romantiker" in the sense of a self-designation. [...] Goethe and Schiller never saw themselves as classics' ('What is Classicism?', in *The Literature of Weimar Classicism*, ed. by Simon Richter (New York: Camden House, 2005), pp. 45–61 (p. 48)).

40. Charles A. Grair, 'Antiquity and Weimar Classicism', in *The Literature of Weimar Classicism*, pp. 63–88 (p. 63).

41. Brown, *Goethe's Faust*, p. 191.

42. Ibid., p. 193.

43. Goethe's diary, 24 March 1830; quoted in Schöne's commentary, *FA* VII.2, 438.

44. See Katharina Mommsen: 'Aus der immer deutlicher [i.e. through the various drafts of this act] werdenden Abhängigkeit vom Orkus resultiert dann ein neuer Wesenszug: mehr und mehr nehmen die ursprünglich der griechischen Dichtung entstammenden Gestalten schemenhaften Charakter an' (*Natur- und Fabelreich in Faust II* (Berlin: de Gruyter, 1968), p. 30).

45. 'In the palinodic *Helen*, Euripides follows Stesichorus, claiming that Helen never went to Troy but remained in Egypt with Proteus and that it was over her *eidolon*, a phantom created by Hera, that the Trojan War was fought: the *eidolon* taunted the warriors for their folly, while Helen [...] waited chastely at home for Menelaus to reclaim her.' (*The Classical Tradition*, ed. by Anthony Grafton, Glenn W. Most, and Salvatore Settis (Cambridge, MA and London: Belknap, 2010), p. 422)

46. Brown, *Goethe's Faust*, p. 203.

47. John R. Williams, *Goethe's Faust* (London: Allen and Unwin, 1987), p. 165.

48. *FA* XIV, 852.

49. This interpretation might appear to be at odds with Goethe's own comment to Eckermann, on 16 December 1829, that his intention in Act III was for 'beide Dichtungsformen [das Klassische und das Romantische] entschieden hervor[zu]treten und eine Art von Ausgleichung [zu] finden' (*MA* XIX, 340.). Yet, even if we consider the conversations with Eckermann to be a reliable record of Goethe's opinions (a question which has been debated since Julius Petersen's study *Die Entstehung der Eckermannschen Gespräche und ihre Glaubwürdigkeit* (Frankfurt am Main: Diesterweg, 1925)), it does not follow that Euphorion must be the locus of the equilibration referred to here. My own view, which I develop in more detail below, is that the true, and transient, moment of 'Ausgleichung' is the moment of poetic transport in 'Innerer Burghof', just prior to the intrusion of Mephistopheles-Phorkyas. Moreover, the identification of Euphorion with Byron, glowingly described by Goethe in Eckermann's report as 'das größte Talent des Jahrhunderts [...] nicht antik und nicht romantisch, sondern [...] wie der gegenwärtige Tag selbst' (*MA* XIX, 231), need not contradict the understanding of the character as a figure of imbalance. Goethe's admiration for Byron is not wholly without reservation: Byron's genius, he goes on to imply, is inseparable from his 'unbefriedigten Naturell [...] und seiner kriegerischen Tendenz, woran er in Missolunghi zu Grunde ging. Eine Abhandlung über Byron zu schreiben', he concludes, 'ist nicht bequem und rätlich, aber gelegentlich ihn zu ehren und auf ihn im Einzelnen hinzuweisen werde ich auch in der Folge nicht unterlassen'.

50. *MA* XI.2, 259.

51. Stuart Atkins, 'The Evaluation of Romanticism in Goethe's *Faust*', in *Essays on Goethe*, ed. by Jane K. Brown and Thomas P. Saine (Rochester, NY: Camden House, 1995), p. 312.

52. Mommsen, *Natur- und Fabelreich*, pp. 53–54.

53. Ibid., p. 25.

54. Eudo C. Mason, *Goethe's Faust: Its Genesis and Purport* (Berkeley: University of California Press, 1967), p. 324.

55. Stuart Atkins's notion of the 'Klassische Walpurgisnacht' and Act III as dream-plays conceived and directed by Faust himself is an interesting idea, and almost gets at the strange self-consciousness of the work; but he is, I think, mistaken in attributing the reflexivity of these scenes, in terms of their form and conception, to Faust himself. See *Goethe's Faust*, e.g. p. 192. Only the Arcadia section of Act III can plausibly be seen as Faust's own orchestration: and Atkins's reading of the Euphorion episode as 'the dramatic demonstration of Faust's complete understanding of the nature of man as defined in Prologue in Heaven' (*Goethe's 'Faust'*, p. 225) seems to exaggerate his achievements and sidestep the deficiencies of this Arcadia.

56. See John Williams: 'the highest and lightest form of cirrus represents a spiritual movement towards "salvation"' (*Goethe's 'Faust'*, p. 183).

57. Victor Lange, 'Faust: Der Tragödie zweiter Teil', in *Goethes Dramen: Neue Interpretationen*, ed. by Walter Hinderer (Stuttgart: Reclam, 1980), pp. 281–312 (pp. 303–04).

58. Stuart Atkins makes (I think) a similar point:

> it is only fitting that Faust should pay his final and highest tribute [...] not to the perfection of timeless beauty but to living beauty of soul and character which [...] must always remain the higher value for the good man who knows that the supreme human-divine achievement is to make the best he can of his life here and now. Mephistopheles [...] appears as Faust's thoughts have turned from the ended dream of Helen to a future inspired by the memory of Margarete, and the return to a finite world of waking reality is completed by the reintroduction of flexible rhyming verse. (*Goethe's 'Faust'*, p. 234)

However, the distinction between the moment of Faust's 'highest tribute' and the events subsequent to his monologue is not, I think, made sufficiently clear. The vision of a future 'inspired by the memory of Margarete' is strictly confined to the monologue, and the departure of the Margarete-cloud and the intrusion of Mephistopheles signify that Faust is already forgetting the 'higher value' which he had just remembered.

59. Mason, *Goethe's 'Faust'*, p. 329.

60. The destructive effect of an absence of memory can also be seen, as R. H. Stephenson observes, in 'the kind of stupidity that the "Lemuren" represent in the final act: devoid of memory, they lack any sense of direction' (*Studies in Weimar Classicism: Writing as Symbolic Form* (Berne: Peter Lang, 2010), p. 195).

61. See Ulrich Gaier, *Fausts Modernität: Essays* (Stuttgart: Reclam, 2000), p. 51: 'auch Faust wird gründlich betrogen. Von den großen Taten [...] leistet er gar nichts [...] es ist Mephistos Herrschaft, und Mephisto war der Oberfeldherr'.

62. 'Das Handeln und Schaffen des neuzeitlichen Menschen, je umfassender es angelegt sein soll, ist umso abhängiger von den technischen Mitteln' (ibid.).

63. Act IV has been interpreted in various ways, but here I follow the reading offered by John Williams: 'the conditions are [close] to the situation in Germany in the first fifteen years of the nineteenth century, to the Napoleonic invasion and occupation, the Wars of Liberation and the restoration of a feudal regime after 1815' (*Goethe's 'Faust'*, p. 187).

64. See Michael Jaeger:

> Das Beten der Alten bedeutet Innehalten, Nachdenken, Zurückbleiben, Erinnerung, Selbst- und Weltreflexion. Diese Reflexivität geht einher mit dem bescheidenen, ruhigen und glücklichen Leben. Die europäische Überlieferung kennt Philemon und Baucis als die unübertroffenen Vorbilder der Vita beata, in der Vita activa und Vita contemplativa im Gleichgewicht sind. Von dem besonderen Glück ihrer reflektierten Existenz fällt ein helles und zugleich grelles Licht auf das Unglück der besinnungslos-ungeduldigen Existenz Fausts. (Jaeger, *Fausts Kolonie*, pp. 403–04)

65. Ibid., p. 401.

66. Ibid., p. 405.

67. Günther Mieth, 'Fausts letzter Monolog: Poetische Struktur einer geschichtlichen Vision', *GJb*, 97 (1980), 90–102 (p. 99).

68. See Williams, *Goethe's 'Faust'*, p. 204; Mason, *Goethe's 'Faust'*, p. 345. For Victor Lange, the process begins with the lines 'Und zieht das Beste meines Innern mit sich fort': 'Von jetzt an gilt es, im verantwortlichen Handeln für andere alles Subjektive, alles Zeitbedingte zu überwinden, die geleistete Tat gegen alle inneren und äußeren Bedrohungen auszuspielen' ('Faust: Der Tragödie zweiter Teil', p. 304). Although I can see a case (albeit one I do not share) for interpreting Faust's final speech in this way, I cannot accept that it is a consistent development from the beginning of Act IV. Geza von Molnár offers a particularly interesting interpretation in 'The Conditions of Faust's Wager and its Resolution in the Light of Kantian Ethics', *PEGS*, 51 (1980–81), 48–80. He interprets Faust's career as the stumbling progression towards an understanding of 'the positive function of freedom through which human value may be imposed on the otherwise meaningless flux of being' (p. 64), and concludes that, in his final speech,

> Faust [...] does not [...] develop into a moral agent — his deeds preclude this contention — [...] [but] [h]is last act and legacy is an artistic rendition symbolic of the same human self-comprehension that inspired Kant to proclaim the reality of

a free realm populated by free beings whose existence would remain a noumenal fiction, however, were they to cease enacting their freedom in nature's domain. (pp. 77–78)

Molnár's solution, though elegant, still fails to convince: for even if, as he claims, the seeds of Faust's commitment to freedom (in the Kantian sense) are sown in the wager, there is so little evidence in the intervening episodes of real progress towards the 'human self-comprehension' which Faust allegedly demonstrates in his final speech, that even this has the air of a dubious eleventh-hour conversion.

69. Nicholas Boyle also disputes the notion of any causal link between Faust's last speech and the image of salvation in 'Berschluchten':

Faust represents his age, and any specific hope he might express would be a part of his age's pathology, sharing its subjectivity and its violence. [...] Faust's final vision is still *a part* of his tragedy. His last speech is simply the logical culmination of his career and introduces no new element that might redeem him in the last moment. (Nicholas Boyle, 'The Politics of *Faust II*: Another Look at the Stratum of 1831', *PEGS*, 52 (1981–82), 4–43 (p. 39))

70. R. H. Stephenson contends that:

[i]n Part Two, where a wealth of mythological material amplifies the unique and personal to the point where it becomes blatantly typical in nature, we find ourselves in a world of sophisticated awareness, on the characters [sic] part, of the forms and symbols that shape experience. It is a world of self-conscious retrospection [...]. (Stephenson, *Studies in Weimar Classicism*, p. 171)

This is relatively unproblematic in relation to some of the figures in the 'Klassische Walpurgisnacht', or to Helena, but requires some qualification where Faust is concerned: for, as we have seen, 'self-conscious retrospection' is something of which he is only capable, or only chooses to engage in, sporadically.

71. Ibid., p. 390.

72. Harold Jantz, *The Form of Faust: The Work of Art and its Intrinsic Structures* (Baltimore: Johns Hopkins University Press, 1978), p. 136.

73. Atkins, *Goethe's 'Faust'*, p. 167.

74. Ibid., p. 219.

75. Ibid., p. 139.

76. Charlie Louth, 'Reflections: Goethe's "Auf dem See" and Hölderlin's "Hälfte des Lebens"', *Oxford German Studies*, 33 (2004), 167–75 (p. 170).

77. Nicholas Boyle, 'Goethe's Theory of Tragedy', *MLR*, 105 (2010), 1072–86 (p. 1083).

78. Mephisto's periodic complicity in the self-consciousness of the text does not, of course, make him the bearer of truth in the work. As Nicholas Boyle observes:

His judgements of Faust often seem shrewd and realistic, and many readers have shared them [...], but he always leaves a feeling that there is more to be said. We know that this is not quite all that it amounts to — that if we allow this voice to speak for us we are being manipulated by a party to the action. (ibid., pp. 1083–84)

Mephisto's occasionally insightful input tightens the moral maze for the audience or reader, and ensures that the play's questions are not worked out in black and white; but his judgement is hamstrung by his inveterate and destructive cynicism, and he is just one element in a work whose 'knowingness' is far greater, and far more effective, than his.

79. See Hagen and Mahlendorf, 'Commitment, Concern and Memory', pp. 479–80.

80. Brown, *Goethe's 'Faust'*, p. 206.

81. Atkins, *Goethe's 'Faust'*, p. 234.

82. Brown, *Goethe's 'Faust'*, p. 245.

83. Albrecht Schöne, *Fausts Himmelfahrt: Zur letzten Szene der Tragödie* (Munich: Carl Friedrich von Siemens Stiftung, 1994), p. 13. The text of this published lecture is, with some minor additions and alterations, broadly the same as that of Schöne's commentary on the scene in the FA, vol. VII.2, pp. 778–95.

84. *Zur Morphologie* (1817), Erster Band: 'Die Absicht eingeleitet', *MA* xii, 13.
85. 'Klassiker und Romantiker', *MA* xi.2, 261.
86. See also Reinhard Koselleck:

> Wer hätte so häufig wie er fertige Erstfassungen in ebenso fertige Zweitfassungen umgegossen, Zweitfassungen, an denen er über Jahre und Jahrzehnte hinweg gearbeitet hat? Daß die Geschichte immer wieder umgeschrieben werden müsse, weil mit neuen Lagen neue Fragen auftauchen, war Goethes persönliche Erfahrung [...]. ('Goethes unzeitgemäße Geschichte', *GJb*, 110 (1993), 24–39 (p. 31))

87. In his own article on the subject, 'Some Parallels between Faust's Salvation and the *Walpurgisnacht*', *PEGS*, 41 (1970–71), 91–102, Shalom Weyl provides a brief conspectus of other important scholarly contributions to this theme (see p. 99).
88. *FA* vii.2, 788. See also Philip H. Jackson: 'for Origen redemption is a process where all souls are literally attracted back towards God, reascending the ladder of beings until they once more reach the highest level, from which they initially all fell' ('"Air and Angels", the Origenist Compromise in Haller's *Über den Ursprung des Übels*', *German Life and Letters*, 32 (1979), 273–92 (p. 287)). The notion of the Fall, and the concomitant doctrine of sin, is not one which Goethe would have espoused, even in the form which Origen gave to it (namely, that torment and damnation are not eternal, but part of a divinely led process of healing and purification); but the appeal for Goethe of this almost metamorphic model of 'reascension' is clear, especially if it is released from Christian orthodoxy.
89. *FA* vii.2, 778.
90. Brown, *Goethe's 'Faust'*, p. 245.
91. Peter-André Alt, *Klassische Endspiele: Das Theater Goethes und Schillers* (Munich: Beck, 2008), p. 220.
92. Schöne, *Fausts Himmelfahrt*, pp. 33–34.
93. Hannelore Schlaffer contends that:

> In den vielen Tönen, die [die Schlußszene] anschlägt, scheint Goethe noch einmal sein ganzes poetisches Können auszubreiten. [...] Die Parodie des Paradieses ist das Eingeständnis, daß es ein Paradies nicht gäbe, wenn die Dichtung in der Lage wäre, von ihm zu sprechen. (Hannelore Schlaffer, 'Paradies und Parodie: Die letzten Szenen in Goethes letzten Werken', in *Interpreting Goethe's Faust Today*, ed. by Jane K. Brown, Meredith Lee, and Thomas P. Saine (Columbia, SC: Camden House, 2004), pp. 102–11 (p. 110))

Although this claim is, I think, exaggerated, I agree with its basic premise, namely that the work, and especially the final scene, subtly dramatizes the tension between poetry's potential reach and the limitations of its grasp.
94. *HA* iii, 638. Although the understanding, propagated by, among others, Emil Staiger, of 'unzulänglich' as 'inaccessible' would also fit nicely here, Albrecht Schöne asserts — rightly, I think — that 'die Belege aus dem allgmeinen wie dem Goetheschen Wortgebrauch, die das stützen sollten, sind so untauglich, daß diese Lesart aufgegeben werden muß' (*FA* vii.2, 814).

CONCLUSION

Nun weiß man erst was Rosenknospe sei
Jetzt da die Rosenzeit vorbei.

The end of a long life is marked by a curious duality. The shadow of death looms over every endeavour, and loss — loss of the past, of loved ones, and, for the least fortunate, even of one's sense of self — has picked holes in the life that remains. Yet it can also be a time of wealth. The accumulation of experience reaches an unprecedented level, and it dwarfs the peaks of youth. Except in those whom it deserts completely, memory rises through its imperfections and swells the present moment to an unfamiliar fullness. The potential, at least, for self-knowledge is at its zenith.

That duality is evident in Goethe's very late writing. Death lurks only half-hidden in many images: in the blank mirror of the lake in poem VIII of the *Chinesisch—deutsche Jahres- und Tageszeiten*, or in Felix's narrow escape at the end of the *Wanderjahre*, and the *Wechselweg* which, whilst it brings Felix back from Hades, appears to be sending Wilhelm (Pollux to Felix's Castor) in the opposite direction; and Act III of *Faust II* revolves around the characters' endeavour, and failure, to cheat death. Equally, the degenerative aspect of ageing rears its head periodically: in the heart pains alluded to in 'Dem aufgehenden Vollmonde', in the poet's feeling of infertility — both physical and emotional — in 'Elegie' ('Der Selbstsinn tief in winterlichen Grüften'), or in the frequent allusions in the autobiographical works to the inadequacies of memory. Those doubts and difficulties which are very specific to old age are linked to Goethe's epistemological caution, partly Kantian in nature, which applies to all stages of human life. Yet this is also the period in which some of his most intriguing new work comes to light. Despite the doubts expressed in the autobiographies, and the impossibility of recovering the past which is impressed on us in *Faust*, Goethe's poetry (including *Faust*) and his prose fiction are full of memory. Each memory, however, is at the same time an innovation, and Goethe's writing is both enriched by what has been and spurred on towards what could be. This more affirmative energy is not a denial, or even a contradiction, of the difficulty expressed at other points: both are aspects or consequences of self-consciousness. Indeed, the spirit of radical experimentation which informs the *Wanderjahre* is directly linked, through the theme and compositional principle of the secret, to the concern for self-limitation. Similarly, the motif of ascension, which acquires particular prominence in the final scenes of *Novelle* and *Faust*, accommodates both tendencies (affirmation and limitation): the movement upward suggests improvement and hope but, in a reminder of the infinite nature of our search for understanding, we are never shown its fulfilment.

The striking combination of retrospection and artistic renewal, which has been a prominent theme of this study, is not wholly unique to Goethe. Something like it can be — and has been — discerned in the last works of the most diverse writers, artists, and composers; and its frequent occurrence gives the lie to the excessive emphasis in our society on old age as a time of burden.[1] Art historians, for example, have noted a burst of creative innovation in Cézanne's last years: his late style, while it retains many of the characteristics of his earlier paintings, is also, like that of Goethe, profoundly new and experimental. Writing in 1927, the artist, critic, and member of the Bloomsbury Group Roger Fry suggested that there is something *unzeitgemäß* about these works:

> If, for us, the great masterpieces of the penultimate period [...] remain the supreme achievements of Cézanne's genius, one may none the less have a suspicion that for certain intelligences among posterity, the completest revelation of his spirit may be found in these latest creations.[2]

Fry's suggestion that the level of innovation in these works is such that only later generations, for whom posterior developments will have rendered his new style less surprising, will be able to appreciate them fully, is equally applicable to Goethe's last works. Our appreciation of them has certainly been enhanced by familiarity with the practices of modernist and post-modern writing. Moreover, the distinction which he makes between the 'penultimate' and the 'latest' periods resonates with the notion, for which I have been arguing in relation to Goethe, of discrete phases within the much broader sweep of 'lateness'.

A particularly rich parallel is that between Goethe and Shakespeare. The last works[3] of both have a quality of strangeness in familiarity: familiarity because, with Shakespeare as with Goethe, '[i]t is notable that in the late plays innovation is based on recapitulation';[4] strangeness because, at the end of their careers, both Shakespeare and Goethe tease the audience or the reader with scenarios that demand both belief and disbelief in greater measure than in their earlier work. In a recent study of Shakespeare's late works, Raphael Lyne writes: 'In the end the vital thing is that the romances excite both wonder and reason, defying the possibility that they exclude one another'.[5] The final scene of *The Winter's Tale*, for example, both presents a moving, breath-taking miracle and challenges the 'willing suspension of disbelief'. No sooner is the wonder of Hermione's resurrection revealed than it is cast into doubt: Paulina seeks to account for the appearance of reality by appealing to artifice ('The ruddiness upon her lip is wet; | You'll mar it if you kiss it, stain your own | With oily painting'[6]), then artifice and illusion are abandoned with an apparent return to reason, though the explanation which is given is in substance improbable ('thou shalt hear that I, | Knowing by Paulina that the oracle | Gave hope thou wast in being, have preserved | Myself to see the issue'[7]). Yet the equivocation about how Hermione has come to be there also has the function of turning doubt on its head. No single explanation for Hermione's restoration to life is adequate, and therefore no definitive one is offered: what matters is the possibility, here made manifest, that she may live again, and truth and happiness be restored; and that has the value of a wonder precisely because of the coils of doubt and, occasionally, despair through which both the characters and the audience have had to struggle. This dynamic is one which we have seen in the very late Goethe. The figure of Makarie and the final scene of *Faust II* are more bizarre than anything in Shakespeare: yet they are the loci of faith, faith in the ideal, and it is only because they stimulate so much questioning that they can be charged with that responsibility.[8]

There is, however, a crucial difference between the late Shakespeare and the very late Goethe, and that is the degree of self-consciousness in their works. Metatheatrical techniques, such as the play within the play, are as prominent in *The Tempest* as in *Faust*; and in both cases, that reflexive form brings the slipperiness of reality in the fingers of human understanding to the attention of the audience or reader. There is even evidence that Shakespeare deliberately and self-consciously revised works which, with hindsight, seemed to anticipate the last plays: John Jones points to the excision which he made, and which was retained in the Folio edition, of part of Act IV, scene 3 of the quarto text of *King Lear* — a 'work which had got out of phase'[9] — as a sign of Shakespeare's concern to forge a distinction between Tragedy and Romance (or Tragicomedy, as the last plays are sometimes called), and to retain a distinct aura for the different phases of his œuvre. Nonetheless, the fact remains that 'lateness' in Shakespeare's case is largely a retrospective construction. The last plays share many distinctive qualities, which may be a reflexive function of maturity; but

> we misrepresent the Shakespeare canon if we imagine that Shakespeare can be treated as if he were a laureate-style poet consciously carving out a career [...] rather than a professional playwright working within the conditions, physical and institutional, of the early modern theatre.[10]

Whereas, in Shakespeare, self-reference is usually implicit — imagine the absurdity of a sonnet entitled 'To Hamlet'! — it is open and pronounced in Goethe. The popular understanding of Prospero's renunciation of magic as an allegory of Shakespeare's own retirement from writing can never be more than speculative — indeed, it borders on the inaccurate, given that Shakespeare continued to collaborate with John Fletcher after he had finished *The Tempest*. In Goethe's last works, by contrast, very-lateness is not a subsequent invention, but an overt quality: it is the sense of borrowed time which permeates his works, the awareness that his unusually long life must end soon, and the particularly intense preoccupation with the course of his career and with his legacy that that awareness breeds. The fundamental difference between the two is that, whilst Shakespeare was in his mid-forties when he wrote his last plays, Goethe was an old man.

Very-lateness, then, is the quality within Goethe's work which says of the writer 'I am old'. It is the understanding of the imminence of natural death; it is the fullness of memory and the fragility of memory; it is at once the sense of being out of step with modernity and the ability to look beyond the unfamiliar present, to produce literary innovations which project far into the future. As a subset of lateness, it may have parallels in the works of other writers, composers, and artists; but it is also a highly specific period in Goethe's own career, about which there is something unique at every stage. Self-consciousness, for its part, becomes a feature of his writing much earlier, though there is no absolute consensus as to when;[11] yet it is in this very late period that it ramifies most fully. Allusions to the work of other writers and reflections on *poiēsis* in general are now accompanied by overt references to his own writing: the history of poetry and the history of *Goethe's* poetry are equal preoccupations in the very late period. Self-consciousness also feeds into self-limitation: reflections on the nature of human understanding tend in this phase to come to rest in the knowledge that no knowledge is total, just as meditations on selfhood lead for the very late Goethe to the question of whether there is or can be such a thing as a fully unified self. Self-limitation never slips into nihilism for Goethe, however; on the contrary, self-reflection is the more energetic and the more necessary because of it. The connecting arc between self-consciousness and very-lateness is memory; and in Goethe's last works, the question of what makes art and the question of what makes a life slide over into one another more than anywhere else in his oeuvre.

This book began with the question of the relationship between Goethe's life and work: the extent to which they converge, and the point at which they must be considered as separate. Such was Goethe's prominence in the public sphere, above all in Weimar, and so apparently comprehensive was the publication of his letters, diaries, and conversations, that it would be easy to imagine that everything he thought can be known. Yet, as we saw in the Introduction, his commentary on 'Harzreise im Winter', though it has the role of a public utterance and the semblance of a revelatory one, is in fact concerned above all to maintain an element of privacy, even of secrecy, about his life and his work. This dialectic of public and private is not confined to the very late period: it extends at least as far back as the *Römische Elegien*. Nicholas Boyle observes that, 'in the poetry into which the heart of a mature man overflows there will always be a 'secret' (the word occurs five times in Elegy XX), an awareness that the poem leaves some things unsaid'.[12] In the *Elegien*, this is occasioned by the presence of another, a beloved, whom the verses 'contain [...] but do not depict'.[13] Later on, however, as in the 'Harzreise' commentary, his concern is with the protection of his own motivations from the prying public eye. The circumstances of Goethe's life press against his very late work, giving it its distinctive shape, and the course of his *career* is an open and persistent theme; but (with the possible exception of 'Elegie') his most interior *feelings* for the most part remain veiled. This does not make his very late work *unfeeling*, or even impersonal — it simply makes it private, even though much of it emerged contemporaneously with preparations for his most permanent public statement, the *Ausgabe letzter Hand*. This, once again, is the achievement of literary self-consciousness, which after all involves both reflection on the self and the creation of a persona. The pervasive practice of self-reference secures Goethe's distinctive poetic style and legacy, for these cannot be the works of anyone else; yet it also lends an iridescent coating to his personal life, which, though always and complexly present in his writing, is also ultimately opaque to the reader. It is, then, not just nature, not just the self, but Goethe who is the 'offenbares Geheimnis' in his last works.

Notes to the Conclusion

1. 'Depictions of older people remain stereotyped and generalized, distorting public opinion and skewing policy debates. For example, the use of economic dependency ratios, one of the commonest measures of ageing, assumes that anyone aged 65 years or older is unproductive. Similarly, the use of disability-adjusted life years to capture the health of a population explicitly views older people as a social and economic burden. Yet many older people continue to make substantial social, economic, and cultural contributions, which can be enhanced by measures that improve their health and functional status.' Peter Lloyd-Sherlock and others, 'Population Ageing and Health', *The Lancet* 397, Issue 9823 (7 April 2012), pp. 1295–96 <> [accessed 23 August 2012]

2. Roger Fry, *Cézanne: A Study of his Development* (London: Hogarth, 1952, first published 1927), p. 79.

3. In Shakespeare's case, I refer to the last single-authored plays.

4. Raphael Lyne, *Shakespeare's Late Work* (Oxford: Oxford University Press, 2007), p. 138. Lyne draws a number of comparisons, including the jealousy of Othello and that of Leontes in *The Winter's Tale*, and the magical atmosphere of *A Midsummer Night's Dream* and *The Tempest*, emphasizing in each case that the parallels are revisions as much as recapitulations, the late plays as different from as they are similar to the early ones. A similar tendency has been noted in the late works of other creative artists. Daniel Grimley, for example, comments that Sibelius's own *Tempest* composition, one of his last works, both acts as 'a focal point for gathering together and summarizing many of the ideas and processes Sibelius had so strenuously sought to develop in his symphonies from the Fourth onward', and displays a 'stylistic diversity and range of expression [which], in [its] contrast with the celebrated unity and concision of works such as the Seventh Symphony, has often puzzled and divided critics' (Daniel M. Grimley, 'Storms, Symphonies, Silence: Sibelius's *Tempest* Music and the Invention of Late Style', in *Jean Sibelius and his World*, ed. by Daniel M. Grimley (Princeton: Princeton University Press, 2011), pp. 186–226 (pp. 191, 187)).

5. Lyne, *Shakespeare's Late Work*, p. 43.

6. William Shakespeare, *The Winter's Tale*, ed. by Stephen Orgel (Oxford: Clarendon Press, 1996), p. 228.

7. Ibid., p. 230.

8. I also treat the interrelation of illusion and reality, of wonder and disbelief, in 'Durch Wunderkraft erschienen: Affinities between Goethe's *Faust* and Shakespeare's *The Tempest*', *MLR*, 107 (2012), 198–210.

9. John Jones, *Shakespeare at Work* (Oxford: Clarendon Press, 1995), p. 210.

10. Gordon McMullan, 'What is a Late Play?', in *The Cambridge Companion to Shakespeare's Last Plays*, ed. by Catherine M. S. Alexander (Cambridge: Cambridge University Press, 2009), pp. 5–27 (p. 19).

11. According to David Wellbery in *The Specular Moment*, self-reflexive practice starts with the early lyric, whereas Nicholas Boyle locates its beginning somewhat later, in the *Römische Elegien* (see *Goethe: The Poet and the Age*, p. 635).

12. Boyle, *The Poet and the Age*, 1, 639.

13. Ibid., p. 640.

BIBLIOGRAPHY

Primary Literature

Editions of Goethe's Works

Goethes Werke. Hrsg. im Auftrage der Großherzogin Sophie von Sachsen (Weimar: H. Böhlau, 1887–1919)

Goethes Werke: Hamburger Ausgabe in 14 Bänden, XIII, ed. by Erich Trunz (Munich: Beck, 1981)

Sämtliche Werke. Briefe, Tagebücher und Gespräche, ed. by Dieter Borchmeyer and others (Frankfurt am Main: Deutscher Klassiker Verlag, 1985–99)

Sämtliche Werke nach Epochen seines Schaffens. Münchener Ausgabe, ed. by Karl Richter and others (Munich: Hanser, 1985–98)

Goethes Werke. Nachträge zur Weimarer Ausgabe, ed. by Paul Raabe (Deutscher Taschenbuch Verlag, Munich, 1990)

Other Works Cited

AUSTEN, JANE, *Mansfield Park*, ed. by Claudia L. Johnson (New York and London: Norton, 1998)

HEGEL, GEORG WILHELM FRIEDRICH, *Werke*, ed. by Eva Moldenhauer and Karl Markus Michel (Frankfurt am Main: Suhrkamp, 1970–99)

KANT, IMMANUEL, *Immanuel Kants Werke*, ed. by Ernst Cassirer and others (Hildesheim: Gerstenberg, 1973)

SHAKESPEARE, WILLIAM, *The Winter's Tale*, ed. by Stephen Orgel (Oxford: Clarendon Press, 1996)

Secondary Literature

ALT, PETER-ANDRÉ, *Klassische Endspiele: Das Theater Goethes und Schillers* (Munich: Beck, 2008)

AMERIKS, KARL, ed., *The Cambridge Companion to German Idealism* (Cambridge: Cambridge University Press, 2000)

AMMERLAHN, HELMUT, 'Wilhelm Meisters Mignon — ein offenbares Rätsel: Name, Gestalt, Symbol, Wesen und Werden', *Deutsche Vierteljahrsschrift für Literaturwissenschaft und Geistesgeschichte*, 42 (1968), 89–116

AMRINE, FREDERICK, 'Romance Narration in Wilhelm Meisters Wanderjahre', *The German Quarterly*, 55 (1982), 29–38

——'Goethean Intuitions', *Goethe Yearbook*, 18 (2011), 35–50

ATHILL, DIANA, *Somewhere towards the End* (London: Granta, 2008)

ATKINS, STUART, *Goethe's 'Faust': A Literary Analysis* (Cambridge, MA: Harvard University Press, 1958)

——*Essays on Goethe*, ed. by Jane K. Brown and Thomas P. Saine (Columbia, SC: Camden House, 1995)

BAHR, EHRHARD, *Die Ironie im Spätwerk Goethes* (Berlin: Schmidt, 1972)

——'Wilhelm Meisters Wanderjahre oder die Entsagenden (1821/1829)', in *Interpretationen: Goethes Erzählwerk*, ed. by Paul Michel Lützeler and James E. McLeod (Stuttgart: Reclam, 1985), pp. 363–95

——*The Novel as Archive: the Genesis, Reception, and Criticism of Goethe's 'Wilhelm Meisters Wanderjahre'* (Columbia, SC: Camden House, 1998)

BARTHES, ROLAND, 'The Death of the Author', in *Image, Music, Text: Essays selected and translated by Stephen Heath* (London: Fontana, 1977), pp. 142–48

BAUMGART, REINHARD, 'Das erotische Gestirn', in *Johann Wolfgang Goethe, Verweile Doch: 111 Gedichte mit Interpretationen*, ed. by Marcel Reich-Ranicki (Frankfurt am Main: Insel, 1992), pp. 461–62

——'Magie und Vernunft', ibid., pp. 469–70

BEISER, FREDERICK, *German Idealism: The Struggle against Subjectivism, 1781–1801* (Cambridge, MA: Harvard University Press, 2002)

BENNETT, BENJAMIN, *Goethe's Theory of Poetry: 'Faust' and the Regeneration of Language* (Ithaca: Cornell University Press, 1986)

——*Beyond Theory: Eighteenth-Century German Literature and the Poetics of Irony* (Ithaca: Cornell University Press, 1993)

BESSERMAN, LAWRENCE, 'The Challenge of Periodization: Old Paradigms and New Perspectives', in *The Challenge of Periodization: Old Paradigms and New Perspectives*, ed. by Besserman (New York: Garland, 1996), pp. 3–27

BINDER, WOLFGANG, 'Das 'offenbare Geheimnis': Goethes Symbolverständnis', in *Welt der Symbole: interdisziplinäre Aspekte des Symbolverständnisses*, ed. by Gaetano Benedetti and Udo Rauchfleisch (Göttingen: Vandenhoeck & Ruprecht, 1988), pp. 146–63

BISHOP, PAUL, ed., *A Companion to Goethe's Faust: Parts I and II* (Rochester, NY: Camden House, 2001)

BLOCK, RICHARD, *Spell of Italy: Vacation, Magic and the Attraction of Goethe* (Detroit: Wayne State University Press, 2006)

BLOD, GABRIELE, *'Lebensmärchen': Goethes Dichtung und Wahrheit als poetischer und poetologischer Text* (Würzburg: Königshausen und Neumann, 2003)

BOERNER, PETER, 'Italienische Reise (1816–29)', in *Interpretationen: Goethes Erzählwerk*, ed. by Paul Michel Lützeler and James E. McLeod (Stuttgart: Reclam, 1985), pp. 344–62

BORCHMEYER, DIETER, *Höfische Gesellschaft und französische Revolution bei Goethe: Adliges und bürgerliches Wertsystem im Urteil der Weimarer Klassik* (Kronberg: Athenäum, 1977)

BOYLE, NICHOLAS, 'Kantian and Other Elements in Goethe's "Vermächtniß" ', *The Modern Language Review*, 73 (1978), 532–49

——'The Politics of *Faust II*: Another Look at the Stratum of 1831', *Publications of the English Goethe Society*, 52 (1981–82), 4–43

——*Goethe: The Poet and the Age*, 2 vols (Oxford: Oxford University Press, 1991–2000)

——'Goethe in Paestum: a Higher-Critical Look at the *Italienische Reise*', *Oxford German Studies*, 20 (1991–92), 18–31

——'Geschichtsschreibung und Autobiographik bei Goethe' (1810–1817), *Goethe-Jahrbuch*, 110 (1993), 163–72

——'Goethe, *Novelle*', in *Landmarks in German Short Prose*, ed. by Peter Hutchinson (Berne: Peter Lang, 2003), pp. 11–27

——'Writing Goethe Writing Goethe', *Journal of Historical Biography*, 1.1 (2007), 5–14

BOWMAN, BRADY, 'Goethean Morphology, Hegelian Science: Affinities and Transformations', *Goethe Yearbook*, 18 (2011), 159–81

BOWMAN, DEREK, *Life into Autobiography: A Study of Goethe's 'Dichtung und Wahrheit'* (Berne: Herbert Lang, 1971)

BRANDT, HELMUT, ed., *Goethe und die Wissenschaften* (Jena: Friedrich-Schiller-Universität, 1984)

BREITHAUPT, FRITZ, *Jenseits der Bilder: Goethes Politik der Wahrnehmung* (Freiburg im Breisgau: Rombach, 2000)

BROWN, JANE K., *Goethe's Cyclical Narratives: 'Die Unterhaltungen deutscher Ausgewanderten' and 'Wilhelm Meisters Wanderjahre'* (Chapel Hill: University of North Carolina Press, 1975)

——*Goethe's 'Faust': The German Tragedy* (Ithaca: Cornell University Press, 1986)

——'Theatricality and Experiment: Identity in *Faust*', in *Goethe's 'Faust': Theatre of Modernity*, ed. by Hans Schulte, John Noyes, and Pia Kleber (Cambridge: Cambridge University Press, 2011), pp. 235–52

BROWN, JANE K., MEREDITH LEE, and THOMAS P. SAINE, *Interpreting Goethe's Faust Today* (Columbia, SC: Camden House, 2004)

BRUFORD, W. H., *The German Tradition of Self-Cultivation: 'Bildung' from Humboldt to Thomas Mann* (Cambridge: Cambridge University Press, 1975)

BUCHWALD, REINHARD, *Führer durch Goethes Faustdichtung* (Stuttgart: Kröner, 1983)

BURGARD, PETER J., *Idioms of Uncertainty: Goethe and Irony* (University Park, PA: Penn-State University Press, 1992)

CHAMPLIN, JEFFREY, 'Hegel's *Faust*', *Goethe Yearbook*, 18 (2011), 115–25

CHEEKE, STEPHEN, *Writing for Art: The Aesthetics of Ekphrasis* (Manchester: Manchester University Press, 2008)

CONRADY, KARL OTTO, *Goethe. Leben und Werk*, 2 vols (Düsseldorf und Zurich: Artemis, 1994)

COOPER, IAN, *The Near and Distant God: Poetry, Idealism and Religious Thought from Hölderlin to Eliot* (London: Legenda, 2008)

DE MAN, PAUL, 'Autobiography as De-facement', *Modern Language Notes*, 94 (1979), 919–30

DOKIC, JÉRÔME, 'Is Memory Purely Preservative?', in *Time and Memory: Issues in Philosophy and Psychology*, ed. by Christoph Hoerl and Teresa McCormack (Oxford: Clarendon Press, 2001), pp. 213–32

DOWDEN, STEVE, 'Irony and Ethical Autonomy in *Wilhelm Meisters Wanderjahre*', *Deutsche Vierteljahrsschrift*, 68 (1994), 134–54

DURRANI, OSMAN, *Faust and the Bible: A Study of Goethe's Use of Scriptural Allusions and Christian Religious Motifs in Faust I and II* (Berne: Peter Lang, 1977)

DYE, ELLIS, *Love and Death in Goethe: 'One and Double'* (Rochester, NY: Camden House, 2004)

EICHHORN, PETER, *Idee und Erfahrung im Spätwerk Goethes* (Freiburg and Munich: Alber, 1971)

EIBL, KARL, *Das monumentale Ich — Wege zu Goethes 'Faust'* (Frankfurt am Main: Insel, 2000)

EMRICH, WILHELM, *Die Symbolik von Faust II: Sinn und Vorformen*, 3rd edn (Frankfurt am Main: Athenäum, 1964)

FISCHER, PHILIP, *Wonder, the Rainbow, and the Aesthetics of Rare Experience* (Cambridge, MA: Harvard University Press, 1998)

FLITNER, WILHELM, *Goethe im Spätwerk: Glaube, Weltsicht, Ethos* (Schöningh: Paderborn, 1983; first published Hamburg: Claaßen, 1947)

FUCHS, ALBERT, *Goethe-Studien* (Berlin: de Gruyter, 1968)

GAIER, ULRICH, *Goethes Faust-Dichtungen: Ein Kommentar* (Stuttgart: Reclam, 1989)

——*Fausts Modernität: Essays* (Stuttgart: Reclam, 2000)

GILG, ANDRÉ, *Wilhelm Meisters Wanderjahre und ihre Symbole* (Zurich: Atlantis, 1954)

GOEBEL, ECKART, *Jenseits des Unbehagens: 'Sublimierung' von Goethe bis Lacan* (Bielefeld: transcript, 2009)

GOLZ, JOCHEN, 'Geschichtliche Welt und gedeutetes Ich in Goethes Autobiographik', *Goethe Jahrbuch*, 114 (1997), 89–100

GOULD, ROBERT, 'The Functions of Non-Literary Quotations in Part 4 of *Dichtung und Wahrheit*', *German Life and Letters*, 44 (1991), 291–305

GRAFTON, ANTHONY, GLENN W. MOST, and SALVATORE SETTIS, eds, *The Classical Tradition* (Cambridge, MA and London: Belknap, 2010)

GRIMLEY, DANIEL M., 'Storms, Symphonies, Silence: Sibelius's *Tempest* Music and the Invention of Late Style', in *Jean Sibelius and His World*, ed. by Daniel M. Grimley (Princeton: Princeton University Press, 2011), pp. 186–226

GRIMM, REINHOLD and JOST HERMAND, eds, *Die Klassik-Legende* (Frankfurt am Main: Athenäum, 1971)

HAAS, STEFANIE, *Text und Leben: Goethes Spiel mit inner- und außerliterarischer Wirklichkeit in Dichtung und Wahrheit* (Berlin: Duncker und Humboldt, 2006)

HACHMEISTER, GRETCHEN L., *Italy in the German Literary Imagination: Goethe's 'Italian Journey' and its Reception by Eichendorff, Platen and Heine* (Columbia, SC: Camden House, 2002)

HAGEN, FRED and MAHLENDORF, URSULA, 'Commitment, Concern and Memory in Goethe's *Faust*', *The Journal of Aesthetics and Art Criticism*, 21 (1963), 473–84

HAILE, H. G., *Invitation to Goethe's* Faust (Alabama: University of Alabama Press, 1978)

HAMM, HEINZ, *Goethes 'Faust': Werkgeschichte und Textanalyse* (Berlin: Volk und Wissen, 1978)

HARDIN, JAMES, ed., *Reflection and Action: Essays on the Bildungsroman* (Columbia: University of South Carolina Press, 1991)

HELLER, ERICH, *Essays über Goethe* (Frankfurt am Main: Insel, 1970)

HERMES, EBERHARD, *Johann Wolfgang Goethe: Novelle* (Stuttgart: Klett, 1995)

HESS, GÜNTER, 'Goethe und die poetische Mondsucht um 1828: DEM AUFGEHENDEN VOLLMONDE', in *Goethe Gedichte: Zweiunddreißig Interpretationen*, ed. by Gerhard Sauder (Munich: Hanser, 1996), pp. 357–67

HILLIARD, KEVIN, 'Römische Elegien XX: Metapoetic Reflection in Goethe's Classical Poetry', in *Goethe at 250: London Symposium. Goethe mit 250: Londoner Symposium*, ed. by T. J. Reed, Martin Swales, and Jeremy Adler (Munich: Iudicium, 2000), pp. 223–32

HUTCHINSON, PETER, 'Introduction', in *Maxims and Reflections by Johann Wolfgang von Goethe*, trans. by Elisabeth Stopp, ed. with introduction and notes by Peter Hutchinson (London: Penguin, 1998), pp. ix–xvi

JAEGER, MICHAEL, *Fausts Kolonie: Goethes kritische Phänomenologie der Moderne* (Würzburg: Königshausen und Neumann, 2004)

——*Global Player Faust oder Das Verschwinden der Gegenwart. Zur Aktualität Goethes* (Berlin: Siedler, 2010)

JACKSON, PHILIP H., '"Air and Angels", the Origenist Compromise in Haller's *Über den Ursprung des Übels*', *German Life and Letters*, 32 (1979), 273–92

JANTZ, HAROLD, *The Form of Faust: The Work of Art and its Intrinsic Structures* (Baltimore: Johns Hopkins University Press, 1978)

JESSING, BENEDIKT, 'Dichtung und Wahrheit', in *Goethe Handbuch*, III, ed. by Bernd Witte and Peter Schmidt (Stuttgart: Metzler, 1997), pp. 278–330

JONES, JOHN, *Shakespeare at Work* (Oxford: Clarendon Press, 1995)

KAIN, PHILIP J., *Schiller, Hegel and Marx: State, Society, and the Aesthetic Ideal of Ancient Greece* (Kingston and Montreal: McGill–Queens University Press, 1982)

KAUFMANN, SEBASTIAN, *'Schöpft des Dichters reine Hand ...': Studien zu Goethes poetologischer Lyrik* (Heidelberg: Winter, 2011)

KELLER, WERNER, *Goethes dichterische Bildlichkeit: Eine Grundlegung* (Munich: Fink, 1972)

——'Faust. Eine Tragödie (1808)', in *Goethes Dramen. Neue Interpretationen*, ed. by Walter Hinderer (Stuttgart: Reclam, 1980), pp. 244–80

KEPPLER, STEFAN, *Grenzen des Ich: Die Verfassung des Subjekts in Goethes Romanen und Erzählungen* (Berlin: De Gruyter, 2006)

KOHL, KATRIN, 'No Escape? Goethe's Strategies of Self-Projection and their Role in German Literary Historiography', *Goethe Yearbook*, 16 (2009), 173–91

KORFF, H. A., *Goethe im Bildwandel seiner Lyrik*, II (Leipzig: Hanau: Dausien, 1958)

KOSELLECK, REINHART, 'Goethes unzeitgemäße Geschichte', *Goethe-Jahrbuch*, 110 (1993), 27–39

KRIEGLEDER, WYNFRIED, 'Wilhelm Meisters Amerika: Das Bild der Vereinigten Staaten in den *Wanderjahren*', *Jahrbuch des Wiener Goethe Vereins*, 95 (1991), 15–31

KUHN, BERNHARD, *Autobiography and Natural Science in the Age of Romanticism: Rousseau, Goethe and Thoreau* (Farnham: Ashgate, 2009)

LANGE, VICTOR, 'Zur Entstehungsgeschichte von Goethes *Wanderjahren*', *German Life and Letters*, 23 (1969), 47–54

——'Faust: Der Tragödie zweiter Teil', in *Goethes Dramen: Neue Interpretationen*, ed. by Walter Hinderer (Stuttgart: Reclam, 1980), pp. 281–312

LEDERER, MAX, 'Noch einmal Schillers Reliquien', *Modern Language Notes*, 62 (1947), 7–12

LEE, CHARLOTTE, '"Wenn ich leben soll, so sei es mit dir!" The Relationship of Father and Son in Goethe's *Wilhelm Meisters Wanderjahre*', *German Life and Letters*, 64 (2011), 489–500

——'Durch Wunderkraft erschienen: Affinities between Goethe's *Faust* and Shakespeare's *The Tempest*', *Modern Language Review*, 107 (2012), 198–210

——'Im flüßgen Element hin und wieder schweifen: Development and Return in Goethe's Poetry and Hegel's Philosophy', *Goethe Yearbook* 20 (2013), 166–77.

——'Mignon and the Idea of the Secret', in *The Present Word: Culture, Society and the Site of Literature. Essays in Honour of Nicholas Boyle*, ed. by John Walker (Oxford: Legenda, 2013), pp. 61–69

LEE, MEREDITH, *Studies in Goethe's Lyric Cycles* (Chapel Hill: University of North Carolina, 1978)

LEMMEL, MONIKA, *Poetologie in Goethes West-östlichem Divan* (Heidelberg: Winter, 1987)

LINDLEY, DAVID, *Lyric* (London: Methuen, 1985)

LLEWELLYN, R. T., 'Parallel Attitudes to Form in Late Beethoven and Late Goethe: Throwing Aside the Appearance of Art', *Modern Language Review*, 63 (1968), 407–16

LLOYD-SHERLOCK, PETER and OTHERS, 'Population Ageing and Health', *The Lancet* 397, Issue 9823 (7 April 2012), pp. 1295–96 <http://www.thelancet.com/journals/lancet/article/PIIS0140–6736(12)60519–4/fulltext> [accessed 23 August 2012]

LOUTH, CHARLIE, 'Goethe's Sonnets', *Publications of the English Goethe Society*, 72 (2003), 15–24

——'Reflections: Goethe's "Auf dem See" and Hölderlin's "Hälfte des Lebens"', *Oxford German Studies*, 33 (2004), 169–75

LUKÁCS, GEORG, *Goethe und seine Zeit* (Berne: Francke, 1947)

LYNE, RAPHAEL, *Shakespeare's Late Work* (Oxford: Oxford University Press, 2007)

MAHONEY, DENNIS, 'Autobiographical Writings', in *The Cambridge Companion to Goethe*, ed. by Lesley Sharpe (Cambridge: Cambridge University Press, 2002), pp. 147–59

MAYER, MATHIAS, *Selbstbewußte Illusion: Selbstreflexion und Legitimation der Dichtung im 'Wilhelm Meister'* (Heidelberg: Winter, 1989)

MASON, EUDO C., *Goethe's Faust: Its Genesis and Purport* (Berkeley: University of California Press, 1967)

MAUTNER, FRANZ H., ERNST FEISE, and KARL VIETÖR, '"Ist Fortzusetzen": Zu Goethes Gedicht auf Schillers Schädel', *Publications of the Modern Language Association*, 59 (1944), 1156–72

MCMULLAN, GORDON, 'What is a Late Play?', in *The Cambridge Companion to Shakespeare's Last Plays*, ed. by Catherine M. S. Alexander (Cambridge: Cambridge University Press, 2009), pp. 5–27

MEHRA, MARLIS HELENE, *Die Bedeutung der Formel 'Offenbares Geheimnis' in Goethes Spätwerk* (Stuttgart: Heinz, 1982)

MIETH, GÜNTHER, 'Fausts letzter Monolog: Poetische Struktur einer geschichtlichen Vision', *Goethe-Jahrbuch*, 97 (1980), 90–102

MINDEN, MICHAEL, *The German Bildungsroman: Incest and Inheritance* (Cambridge: Cambridge University Press, 1997)

MITTERMÜLLER, CHRISTIAN, *Sprachskepsis und Poetologie: Goethes Romane 'Die Wahlverwandtschaften' und 'Wilhelm Meisters Wanderjahre'* (Tübingen: Niemeyer, 2008)

MOLNÁR, GEZA VON, 'The Conditions of Faust's Wager and its Resolution in the Light of Kantian Ethics', *Publications of the English Goethe Society*, 51 (1980–81), 48–80

——*Goethes Kantstudien: Eine Zusammenstellung nach Eintragungen in seinen Handexemplaren der 'Kritik der reinen Vernunft' und der 'Kritik der Urteilskraft'* (Weimar: Böhlaus Nachfolger, 1994)

MOMMSEN, KATHARINA, *Natur- und Fabelreich in Faust II* (Berlin: de Gruyter, 1968)

MOTZKIN, GABRIELE, 'Goethe's Theory of Memory', in *Goethe und das Zeitalter der Romantik*, ed. by Walter Hinderer (Würzburg: Königshausen und Neumann, 2002), pp. 151–62

MUENZER, CLARK E., *Figures of Identity: Goethe's Novels and the Enigmatic Self* (University Park: Pennsylvania State University Press, 1984)

NESSELER, OLGA and THOMAS NESSELER, *Auf des Messers Schneide. Zur Funktionalisierung literarischer Kreativität bei Schiller und Goethe. Eine psychoanalytische Studie* (Würzburg: Königshausen und Neumann, 1994)

NEUMANN, GERHARD, *Ideenparadiese: Untersuchungen zur Aphoristik von Lichtenberg, Novalis, Friedrich Schlegel und Goethe* (Munich: Fink, 1976)

NICHOLLS, ANGUS, *Goethe's Concept of the Daemonic: After the Ancients* (Columbia, SC: Camden House, 2006)

——'Goethe and Twentieth-Century Theory: An Introduction', *Goethe Yearbook*, 16 (2009), 163–72

NISBET, H. B., '*Das Dämonische*: On the Logic of Goethe's Demonology', *Forum for Modern Language Studies*, 7 (1971), 259–81

OLNEY, JAMES, *Memory and Narrative: The Weave of Life-Writing* (Chicago: University of Chicago Press, 1998)

OSWALD, STEFAN, *Italienbilder: Beiträge zur Wandlung der deutschen Italienauffassung 1770–1840* (Heidelberg: Winter, 1985)

PASCAL, ROY, *Design and Truth in Autobiography* (London: Routledge and Kegan Paul, 1960)

PERLOFF, MARJORIE G., 'The Autobiographical Mode of Goethe: *Dichtung und Wahrheit* and the Lyric Poems', *Comparative Literature Studies*, 7 (1970), 265–96

PESTALOZZI, KARL, 'Goethes Darstellung des Alters im Gedichtzyklus *Chinesisch-deutsche Jahres- und Tageszeiten*', in *Goethe. Freiburger Literaturpsychologische Gespräche: Jahrbuch für Literatur und Psychologie*, XXIX, ed. by Wolfram Mauser, Joachim Pfeiffer, and Carl Pietzscher (Würzburg: Königshausen und Neumann, 2010), pp. 219–37

PETERSEN, JULIUS, *Die Entstehung der Eckermannschen Gespräche und ihre Glaubwürdigkeit* (Frankfurt am Main: Diesterweg, 1925)

REED, T. J., *Goethe* (Oxford: Oxford University Press, 1984)

——*The Classical Centre: Goethe and Weimar 1775–1832* (Oxford: Clarendon Press, 1986)

REIBENSTEIN, CHRISTIANE, *Bibliotherapeutische Aspekte in ausgewählten Werken Goethes* (Aachen: Shaker, 1996)

REICH-RANICKI, MARCEL, ed., *Johann Wolfgang Goethe, Verweile Doch: 111 Gedichte mit Interpretationen* (Frankfurt am Main: Insel, 1992)

REISS, HANS, 'Wilhelm Meisters Wanderjahre: Der Weg von der ersten zur zweiten Fassung', *Deutsche Vierteljahrsschrift für Literaturwissenschaft und Geistesgeschichte*, 39 (1965), 34–57

REISS, TIMOTHY J., 'Perioddity: Considerations on the Geography of Histories', *Modern Language Quarterly*, 62 (2001), 425–52

REMAK, HENRY H. H., 'Autobiography or Fiction? Johann Wolfgang and Johann Caspar Goethe's "Schöne Mailänderinnen" and the "Frankfurter Gretchen" as Novellas', in *Goethe in Italy*, ed. by Gerhart Hoffmeister (Amsterdam: Rodopi, 1988), pp. 21–54

RICHTER, KARL, 'Naturwissenschaftliche Voraussetzungen der Symbolik am Beispiel von Goethes Alterslyrik', *Jahrbuch des Wiener Goethe Vereins*, 92–93 (1988–89), 9–24

RICHTER, SIMON, ed., *The Literature of Weimar Classicism* (Rochester, NY: Camden House, 2005)

ROHDE, CARSTEN, *Spiegeln und Schweben: Goethes autobiographisches Schreiben* (Göttingen: Wallstein, 2006)

RÜDIGER, HORST, 'Weltliteratur in Goethes "Helena"', *Jahrbuch der deutschen Schillergesellschaft*, 8 (1964), 172–98

SACHERS, REGINA, 'Context and Composition: The Making of Goethe's *Gott und Welt*' (Dissertation: University of Cambridge, 2009)

SAID, EDWARD, *On Late Style: Music and Literature against the Grain* (New York: Pantheon Books, 2006)

SASSE, GÜNTER, *Auswanderung in die Moderne: Tradition und Innovation in Goethes Roman 'Wilhelm Meisters Wanderjahre'* (Berlin: De Gruyter, 2010)

SAUDER, GERHARD, ed., *Goethe Gedichte: Zweiunddreißig Interpretationen* (Munich: Hanser, 1996)

SAX, BENJAMIN C., *Images of Identity: Goethe and the Problem of Self-Conception in the Nineteenth Century* (New York: Peter Lang, 1987)

SCHADEWALDT, WOLFGANG, 'Zur Entstehung der Elfenszene im 2. Teil des Faust', *Deutsche Vierteljahrsschrift für Literaturwissenschaft und Geistesgeschichte*, 29 (1955), 227–36

SCHEIBE, SIEGFRIED, 'Der vierte Teil von "Dichtung und Wahrheit": Zur Entstehungs-geschichte und Textgestalt', *Jahrbuch der Goethe-Gesellschaft* (1968), 87–115

SCHLAFFER, HANNELORE, *Wilhelm Meister: Das Ende der Kunst und die Wiederkehr des Mythos* (Stuttgart: Metzler, 1989)

——'Paradies und Parodie: Die letzten Szenen in Goethes letzten Werken', in *Interpreting Goethe's Faust Today*, ed. by Jane K. Brown, Meredith Lee, and Thomas P. Saine (Columbia, SC: Camden House, 2004), pp. 102–11

SCHLAFFER, HEINZ, 'Exoterik und Esoterik in Goethes Romanen', *Goethe Jahrbuch*, 95 (1978), 212–26

——*Faust Zweiter Teil: Die Allegorie des 19. Jahrhunderts* (Stuttgart: Metzler, 1981)

SCHMIDT, JOCHEN, *Die Geschichte des Genie-Gedankens 1750–1945*, I: *Von der Aufklärung bis zum Idealismus* (Darmstadt: Wissenschaftliche Buchgesellschaft, 1985)

SCHMITZ, HERMANN, *Goethes Altersdenken im problemgeschichtlichen Zusammenhang* (Bonn: Bouvier, 1959)

SCHNUR, HARALD, 'Identität und autobiographische Darstellung in Goethes "Dichtung und Wahrheit"', *Jahrbuch des Freien Deutschen Hochstifts* (1990), 28–93

SCHÖNE, ALBRECHT, '"Regenbogen auf schwarzgrauem Grunde": Goethes Dornburger Brief an Zelter zum Tod seines Großherzogs', *Jahrbuch des Wiener Goethe Vereins*, 81–83 (1977–79), 17–35

——*Goethes Farbentheologie* (Munich: Beck, 1987)

——*Fausts Himmelfahrt: Zur letzten Szene der Tragödie* (Munich: Carl Friedrich von Siemens Stiftung, 1994)

——*Schillers Schädel* (Munich: Beck, 2002).

SCHULTE, HANS, JOHN NOYES, and PIA KLEBER, *Goethe's Faust: Theatre of Modernity* (Cambridge: Cambridge University Press, 2011)

SCHULZ, GERHARD, 'Goethe's *Italienische Reise*', in *Goethe in Italy 1786–1986*, ed. by Gerhart Hoffmeister (Amsterdam: Rodopi, 1988), pp. 5–19

SEITZ, ERWIN, *Talent und Geschichte: Goethe in seiner Autobiographie* (Stuttgart: Metzler, 1996)

SHARPE, LESLEY, ed., *The Cambridge Companion to Goethe* (Cambridge: Cambridge University Press, 2002)

STAIGER, EMIL, *Goethe*, 3 vols (Zurich: Atlantis, 1952–59)

STELZIG, EUGENE, *The Romantic Subject in Autobiography: Rousseau and Goethe* (Charlottesville, VA: University Press of Virginia, 2000)

STEPHENSON, R. H., *Goethe's Conception of Knowledge and Science* (Edinburgh: Edinburgh University Press, 1995)

——*Studies in Weimar Classicism: Writing as Symbolic Form* (Berne: Peter Lang, 2010)

STERN, J. P. and J. J WHITE, eds, *Paths and Labyrinths: Nine Papers Read at the Franz Kafka Symposium Held at the Institute of Germanic Studies on 20 and 21 October 1983* (London: Institute of Germanic Studies, University of London, 1985)

STÖCKLEIN, PAUL, *Wege zum späten Goethe. Dichtung — Gedanke — Zeichnung: Interpretationen um ein Thema*, 2nd edn (Hamburg: Schröder, 1960)

SWALES, MARTIN, 'Goethe's *Faust*: Theatre, Meta-Theatre, Tragedy', in *Goethe's Faust: Theatre of Modernity*, ed. by Hans Schulte, John Noyes, and Pia Kleber (Cambridge: Cambridge University Press, 2011), pp. 197–208

SWALES, MARTIN and ERIKA SWALES, *Reading Goethe: A Critical Introduction to the Literary Work* (Rochester, NY: Camden House, 2002)

TRUNZ, ERICH, ed., *Studien zu Goethes Alterswerken* (Frankfurt am Main: Athenäum, 1971)

——'Goethes späte Lyrik', *Deutsche Vierteljahrsschrift für Literaturwissenschaft und Geistesgeschichte*, 23 (1949), 409–32

UTZ, PETER, *Das Auge und das Ohr im Text* (Munich: Fink, 1990)

VAGET, HANS RUDOLF, 'Johann Wolfgang Goethe: *Wilhelm Meisters Wanderjahre*', in *Romane und Erzählungen zwischen Romantik und Realismus: Neue Interpretationen*, ed. by Paul Michael Lützeler (Stuttgart: Reclam, 1983), pp. 136–64

VIETÖR, KARL, 'Goethes Gedicht auf Schiller's Schädel', *Publications of the Modern Language Association*, 59 (1944), 142–83

——*Geist und Form: Aufsätze zur deutschen Literaturgeschichte* (Berne: Francke, 1952)

VINCENT, DEIRDRE, 'Text as Image and Self-Image: The Contextualization of Goethe's *Dichtung und Wahrheit* (1810–1813)', *Goethe Yearbook*, 10 (2001), 125–53

WAGNER, IRMGARD, 'Goethe's Bohemian Traces or: Marienbad Mirrorings', *Modern Language Studies*, 31 (2001), 151–62

WAGNER-DITTMAR, CHRISTINE, 'Goethe und die chinesische Literatur', in *Studien zu Goethes Alterswerken*, ed. by Erich Trunz (Frankfurt am Main: Athenäum, 1971), pp. 122–228

WEIMAR, KLAUS and DAVID E. WELLBERY, *Goethe, 'Harzreise im Winter': Eine Deutungskontroverse* (Paderborn: Schöningh, 1984)

WELLBERY, DAVID E., *The Specular Moment: Goethe's Early Lyric and the Beginnings of Romanticism* (Stanford: Stanford University Press, 1996)

——'Afterword', in *The Sorrows of Young Werther; Elective Affinities; Novella/Johann Wolfgang von Goethe*, trans. by Judith Ryan and Victor Lange, ed. by David E. Wellbery (New York: Suhrkamp, 1988), pp. 283–96

——'Wahnsinn der Zeit: Zur Dialektik von Idee und Erfahrung in Goethes *Elegie*', in *Die Gabe des Gedichts: Goethes Lyrik im Wechsel der Töne*, ed. by Gerhard Neumann and David E. Wellbery (Freiburg im Breisgau: Rombach, 2008), pp. 319–52

WEYL, SHALOM, 'Some Parallels between Faust's Salvation and the *Walpurgisnacht*', *Publications of the English Goethe Society*, 41 (1970–71), 91–102

WIESE, BENNO VON, *Die deutsche Novelle von Goethe bis Kafka: Interpretationen*, II (Düsseldorf: Bagel, 1956)

WILD, GERHARD, *Goethes Versöhnungsbilder: Eine geschichtsphilosophische Untersuchung zu Goethes späten Werken* (Stuttgart: Metzler, 1991)

WILKINSON, ELIZABETH M., '"Tasso: ein gesteigerter Werther" in the Light of Goethe's Principle of Steigerung', *Modern Language Review*, 44 (1949), 305–28

——'The Theological Basis of Faust's "Credo"', *German Life and Letters*, 10 (1956–57), 229–39

——'Goethes "Trilogie der Leidenschaft" als Beitrag zur Frage der Katharsis', *Freies Deutsches Hochstift: Reihe der Vorträge und Schriften*, 18 (1957)

WILKINSON, E. M. and L. A. WILLOUGHBY, *Goethe: Poet and Thinker* (London: Edward Arnold, 1962)

WILLIAMS, JOHN R., *Goethe's 'Faust'* (London: Allen and Unwin, 1987)

——*The Life of Goethe: A Critical Biography* (Oxford: Blackwell, 1998)

WITTE, BERND and others, eds, *Goethe Handbuch*, 4 vols (Stuttgart: Metzler, 1996–99)

WRIGHT, JOAN, *The Novel Poetics of Goethe's 'Wilhelm Meisters Wanderjahre': Eine zarte Empirie* (Lewiston, NY: Edwin Mellen Press, 2003)

ZASTRAU, ALFRED, ed., *Goethe Handbuch. Goethe, seine Welt und Zeit in Werk und Wirkung*, I (Stuttgart: Metzler, 1961)

INDEX